A Bureaucrat Speaks

Attention Authors

'We Convert Fighters into Writers'. That's the motto of Manas Publications since more than four decades. Our message to the world is that India can win the battle not only by the bullet but also by the pen. There is no dearth of intellectuals in our country, but their knowledge is confined to them only. No sincere effort has been made by any other publisher to channelise their knowledge in national interest. That is why the talent of a large number of intellectuals remains latent. An author transforms his knowledge into a manuscript, and it is our job to spread his/her knowledge by converting it into a beautiful book. For over four decades, Manas has been motivating the intellectuals by publishing their manuscripts and would like to publish your manuscript too. If you or your colleagues have any manuscript ready for publication or are working on it, kindly contact us with detailed synopsis and list of contents. We will transform your work into a valuable publication. If you wish, we can also suggest you the suitable subjects for writing the books related to your area of expertise. Manas is known for its publishing quality and commitments. We take utmost care in production and give wide publicity to the book as well as its author through our national and international distribution network.

A Bureaucrat Speaks

Sovan Kanungo, IAS

Manas Publications
(We Convert Fighters into Writers)
(New Delhi-110002 (INDIA)

MANAS PUBLICATIONS

(We convert Fighters into Writers)

(Publishers, Distributors, Importers & Exporters)
4402/5-A, Ansari Road (Opp. HDFC Bank)
Darya Ganj, New Delhi-110 002 (India)
Off. 23260783, 23265523, Res. 23842660
Fax: 011-23272766
E-mail: manaspublications@gmail.com
manaspublications@yahoo.com

ISBN 978-81-7049-473-7
₹ 695/-

Designed at
Manas Publications

Printed in India at
RK Offset, Delhi and published by Mrs Suman Lata for
Manas Publications, 4402/5-A, Ansari Road,
(Opp. HDFC Bank),
Darya Ganj, New Delhi-110 002 (INDIA)

Contents

Preface

After more than six decades of the independence we still wonder if a good governance will remain an elusive dream for our country. Political opportunism, nepotism and corruption have eroded the whole governance, making people despondent and cynical. The prophetic words of C Rajagopalachari, the 'Chanakya' of our freedom movement, who later became the first and last Indian Governor-General of independent India, seem to have come true. He had written in his *Jail Diary* on 24 January 1922:

> "....Swaraj will not at once, or I think even for a long time to come, mean better government or greater happiness for the people. Elections and their corruptions, injustice, and the power and tyranny of wealth, and inefficiency of administration will make a hell of life.... Men will look regretfully back to the old regime of comparative justice, and efficient, peaceful, more or less honest administration."

How did the colonial government manage to ensure justice, peace, efficiency and honesty in administration? Not that there was no corruption or nepotism in those days, but the government was able to function by instituting suitable structures and systems, investing adequate powers at different levels, and providing for close monitoring and supervision to ensure that these powers were exercised judiciously. Higher policy was no doubt dictated by the political masters at Whitehall, but they neither interfered nor micromanaged the local administration. The Governor-General and Provincial Governors must have ensured that district officials, who operated in the field, close to the people, had ample power and authority to decide issues. They were made to exercise their powers and use their position in the interest of good governance. Close supervision, effective superintendence and strict enforcement of accountability were the key elements that kept the administration alert and minimised errant behaviour.

When we achieved independence, we inherited the structure and systems through which the British had governed us. By and large, they still are in place; the difference lies in their working. The colonial rulers in London came to be replaced by our own leaders in Delhi and at state capitals. For a while they conducted themselves with dignity and devotion to larger national interest, but gradually discovered that it was more interesting as well as profitable to dabble in micro-management rather than confine themselves to issues of higher governance, such as policy formulation, programme evaluation and enforcement of accountability. Transfer of officers, award of contracts and doling out favours became preoccupations of the political executive. Unscrupulous officers found it convenient to make common cause in this. Governance suffered as devolution of power and enforcement of accountability eroded.

Over time, governance deficit assumed frightening proportions. Practically one-third of the districts have now become ungovernable due to insurgency. Terrorist violence, growing power of the underworld, unbridled criminal activity and corruption have rudely shaken the foundation of the world's largest democracy. There is a pervasive feeling of insecurity. Faith in the criminal justice system has been severely eroded and administration is held largely in contempt. It was not so when I joined the Indian Administrative Service.

A couple of years ago a friend and a relative, Professor Bikram K Das and his wife Lilu took my wife and me on a visit to their farm house near Bhubaneswar. After a sumptuous lunch there, we were chatting over coffee when I narrated some incidents of my past civil service days. Bikram suggested that I should write my memoirs. Not only did he insist but was also joined by Lilu. On my declining the suggestion saying that I had no talent as a writer, it was Lilu who kept insisting that I must write and assured that Bikram would make good any deficiency in the draft. I was still reluctant. Sadly, Lilu passed away a few months later. But Bikram kept enquiring about the progress of my writing which had not even commenced. She was my cousin, darling of all who knew her well; I decided to start and haltingly progressed. Bikram pursued me like a teacher chases a lazy student. He not only ensured that I completed the task but did me enormous favour of going through the entire draft and improving it substantially. I would also like to acknowledge the contributions made by my daughter Priya Kanungo, a journalist by profession, who gave valuable editorial inputs.

The reminiscences that follow relate mostly to matters concerning public administration; I have deliberately avoided reference to my family and friends as they may be of little concern to others.

Sovan Kanungo

Chapter 1

Early Years in Service

Administration was reasonably clean and efficient when I joined the Indian Administrative Service as a recruit in 1960. Malefic influences at the time were already in evidence but tall leaders like Pandit Jawaharlal Nehru and Lal Bahadur Shastri were able to keep those forces in check through their character, integrity and vision. After the exit of leaders of that calibre, two deleterious influences have worked unhindered to land us in the present mess. One is the pernicious interference by the political executive in routine administration, which has steadily weakened the governance structure, and the other, a vast increase in new government programmes without ensuring that the agencies implementing them remain sound and adequate. Commission after Commission has been set-up to recommend measures to tone up and reorganise the administration but nothing much done to arrest the decline. Politicians alone have not been the culprit. They were successful in enlisting the active cooperation of over-ambitious bureaucrats in pursuit of short-term objectives at the cost of prudence and administrative ethics. The rot came in rather insidiously over a long period. Not that the bureaucracy, the higher civil services in particular, lacked officers committed to maintaining the highest standards of service; but their number progressively dwindled over time as many preferred to swim with the current.

When I look back to the half century that has passed since I joined the IAS, there is a deep sense of regret that administration, of which I was a miniscule part, deteriorated even while I was serving. In the pages that follow I recapitulate some events of my service career, marked by no extraordinary ability or attainment, but was informed by a strong desire to serve the public interest with dignity.

The first posting of an IAS officer, after training, is generally as officer-in-charge of a sub-division, with varying designations such as SDO, SDM or Sub-Collector, depending upon the practice prevalent in different states. But my batch of IAS recruits allotted to the Orissa cadre was put through a year-long assignment as Block Development Officers (BDOs). It was treated as a part of training but was no different from a duty post as we each held full charge of a Block. Those were the early days of the Community Development movement which, together with the Panchayati Raj system for devolution of power, became the flagship programme of national policy, inspired by leaders imbued with a passion for integrated rural development. Orissa was among the first few states that adopted Panchayati Raj in early 1960s. The three-tier structure of development administration had Gram Panchayat at the village level, Panchayat Samiti at the Block level and Zila Parishad at the district level. Of these, the Block was by far the most critical agency on which devolved the responsibility of execution of development programmes. Block Offices headed by BDOs were already in operation as vehicles of rural development.

With the introduction of Panchayati Raj an elected body of Panchayat Samiti, with its elected Chairman, was superimposed on the Block administration to oversee programme implementation; the BDO became chief executive officer of the Panchayat Samiti. The prospect of working on duty post at that level did not hold much attraction but in retrospect it turned out to be a great opportunity to gain experience of development administration at the grass-root level under democratic decentralisation. The relationship between the Chairman and the BDO in that set-up was a delicate one, with plenty of scope for ego clash. But luckily I had no problem. Ramnath Dash, an advocate and a fine gentleman with a clean image, was the Chairman of the Panchayat Samiti at Aska where I was posted as BDO. He never interfered in my work. I gave him full support and respect and spent a highly rewarding year as BDO.

Thereafter, I was posted as Sub-Divisional Officer (SDO) of Talcher, a former princely state, constituted into a sub-division following merger after Independence of over 500 princely states into the Indian Union. There was little that Talcher had to show by way of public services. People lived largely on rain-fed farming, with abysmally low productivity. Apart from some collieries and a railway line laid by the British mainly for the transportation of coal, the sub-division could boast of no industrial activity. It had large deposits of coal, yet to be developed in a big way; the National Coal Development Corporation, a public sector company, had just begun open-cast mining operations there. They had set-up a small township with facilities like piped water, electricity, a school and a hospital and also a fine club. But Talcher, the sub-divisional headquarters, was a sleepy little place.

During my training period, particularly during land revenue settlement operations, I realised that in a rural economy with acute poverty and lack of communication we could serve the people best by moving as close to them as possible rather than getting them to travel long distances to reach the administration. As a SDO I therefore, held camp-court frequently at different locations, to dispose of cases which related mostly to land administration. While settling some of the cases I was not averse to encroaching on matters that were not strictly within my jurisdiction, provided the parties agreed to settle amicably. I was only too happy to record as my decision the mutually agreed conclusion which was accepted as binding (if lawyers were not involved).

While I exercised discretion to provide justice to the weak, I made it a point to act strictly in accordance with the law when dealing with people who had power or influence. One day the manager of a circus company met me with an application seeking permission to set-up his camp to hold performances for a month or so. Soon after his arrival I got a call from a minister in Bhubaneswar recommending the case. Had that call not come, I might have simply endorsed the application to the local police for disposal. But the synchronisation of the call with the applicant's visit made me suspicious. I called my Head Clerk and gave him the application, asking him to let me know immediately under which provision of law the SDO's permission was required. I was informed that there was no such legal requirement, but over the years a practice had developed of the SDO's permission being sought and given. I was also informed that on the strength of such permission, the same company had performed circus shows for 60 days and then pushed off without paying to the Notified Area Council (a smaller version of Municipality) the rent due for the use of its land.

The dues together with penalty and interest had mounted to about a lakh of rupees, which the circus company was trying to avoid by seeking the SDO's permission directly. I immediately issued an order asking the company to clear the dues first, to the satisfaction of the Notified Area Council, and thereafter seek the Council's permission to use the land for circus shows, after obtaining a 'No-Objection Certificate' from the police. Soon, another phone call came from the minister. I politely explained the situation to him. He did not pursue the matter further nor did he hold it against me in future as a long-serving minister and later Deputy Chief Minister. This incident taught me a lesson which was to guide me all through my service career: fair and prompt exercise of decision is the most effective weapon against extraneous pressure, either ministerial or otherwise.

In those days the SDO Talcher had the additional responsibility of being the Administrator of a coal mine, that had been taken over by the government as it had become unsafe after it got flooded. While handing over charge, my predecessor had cautioned me that the manager of the mine needed firm handling as he had a tendency to function arbitrarily, ignoring instructions. An occasion soon arose for me to tackle him. My Head Clerk came to me one day with a grievance that the manager had sent in a bunch of bills along with the cash receipts, without affixing the mandatorily required revenue stamps. I asked the Head Clerk to speak to the manager and told him to affix revenue stamps on the receipts, which he might have neglected to do through oversight. The Head Clerk reported back after a fortnight that the manager had not bothered to carry out my instructions despite a telephonic reminder. He added that this was not the first time that such a lapse had occurred and that there was a history of repeated irregularities. On receipt of the report I spoke to the manager over the phone and advised him to rectify the omission, which he never did.

After referring to the Indian Stamp Act I then issued a formal notice to the manager that since a deliberate violation of the Act had come to my notice, I had impounded the documents and intended to proceed in accordance with the law, unless I received a satisfactory response within a specified period. This had an electrifying effect, though not by way of response from the manager. I got a phone call from my Collector, a mild person, asking me in panic what had happened as the Secretary in the Mining Department had asked him to intervene. I gave full account of the case, added that a copy of my self-explanatory notice had been sent to him as well as the Mining Secretary for information. The Collector was aware of the manager's conduct, about which my predecessor had briefed him too. It was not difficult for me to convince him that the manager needed to be disciplined and to do so, I had already started a quasi-judicial process. I assured the Collector that I would not transgress the law and he agreed to keep off. But the manager showed no sign of remorse.

A couple of days later the Mining Secretary landed up at Talcher on an unscheduled visit. Apparently, some people in Bhubaneswar were keen to protect the manager. There was visible relief when I explained that all I desired was rectification of the continuing violation of the Stamp Act; the case would be closed as soon as it was remedied. This was done the very next day and the manager came to realise that his cosy relationship at the state headquarters was no shield. This case gave me the opportunity, at a young age, to develop healthy irreverence towards undue interference in the exercise of administrative discretion. While I found nothing wrong in my Collector enquiring about the matter to discharge his general superintendence, I was clear in my mind that the Mining Secretary had no business to come down all the way from Bhubaneswar to interfere in a matter like this.

Another experience of my SDO days also illustrates how administrative norms are thrown to the winds through the supercilious conduct of extra-constitutional authorities. Prime Minister Jawaharlal Nehru was scheduled to lay the foundation stone of a major thermal power plant in Talcher. According to the official programme he was to leave Delhi early in the morning by a special plane for Charbatia Airport, travel by helicopter to Talcher to lay the foundation of the thermal power plant and then proceed to Tikarpara where a multi-purpose dam was to come up, return to Charbatia and go on to Bhubaneswar for an important meeting of the All-India Congress Committee. Chief Minister Biren Mitra was to receive the Prime Minister at Talcher where the function was scheduled for 9 a.m. Biju Patnaik, who had resigned as the previous Chief Minister and used to be referred to as 'Super Chief Minister' because of the enormous influence he had over the Chief Minister, was to receive the PM at Charbatia and accompany him to Talcher. I was responsible for the arrangements at Talcher and the Collector of the district was to be present at Tikarpara.

A group of officials, headed by the Chief Minister, had lined up at the helipad to receive the PM. I suddenly noticed the officer-in-charge of the local police station rushing desperately towards us on his bicycle. Police Stations had no motor vehicles, not even a motorcycle, in those days and cell phones were not invented. As I went up to him, he mumbled breathlessly, even before dismounting, that the PM's visit to Talcher had been cancelled. When I asked him for the source of the message, he told me that the Chief Secretary had rung up the Police Station from Bhubaneswar and asked him to inform me. I was perplexed. The Chief Minister had driven down from Bhubaneswar that very morning and arrived a short while ago to receive the PM and now here was this message! My first impulse was to ring up Bhubaneswar for confirmation, before passing on the information to the Chief Minister for which purpose I would have to drive some distance to the nearest phone. As I was about to start, I was startled by the noise and then the sight of an approaching helicopter. I rushed back to the reception line and assumed that some prankster had tried to fool us with that telephonic message.

The Prime Minister's programme passed off well. After laying the foundation stone of the thermal power plant he addressed a massive public meeting, for which men and women had come from villages far and wide. I was deeply moved to see common villagers camping overnight near the venue lest they be late for the 9 a.m. meeting to be addressed by the charismatic leader. Most of them could not have understood much of what he said; but a glimpse of him was all they wanted. But those of us who were privileged to be in the close proximity of the PM did not fail to notice the tired look on his face and a distinct drag in his left foot. He was clearly not well.

My days in Talcher ended with the high point of the Prime Minister's visit. The government had already issued an order posting me to the state secretariat as Under Secretary in the Finance Department, but the order was kept in abeyance until the PM's visit to Talcher was over. Soon thereafter, I moved to Bhubaneswar and took up my new post. While on a courtesy call to the Chief Secretary I mentioned how an imposter pretending to be the Chief Secretary had almost succeeded in de-railing the PM's visit to Talcher. He cut me short and told me, to my utter surprise, that it was he (the Chief Secretary himself) who had asked the police officer to convey me the cancellation of the Prime Minister's visit so that I could inform the Chief Minister. He went on to say that on the previous night the PM had felt uneasy in Delhi and his personal physician had prevailed on him to cancel the strenuous visit to Talcher and Tikarpara. Accordingly, the programme was revised and the PM was to proceed to Bhubaneswar, skipping Talcher and Tikarpara. The PM's office had conveyed the revised programme to the Chief Secretary who, in turn, transmitted the message to Talcher. It was Biju Patnaik who had forced the PM at Charbatia to go ahead with the earlier programme. He told the PM that lakhs of people waiting to see him would be disappointed if he failed to turn up; the PM yielded. That explained the tired look I saw on his face. He died a couple of months later.

Biju Patnaik was not authorised to overturn the medical advice given to safeguard the Prime Minister's health. He was also not a member of the Prime Minister's family. Yet he was allowed to force a course of action that had severe repercussion on the Prime Minister's life? In better health the PM could of course have decided for himself but his health was known to be failing. Medical advice was clear that the helicopter ride needed to be dropped. Those in charge of the PM's security were duty bound to ensure it but they failed to do so. Does this not highlight the enormous harm that can be caused by interference of extraneous forces?

Chapter 2

In the Secretariat: Finance Department

The order transferring me to the Secretariat carried a caveat that I should move to Bhubaneswar immediately after the Prime Minister's visit in January 1964 without availing the usual joining time of ten days or so. On receiving the order, my sense of importance had shot up. I imagined that I had been specially chosen to undertake a key assignment which required my urgent attention. With an inflated ego I reported to the Finance Secretary, driving down straight to Bhubaneswar, only to face an anti-climax. No work awaited me nor was there a room where I could set-up my office. A room was eventually found at one end of the corridor after a week or so but allocation of work took much longer. My predecessor having gone out of the Department on promotion a month before my arrival, the work had been redistributed among the remaining officers and his room taken over by someone who had just returned from leave. As I look back I feel that the experience of being without work and a room for some time had a salutary effect in puncturing my inflated ego.

The work allotted to me initially was Efficiency Audit—a relatively new type of work in the government, intended to assess the efficacy of programmes implemented by executing agencies. The objective was to evaluate physical achievements rather than focus only on financial outlays and expenditure, which the Audit Departments traditionally did since the British Government days. No IAS officer before me had been assigned charge of the Efficiency Audit Cell. The work was considered unattractive and I was appointed there simply because it was the only slot lying vacant. I was a little disappointed initially but found it immensely interesting as I applied myself to the work. I was able to produce some reports which brought me to the notice of the Chief Secretary, B Sivaraman, an outstanding officer of the ICS who had a profound influence on me throughout my career.

I was soon placed, along with my batch-mates elsewhere, in the senior scale and made a Deputy Secretary. The work assigned to me was to prepare the state's case for presentation before the Fourth Finance Commission. It was an onerous task, often exasperating, but I benefited from it immensely. It gave me the opportunity to study and understand the activities of all departments of the government and to interact closely with them so as to be able to project, adequately and justifiably, their requirement of funds for the next five years, in order that the state might get a favourable devolution of funds from the Union Government. I not only got a comprehensive picture of the activities of the entire government but also a good understanding of the budgetary process. The work brought me much closer to the Chief Secretary than ordinarily possible for an officer with only four years of service, of which two had been spent in training. In a remarkably short time Sivaraman discovered that he could get quicker and better results from direct interaction with me rather than relying only on hierarchical movement of papers. At the concluding round of discussion with the Finance Commission the state team was led by the Chief Minister accompanied by a large body of senior officers, headed by the Chief Secretary.

I was the junior most and the only Deputy Secretary there. Though all the Secretaries were present, it was the Chief Secretary, who answered all queries and explained all issues that came up. He argued our case so convincingly, asking me in between to fill in the details, that at the end of the proceedings the Chief Minister was overwhelmed and complemented him profusely; the Chairman and Members of the Commission also joined in. To my pleasant surprise the Chief Secretary called me out and was generous in saying that much of the credit was due to the 'young man' for excellent preparation of the case. That undoubtedly was an exaggeration because even at the stage of preparation it was he who had guided me. Not only those kind words but also the handsome award which the state got from the Finance Commission came as a huge reward for hard work.

I must add that in those early days when I was in the Secretariat, two persons who gave me enormous encouragement were CG Somiah, who was Additional Secretary in my department and Gian Chand, who too was Additional Secretary, but in a different department. I formally reported to neither of them but whenever I felt a little lost in direct line of Sivaraman's fire, my confidence revived by the soothing words of those two seniors. Another officer, much more senior, who encouraged me and helped in honing my meagre skill in drafting and noting was SK Bose, a former Professor who had been recruited to the IAS at the time of initial constitution of the service and with whom I came in close contact while in the state administrative officers training school (those days at Hirakud), of which he was the Principal.

I had no prior inkling of the nature or content of either of the assignments mentioned above that were given to me or in the Finance Department. No one in the department was keen to do those jobs. Being the junior-most Deputy Secretary I had no choice left. But once started on the job, I plunged in with all sincerity. Soon, I started liking the work and gave it my best effort. What had appeared unattractive initially gave me, in course of time, not only job satisfaction but personal recognition as well. The result was highly rewarding. Later in my career too I had several such experiences that made me wonder why officers lobbied for what they considered attractive assignments and compromised themselves unnecessarily.

This first spell in the Finance Department—two more tenures were to come later—gave me the opportunity also to examine comprehensively the pay structure of the state with a view to removing anomalies that had crept in. I immediately realised that this could not be done without addressing some basic issues. If two groups of officials or even two isolated posts in different organisations had equal pay scales in the past and for some reason the parity was disturbed later, those who fell behind nursed a sense of grave injustice and felt that the situation had become anomalous. In the process of removing that anomaly other anomalies came to be created, resulting in a bigger mess. However, I dealt with the grievances that had piled up and was pleasantly surprised to see that my proposals were approved and implemented without any significant modification.

Even in those early days, I had formed a view that there was no need for too many pay scales in the government. There could be just a few scales of pay for all the services and officers of different services could be fitted into different grades depending upon the level of responsibility entrusted to them. That I thought would contribute towards abolition of 'caste system' which ran as an undercurrent among officials of different services creating divisions and discontent. I discussed this matter with senior officers who felt, however, that it would be futile to pursue an idea which had found no favour in the past with either the Central Government or in any state. Accordingly, I gave up the idea of putting across my view formally. After decades I was glad to find that the view I held had gained acceptance through recommendations of successive Pay Commissions at the Centre.

I am tempted to recall how, in an unrelated context, a

light-hearted remark by me in course of a chat with a friend developed into a potentially explosive situation. A close friend of mine, working in the Secretariat, used to drop in for tea in my room. He noticed that a letter from Morarji Desai, then Union Finance Minister addressed to the Chief Minister and marked down to me, was lying on my table for some time. It was on a major issue of federal finance on which the Union Finance Minister had sought the views of state governments. My friend felt concerned that I had not taken prompt action on the letter and submitted the case to the Chief Minister. He was new to the Secretariat whereas I had already watched from close quarters some Ministers and their idiosyncrasies. I made some irreverent remark on Ministers in general and asked my friend why he assumed that Ministers had interest in abstruse issues of federal finance. He responded by enquiring what, in my view, were matters of interest to them.

Those were the days of long periods of waiting for motor cars of which only three models were available in India and getting a car allotted from the government quota was a privilege. Likewise, living accommodation in Bhubaneswar was limited and an officer anxiously looked forward to priority allotment of a suitable house. I blurted out that Ministers' interests lay in matters like allotment of cars and houses. Both of us had a hearty laugh, thought that a good joke had been cracked and I took the matter as closed. Little did I know that my friend had narrated it to many other colleagues!

Several months later, an officer much senior to me dropped in and surprised me saying that he had come straight from the Chief Minister's room to upbraid me for my indiscrete reference to Ministers. He told me that the Chief Minister had sent for him in some connection and as he entered his room the Transport Minister barged in and remonstrated that I was maligning Ministers by making derogatory remarks concerning their preoccupation with the allotment of cars and houses. Luckily for me, the Chief Minister Sadashiva Tripathy, was a kind and mature person. He made light of the situation and persuaded the Minister to enjoy the joke which indeed it was. Since the joke had been shared with many it would have gathered much embellishment by the time it reached the Transport Minister. He had every reason to be upset as he was known to be in the habit of liberally exercising his discretion in the allotment of cars from the government quota. Had the Chief Minister not been endowed with a sense of humour, I would surely have landed in serious trouble. This early warning should have been enough for me to exercise caution in making remarks in future but alas, I failed miserably in restraining myself. There were to be many more occasions in my service career in which I made irreverent remarks about seniors. Luckily no one took serious exception to them and I escaped unhurt.

My early brush with corruption at high places occurred during this tenure in the Finance Department. This was soon after I had substantially completed my special assignments and was handling a part of the normal work of the department. One day a file of the Irrigation Department came to me in normal course with their proposal to purchase 12 crawler-tractors at a cost of about Rs. 25 lakh—an amount that may appear small now but was quite a large sum in the mid-1960s. Examination of the proposal in the Finance Department had revealed that the approved budget of the Irrigation Department had no financial provision for the proposed purchase. I suggested that the proposal be turned down because no case had been made out to treat it as unforeseen or emergent.

My Secretary tried to strike a compromise by suggesting purchase of six instead of twelve units. He submitted the file to higher-ups and the proposal to purchase all the twelve units was ultimately agreed to. Soon thereafter the file came back to us, this time with the condition for the payment of 90% of price as an advance. On scanning the papers I founded that even the supplier had not asked for any advance payment; instead his offer letter in the file had stipulated that 90% of the price should be released by the government once the crawler-tractors were actually supplied. I highlighted that portion of the supplier's letter and recorded my view that no advance payment was necessary. Since I differed with the proposal of Secretary (Irrigation), a much senior officer, I submitted the case to my Secretary (or perhaps the Additional Secretary) for approval and he agreed with me. In spite of this, the supplier was favoured with the advance payment which ultimately became a total loss to the government as no supply was ever made. On getting the advance payment the supplier celebrated at a party (perhaps in his home town, Vijayawada) and losing restraint under the influence of liquor, boasted loudly to friends how he had managed to befool the Government of Orissa. This was overheard by some political activists who alerted opposition leaders in Bhubaneswar and the matter was raised in the Assembly which was in session. There was severe criticism of the government over what appeared to be a big scandal. After a lot of dilly-dallying, the Government of Orissa was forced to ask for a CBI enquiry. It was only when the Investigating Officer showed me the file and revealed to me the background to the entire matter, after he had made sure that I was not a part of the scandalous deal, that I came to know of the involvement of high functionaries.

A dinner hosted by the Chief Minister in honour of a visiting Union Cabinet Minister (who hailed from Andhra Pradesh) apparently provided the forum to kick start the process that ended up in the scandal. All the senior officers who had given a helping hand were present at that dinner; I was not senior enough to come to reckoning. Those who did the paper work in the Irrigation Department found the demand for the advance payment so compelling that the payment was made by them despite the Finance Department's disagreement recorded in my note, which had the approval of my Secretary. To cover up this grave irregularity they hit upon a strategy to misrepresent things by saying that notwithstanding my written disagreement, I had orally agreed to the advance payment subsequently.

That obviously was a lie. I was not even competent to overturn our recorded advice which had the approval of my senior and even if I did exceed my limit, rules of procedure required my written confirmation. Be that as it may, the CBI found adequate material to prosecute a number of persons including the Secretary (Irrigation) on a number of charges. That case, in which I was called upon to give evidence, dragged on for years. The officers involved suffered long periods of suspension and severe indignity but the Ministers remained unscathed. Giving evidence against a senior officer charged in a criminal case was by no means a pleasant task. I had to face stiff cross examination by the defence counsel who was a well known criminal lawyer and a former Minister. Luckily no pressure was exerted on me outside the court room to tone down my evidence which was crucial.

Before moving to the next phase of my experience I would like to recall a series of events which I was fortunate to have witnessed in my early days in the Finance Department. Biju Patnaik, after demitting the office of Chief Minister under the Kamraj Plan, had become Chairman of the newly constituted State Planning Board. His close friend and confidant, Biren Mitra, who succeeded him as Chief Minister, had willingly ceded to Patnaik the position of pre-eminence in the administration, for which reason Patnaik was being referred to as 'Super Chief Minister'. As Chairman Planning Board, he found the Third Five Year Plan of the state, already settled with the Planning Commission during the preceding President's Rule, inadequate for the state's development needs. He asked senior officers to get down to the job of having the size of Orissa's State Plan doubled. The initial official response predictably was that the Planning Commission would not approve it and Orissa was not in a position to mobilise more funds. Patnaik's reaction was characteristically reflective of his phlegmatic personality. He shot back a note mentioning that he was not willing to accept defeat even before an attempt. The Planning Commission refused to assist. But Patnaik was determined. He kept pushing the officers and ultimately achieved a substantial increase in the State's Third Plan outlay.

He also took the bold initiative of starting construction of

Paradip Port in the state sector when Government of India declined to support our proposal for a major port at Paradip.

The Railways refused to provide a rail link between the port and the mining area in the state to enable export of iron ore. But Patnaik was undeterred; he got a 150-kilometre long Expressway constructed entirely by the state to move ore to Paradip in large trucks specially designed for the purpose. Only long after the project was made operational, the Centre took over Paradip Port and turn it into a major port with supporting facilities including rail link with the hinterland. The fully functional port and several other projects and institutions that Biju Patnaik set-up first as Chief Minister and thereafter as Chairman Planning Board now stand testimony to his dynamic leadership. But did he do it all by himself? He certainly gave the lead and the vision. It was the bureaucracy headed by an exceptionally competent Chief Secretary that not only had the ideas translated into feasible programmes but also ensured attainment of the objectives. As a young officer I had the privilege of watching all this from close quarters in the state Secretariat.

Thirty years later, the same Biju Patnaik became Chief Minister once again and remained in that position for five years. But this time he hardly left any footprint on Orissa's development, despite having acquired not only enormous administrative experience and political clout but also a tall national stature. What then was the reason for that lack of success? Had his governance skills declined or was it the bureaucracy that did not measure up; perhaps both. It is therefore no wonder that a mega project intended to be set-up by POSCO of South Korea in the vicinity of Paradip, which could have brought a massive investment of US $ 12 billion, has languished for years.

I have gone too far ahead in my narrative and must get back. After spending over three years in the Finance Department I was pleasantly surprised one day to get orders for my District posting.

Chapter 3

As District Magistrate

The assignment to which a young administrator looks forward most keenly is that of District Magistrate. I was also not an exception. The district which had been given under my charge was Sambalpur, a large and important district, now split into four. A piquant situation arose soon after I joined. The district headquarters town, also named Sambalpur, had a local tradition of celebrating the annual Rath Yatra of Lord Jagannath, perhaps in a manner different from that observed in Puri, the seat of the main Jagannath temple. This festival came so close to my joining the district that I had no time to get briefed on the arrangements made by the administration. The local SDO also was new to the place and not briefed. On the day of the festival, late in the afternoon, I was informed that although the deities had been installed in the ceremonial chariot, tension was building up as organisers had refused to allow the chariot to be pulled by the devotees. I immediately held a meeting with the SP and other officials of the district and was informed that there had been some serious disorder in the previous year, for which the police had filed a criminal case against members of the Organising Committee.

On enquiring into the composition of the Committee, I was surprised to find that it was headed by a distinguished citizen who had retired some years earlier as Additional District Magistrate and was known to me personally. When I spoke to him over the phone he told me that there was strong resentment against the police, which had passed an order under Section 30 of the Police Act, preventing the pulling of the Lord's chariot without prior permission. It was the police, and not the Organising Committee, which was standing in the way of the celebrations by insisting that a fresh application be submitted for permission to conduct the Rath Yatra festival, as Section 30 was in force. The Organising Committee was unwilling to apply as they felt that they had been treated unfairly by the police a year before.

I was aware that Section 30 was a provision intended to be enforced for a short period only and not in perpetuity. Its extension beyond a specified period required the prior approval of the District Magistrate. When I wanted to know the period for which the proclamation under Section 30 had been made, nobody could recall anything clearly, until the officer-in-charge of the police station produced the relevant file. A glance at the papers was sufficient to make one shudder at the casual manner in which the law had been trivialised. The order under Section 30 had been promulgated years earlier, for a purpose which could not be gleaned from that file of dog-eared papers. The law stipulated that any proclamation under Section 30 would remain valid for a period not exceeding thirty days and extension beyond that period required the specific approval of the District Magistrate. In this case, successive Superintendents of Police had gone on extending the period routinely without ever having submitted the papers to the District Magistrate. I was amazed at the cavalier attitude. But soon I realised that the solution to the problem had come effortlessly.

The problem was a creation of the administration itself and obviously it had a duty to provide the requisite solution. I concluded that since the order under Section 30 had been extended without observing due process, it was no longer valid; the organisers of the festival were therefore under no obligation to seek permission of the police to take out the procession. After discussing the implications among ourselves, the SP and myself together went to the place where Lord Jagannath, mounted on his car, had remained stationary while thousands of devotees seethed in anger, squeezed into a narrow road along which the car was to be pulled. They had been held back from pulling the car for hours by a ham-handed administration under a false notion of maintenance of law and order. The anger was justifiable and the tension in the atmosphere was palpable.

Grim faced members of the organising committee hesitantly greeted us not knowing what our next step was going to be. I was first stunned at the size and mood of the crowd but recovered soon and started addressing the congregation using a quickly assembled public address system. The gist of what I said was that judging by the solemnity of the occasion and the disciplined conduct of the congregation that had endured heat and dust for hours, the SP and I had decided that there was no need to be rigid about formalities and that pulling of the Lord's car could commence without further delay. There was a spontaneous roar of approval and the festivities resumed with the usual blowing of conch shells and beating of drums. A major problem, needlessly inflicted by the administration, was diffused. I received my first lesson in a real time management of law and order.

An issue concerning the tenancy rights of villagers around the periphery of the Hirakud Dam reservoir was another opportunity for me to view a problem from the standpoint of the aggrieved. When the dam was constructed in the mid 1950s, the government had acquired all the lands that were going to be submerged, on payment of full compensation. Where inhabited areas would not be submerged even when the water level in the reservoir would be at its highest, the villagers were left undisturbed, although much of their land holdings were acquired to provide an adequate margin of safety, in case of seasonal fluctuations in the reservoir level. Except for a few months during the rainy season, thousands of acres on the periphery would remain fertile for raising crops and villagers were allowed to cultivate them, even though they had no ownership rights over the land. A practice had grown of the local administration giving farmers permission to raise crops on annual lease. This arrangement worked satisfactorily for years but a sense of insecurity and unrest arose when the state government announced that the lands in question would be given away to the Central Government for the establishment of a large seed farm.

Tension grew among the affected villagers. Anticipating possible escalation in unrest I camped in the area, access to which was quite difficult in those days. After extensive interaction with the people I was left with no doubt that the government's decision, taken without ascertaining facts on the ground, would severely affect the livelihood of several thousand families and was patently unjust. I could convince the villagers that sincere efforts would be made for reconsideration of the decision. On return to headquarters a detailed report was sent by me to the government, giving reasons why the well established practice of allowing the villagers to raise crops should continue and the seed farm confined to a limited area which was not in dispute. Later on, I was informed that my report luckily reached the government soon after the Revenue Department had questioned the authority of the Agriculture Department, who had unilaterally announced the government's intention to transfer the periphery land to the proposed Central Seed Farm.

The turf war between the two departments was decided ultimately on the basis of my report which addressed the substantive issue of livelihood of the people of the region. I must add that in this case as well as in the matter of the Rath Yatra, timely action by the administration brought credit to the government and left no scope for politicisation. While the first case demonstrated the efficacy of an alert and assertive district administration willing to defuse a self-created problem without standing on false prestige, the second illustrated how a publicised government decision could be got reversed by a District Officer, reporting authentic realities with conviction, leaving no scope for political exploitation of a potentially explosive situation. A third case, summarised below, will indicate the futility of motivated pressure in the face of a firm and principled stand, irrespective of the relative authority of individuals or institutions.

My biggest problem in handling corruption, as a District Magistrate, was with the Civil Supplies department. The country was facing food shortage and great emphasis was being laid on procurement of food grains in surplus areas such as my district to build up stocks for public distribution. There was a need to prevent stockpiling by unscrupulous traders who indulged in black marketing. The District Civil Supplies Officer (CSO) and staff under him were primarily responsible for enforcing laws and implementing government policy but there was much to be desired in this matter. Tired of their feeble approach, I set the anti-corruption Vigilance police in action. The Superintendent of the Vigilance Police, a friend of mine, personally selected with care some targets where stern deterrent action could be taken. Once the requisite evidence was compiled, I decided that immediate action was warranted in a particular case to take into custody a well known trader under the preventive detention law then in force.

The desired impact was achieved and local response was appreciative. But, the Civil Supplies Department in the secretariat at Bhubaneswar was upset. I started getting telephone calls accusing me first of causing panic in the market. Since I stuck to my position firmly, the accusing tone changed into persuasion to have the trader released. I could clearly see that, short of speaking to me directly, the Minister for Civil Supplies was trying hard to pressurise me through senior officers of his department. The District Magistrate's power to keep a person in preventive custody was, I think, limited to twelve days beyond which the detainee could not be retained in jail without the state government's approval. Despite knowing the Minister's interest in the trader I sent my proposal for continuance of the detention though I did not have much hope for its approval by the government. I have been informed that the Chief Minister, who alone was competent in the matter as the Home Minister, was inclined to approve but ultimately yielded to persuasion by the Civil Supplies Minister. However, I was glad that the Chief Minister did not order the trader's immediate release or curtailment of the period of detention to less than twelve days. After that the CSO and officers under him became a little more alert although they enjoyed powerful support at higher levels in the department.

The related issue of food procurement for public distribution came up for consideration shortly thereafter at a Collectors' Conference in Bhubaneswar. Those days were prior to the Green Revolution, when the country faced severe food shortages and was hugely dependent on imported wheat from USA. Although Orissa was a food surplus state, several pockets were deficit in food grains. Elaborate arrangements were in place to maximise the procurement of rice so that not only could the requirements of the deficit areas be met within the state but surplus grains could be supplied to the central pool administered by the Government of India. A traditional method employed extensively in those days was the establishment of check-gates to control the movement of food grains, to facilitate procurement in surplus areas. Procurement targets were assigned to each district and Collectors were made responsible for fulfilling their respective target.

Sambalpur district was food surplus but the neighbouring district of Sundargarh, with the Rourkela Steel Plant in it, was acutely deficit in food grains. Check-gates had been set-up at the border to prevent movement of paddy from Sambalpur to Sundargarh. Since there was a wide margin of difference in the free market prices of paddy in the two districts, it was highly profitable for traders to move stocks across the border to Sundargarh. Smuggling, and the associated corruption at check-points, had assumed disgusting proportions; particularly at the check-gate near Jharsuguda on the Sambalpur-Sundargarh border. At the conference of Collectors I pleaded for the removal of the check-gates and strongly advocated free movement of paddy between the two districts, so as to ease the supply constraint in Rourkela and eliminate corrupt practices at check-gates. The Chief Minister RN Singh Deo, who was presiding over the meeting, appeared persuaded by my argument that feeding Sundargarh district was also the responsibility of the state government, and since I was confident of fulfilling the procurement target for my district, the government should have no objection to my proposal for abolition of the Jharsuguda check-gate, which had become notorious.

The Minister of Civil Supplies, however, was stubbornly in favour of continuance of the existing practice and my proposal was rejected. I returned disappointed to my district, but determined to render the Jharsuguda check-gate 'unproductive' for people in high position in Bhubaneswar. Instead of staying back at home in Sambalpur, I proceeded straight to the Jharsuguda check-gate and obtained a solemn promise from the staff that, until and unless they received any further orders from me in person, they would have to ensure that not a single truck carrying paddy or rice crossed over to the other side, either with or without a permit. I left after giving them strict instructions that all trucks carrying paddy or rice were to be detained and samples of what they carried were to be sent to me for verification. I was aware that a clandestine practice was rampant of trucks carrying milled rice being allowed to cross over to Sundargarh district at the Jharsuguda check-gate on the strength of permits certifying the product as 'hand-pounded' rice, which was exempt under the Movement Control Order.

To reinforce accountability, I told the staff that I would be specially deputing an officer from the district headquarters to keep a strict watch at the check-gate. Even before I could send any such officer, the first batch of samples arrived with a report that a convoy of trucks carrying rice had been detained at the check-gate. I hurriedly set-up a committee of three officers, including the District Civil Supplies Officer, to examine the samples, secured their report that there was prima facie evidence of violation of the Movement Control Order, and deputed a specially selected officer to Jharsuguda with authority to seize the trucks. What this officer reported to me from Jharsuguda was startling.

He spoke to me over the phone and gave a graphic account which, briefly stated, was the following: before the officer reached the check-gate, an Additional Secretary of the Civil Supplies Department, who had come all the way from Bhubaneswar, had pressurised the check-gate staff to release the trucks. However, they refused to do so, pleading that they were duty bound to keep the trucks detained until the Collector gave them the release order. The arrival of my officer with the seizure order gave the check-gate staff immense relief. The Additional Secretary first tried to brow-beat my officer but backed off after the seizure order was served. I was deeply touched by the loyalty of the staff at the check-gate although I had only a single meeting with them. As for my own officer, there was never a doubt about his loyalty or integrity.

The Additional Secretary was, of course, an interloper who had no business to try to bypass the Collector in approaching the staff at the check-gate, ignoring even the District Civil Supplies Officer. Senior officers like him, too keen to please the powers that be, are the worst offenders who destroy the edifice of governance. He made a hasty retreat from the check-gate saying that he was going to protest to the Collector but never saw me on his way back to Bhubaneswar. This single incident brought to a sudden halt the illicit movement of rice across the check-gate although I knew that after a few days it would be business as usual again because the temptation was too compelling. On further enquiry it transpired that the consigner of the seized rice was a person wielding considerable influence over the Civil Supplies Minister, who was understandably angry that the Collector had the temerity to upset the cosy working of his department. The Minister was shrewd enough not to speak with me. Instead he got me summoned by the Chief Minister, who was heading a coalition government. The Civil Supplies Minister belonged to the party of the coalition partner. I admired the way the CM resolved the problem. He first asked me to send the samples of the seized material to the laboratory at Bhubaneswar for an expert opinion, to confirm whether or not the rice was hand-pounded.

The Civil Supplies Minister was immensely pleased because he was confident that the laboratory, under his department, would give a favourable report. The CM then recalled the discussion at the recently concluded Collectors' Conference and asked the Civil Supplies Secretary to issue orders removing the check-gate at Jharsuguda, on an experimental basis, for three months. The Minister did not object; he was glad that the problem in which his department was enmeshed stood resolved and he was still left with many other check-gates. I too was happy that a totally avoidable obstruction to free movement of food grains, serving as a bottomless pit of corruption, was removed. My procurement target was exceeded sooner than expected. In due course all intra-state check-gates set-up to assist in the procurement of food grains were abolished, though it took a long time.

A major law and order situation which arose during my tenure in the district owing to unrest among engineering students is worth recounting. Those were the days of widespread dissatisfaction among engineering graduates for want of suitable employment opportunities; many graduate engineers had to work as junior engineers for years because there were no vacancies for graduate engineers. This led to an all-India strike by engineering students. Those of the engineering college at Burla, in my district, had predictably joined the strike. After a few days of peaceful demonstration the strike was called off by the all-India Action Committee, to whom some assurance was given by the Central Government. We expected the strike at the local engineering college also to an end. The student-leaders, however, decided to meet the Chief Minister at Bhubaneswar, before returning to their classes and proceeded there. But the Chief Minister declined to see them on the ground that they had not taken prior appointment, with the permission of their Principal. They came back with severely bruised egos and instead of returning to classes, picketed close to the college, bringing traffic on the National Highway, connecting Kolkata and Chennai, to a standstill. The police tried in vain to persuade them to disperse and then informed me.

I proceeded to the spot immediately and found a huge traffic pile-up on both sides of the Mahanadi Bridge where the students were picketing. Instinctively (although some people disapproved it) I mingled with the crowd and was able to reach their leaders. I tried to persuade them to end the agitation so that traffic could move on the busy National Highway. At first they insisted that they would not disperse until the Chief Minister came and apologised for the insult he had inflicted by not meeting them in Bhubaneswar. Later, they softened somewhat saying that they would not insist on an apology but the CM must come to explain what he intended to do to enlarge employment opportunities for them. By then I had already been in their midst for over an hour. Tension was building up as dusk was setting in and it was getting dark. My officers, who were at a distance along with the police force, were apprehensive that the agitating students might have made me captive, which they could easily have done. That also was the concern of a senior officer, held up in the traffic at one end of the bridge, who sent me a message through a local officer asking me to desist from further negotiation and have the crowd dispersed forcibly. But I was unwilling to use force on the students.

They were totally peaceful although with badly bruised egos, and the location of the picketing was such that, if provoked by police action, many would have been seriously injured and some might have fallen over the bars on both sides of the bridge into the river flowing underneath. I continued to engage them and eventually succeeded in getting them to disperse, on the assurance that I would personally convey their feelings to the Chief Minister. Engaging a large number of agitated students for hours was strenuous but I felt rewarded at the end because the protest ended without any police action. On my return home late in the evening I spoke with the Chief Minister who, having been briefed already by his staff, complemented me on my patient handling of the situation. He felt greatly relieved that the protest, directed against him personally, had ended peacefully. He assured me that he would send the Secretary, Planning Department, to Sambalpur to explain to the students what the government was doing for them. The Secretary arrived within a day or two and we had extensive interaction with a representative group of students in a very cordial atmosphere.

We all expected that normalcy would be restored. But our expectation was not realised. A radical section of students prevailed over the others and decided to continue the agitation. For a day or two there was apparent calm but the students did not go back to their classes. They blocked the highway again and also stopped the movement of trains on the railway line running close to the highway. They chose the time of approaching dusk to mount the agitation which clearly indicated pre-meditated action. The Superintendent of Police had already stationed abundant force at the nearby police station and we both proceeded to confront the situation head on. This time I remained at some distance and addressed the students over a public address system. While I was speaking to the students, explaining what the government was trying to do to mitigate the problem of unemployment, to which there could not be any instant solution, the SP deployed the police force to disperse the crowd by force, the moment an order was given. It was already dark and a lot of people from the neighbouring area had assembled as onlookers.

I was keen to ensure that force, when applied, was the minimum necessary and only after giving adequate warning to the agitators and onlookers. The police force had been briefed suitably. I repeatedly called upon the agitators to disperse, failing which police would be forced to act. I also announced that if they did not listen to me, I would withdraw and ask the SDO to deal with them in accordance with law. Finally, I stepped back, ensured that the police unit equipped with firearms remained close to me so that there was no cavalier action by trigger-happy policemen, and instructed the SDO to take the microphone, declare the assembly of agitators unlawful and have them dispersed. The place from where we were addressing the people was well lit. When they saw the SDO holding a microphone, the onlookers went away, anticipating imminent police action. But the agitators remained and started brick-batting, after which the SDO ordered the police to disperse the unlawful crowd. The police then began a Lathi charge. Soon thereafter, I heard the sounds of blast and flashes of light in the night sky, resembling gun shots which, on verification, turned out to be crackers fired by the agitators themselves to send a misleading impression to the people that they had been fired upon by the police.

The agitators who had taken over the leadership had indeed done careful planning to discredit the government even without much of an issue! The dispersal operation did not take much time with hardly a dozen people, students and policemen taken together, sustaining minor injuries. All this happened in the darkness of night, when police action against even a violent crowd is looked upon with suspicion and disapproval. The State Assembly was in session at that time. I had expected severe condemnation of the government, the district authorities in particular, for the action taken. The fact that a low key protest by the Opposition in the Assembly was easily silenced by the government came as a pleasant surprise. People in Sambalpur had realised that the district authorities had dealt with the striking students with patience and restraint. Even the student community in general, at this university town with several other colleges, did not agitate against the police action and refrained from joining a protest which a misguided group of radicals tried to organise, but gave up due to lack of response. Normalcy was restored in the engineering college sooner than expected.

News-reports of police high-handedness, particularly against the weaker sections, always abound. This is by no means new. The colonial administration made extensive use of police power to safeguard its imperial interests. Any challenge to its authority was firmly curbed. But the colonial masters also needed peace and a sense of security among the people over whom they ruled. To that end they provided internal checks and balances within the administration to prevent excesses. District Magistrates, charged with the overall responsibility of governance in their respective districts, were vested with powers to oversee police administration so that they could intervene at the local level to prevent excesses and avoid unnecessary problems. After independence, with greater emphasis laid on welfare and development, District Magistrates became preoccupied with developmental activities and gradually withdrew from general supervision over the police. An impression gained ground that DMs need not bother themselves with police matters. This by no means was the spirit of the law. An incident described below illustrates how a pro-active role by the DM in the vital matter of armed police deployment could prevent an industrial relations issue from escalating into a bigger confrontation in a District.

A large paper mill in a remote part of my district was beset with labour problems which had led to a strike, followed by lock-out by the management. The situation had been further complicated after the murder of a leading labour leader who, the workers believed, had been got killed by the management to frighten them into submission. Antagonism hardened on both sides and conciliation efforts failed. The Conciliation Officer, while briefing me in the matter, gave vent to his feeling that the management was proving unreasonable as they believed that continued lock-out under police protection would break the back of the strike. He added that the mill had a history of repressive management practices, gave me a few instances thereof, and requested me to intervene as he apprehended that the ongoing agitation might turn violent. I advised him to resume conciliation in my presence. On interacting with both parties in the resumed conciliation I found that the management, which was clearly at fault, first tried to prolong the agony of the workers whose demand, apart from a fair and speedy investigation into the murder of their leader, was only for modest improvements in working conditions.

After prolonged discussion the management agreed to lift the lock out and the workers, led by the local Communist MLA, assured full cooperation. It was also agreed between the management and workers that there would be no victimisation or threat. I promised to ensure proper investigation of the murder case to enable early trial of the guilty. Later that day, as I was about to speak with the SP on the progress of investigation of the murder case, I got a cryptic note from him to the effect that there was apprehension of serious labour trouble at the paper mill, for which he had already sent the Armed Police Reserve (APR) to the mill and I was required to depute a Magistrate to be stationed with the police force. I was taken aback because at the meeting in my room only a few hours earlier there was no hint of any breach of peace. I rang up the SP, explained to him in detail what had transpired at the meeting that very morning and told him that the sudden appearance of APR at the mill could vitiate the prevailing peaceful atmosphere and provoke the workers unnecessarily. I advised him to call the APR back or ask them to halt midway at Jharsuguda Police Station.

I found the SP reluctant to go by my advice. I was aware that he had exceeded his powers by ordering the APR to move out of headquarters without the approval of the DM but I refrained from rubbing it in. But when he persisted in his reluctance to cooperate, I told him that he should take my advice as an order of the DM, offered to follow it up with a written order and did so immediately.

I had taken an unusual step; many would consider it even inadvisable. But I had a genuine impression that someone in the police was unfairly taking the side of a management determined to brow beat its workers into abject surrender. I decided that rather than wait passively for further developments, I should take some pro-active measure. I rang up the SDO, gave him a detailed briefing and requested him to proceed to the mill and speak with me from there after assessing the ground situation. He acted promptly, drove through the night, crossing the river by an inspection trolley over the rail bridge, and rang me up from the police station located at the mill gate shortly before daybreak. He assured me that everything was fine and there was no apprehension whatsoever of any breach of peace. The officer-in-charge of the police station also spoke with me. He informed me that far from any tension, there was in fact jubilation among the workers at the prospect of immediate resumption of normalcy at the mill, and there was no need for any additional police force. The SDO stayed on until work at the mill was resumed later in the morning and continued peacefully. The SP, a decent person, realised that he had erred in ordering the APR to move. This event, which followed a few weeks after the Rath Yatra incident narrated earlier, only reaffirmed the utility and importance of the District Magistrate's role in ensuring good governance as mandated by law.

The high point of my days at Sambalpur was a visit by the President of India, Dr. Zakir Hussain who came to lay the foundation of Sambalpur University. A few days before his visit I read in a news magazine that he had a keen interest in roses and fossils. There was a government farm in my district where the Manager, a lover of roses himself, had some beautiful roses. He took charge of floral arrangements at the Guest House, overlooking the Hirakud reservoir, where the President was to stay overnight. I had no worry on that score but could not think of anyone who could help with fossils. The District Mining Officer had fallen far short of my expectation in his normal work and I had written him off as 'Good for Nothing'. There was no point, I thought, in expecting any help from him. Nevertheless I told him half-heartedly about the President's interest in fossils and left it at that, expecting no result. He promptly disappeared and did not surface until the day of the President's visit.

The Governor and the Chief Minister had arrived that morning to receive the President and I had gone to the Guest House in advance. When I arrived there I saw in a side room a beautiful display of a variety of fossils which would impress anyone. I was informed that the Mining Officer had set it up. At the airport I mentioned the President's interest in fossils and roses to the Governor and the Chief Minister. They spoke approvingly of the flower arrangements which they had already noticed at the Guest House but showed complete disinterest in fossils. During the President's drive to the Guest House I travelled with his Military Secretary (MS) and mentioned to him that some fossils had been collected but neither the Governor nor the Chief Minister appeared inclined to present them to the President. Knowing the President's interest, the MS asked me to keep the fossils in readiness and leave the rest to him.

The President had a busy schedule, in the midst of which there was some time for tea at the Guest House. It was there that the MS whispered something to the President. He immediately stood up and was ushered to the room where the fossils had been brilliantly displayed. The President was visibly impressed and made no secret of his child-like joy at seeing the fine collection. The Governor and the Chief Minister were pleasantly surprised. Not only did the President gave me handsome compliments there, and again at the airport when we saw him off the following day, but I also got a letter of appreciation from him. The important lesson I learnt from this episode was never to under-estimate anyone and never consider a person to be 'Good for Nothing'. I got the handsome compliments for presentation of the fossils but I knew that it was entirely on account of the quiet efficiency of the Mining Officer, a self effacing person whose talent I had failed to detect.

Soon after the President's visit I received orders posting me back to the Secretariat, in the Finance Department again.

It did not come as a surprise because I had already received a hint from the Chief Minister, during his brief visit to receive the President, that I might be called back to prepare the state's case for presentation to the Fifth Finance Commission, which had just been constituted.

Chapter 4

Back to Finance Department

The Finance Commission assignment and the related work was by no means new to me. My seniors in the Department had confidence in me and I needed little guidance. We also had a new Chief Secretary, AK Barren, a transparently fair administrator recruited to the IAS on initial constitution of the service at the time of independence. His style of work was entirely different from that of his predecessor, B Sivaraman who was my role model but in retrospect I feel that as Chief Secretary, Barren with his laid back style but sterling character, unimpeachable integrity and admirable fairness, was perhaps as successful as Sivaraman. I was also glad to see that my Secretary in the Finance Department, KS Bawa, a brilliant officer, was still there, giving me the opportunity to work with confidence and autonomy. The result was highly rewarding; the award Orissa got from the Finance Commission was as good as on the previous occasion under the Fourth Finance Commission.

As Joint Secretary, I was also placed in-charge of many other functions of the Finance Department, more importantly the Budget Division. The state budget was still being prepared in accordance with a manual prepared under the colonial regime when government business in the Secretariat could be transacted in a leisurely manner. With the advent of Five Year Plans and emergence of the practice of Annual Plan discussions with the Planning Commission, the finalisation of schemes by different departments of government became a much more elaborate exercise, leaving very little time for scrutiny in the Finance Department at the pre-budget stage. To enable timely presentation of the budget in the State Assembly, budgetary allocations for Plan schemes had come to be made by the departments concerned without adequate financial scrutiny. This had reduced the Budget virtually to a compilation of schemes unexamined by the Finance Department.

To overcome the infirmity, individual Plan schemes were being referred back to the Finance Department for scrutiny after approval of the Budget by the Legislature. Followed by queries and clarifications, a large part of the new financial year was being spent in back-and-forth movement of papers before administrative departments could issue sanction orders after the Finance Department had completed its scrutiny. This practice left much less time for implementation of schemes at the ground level. The result inevitably was shoddy implementation or surrender of budgeted funds and often both. I found this system unacceptable.

After detailed interaction with my colleagues, we prescribed a revised procedure for pre-budget scrutiny of schemes. The new procedure envisaged that for the purpose of budget formulation, details of schemes would be sent to the Finance Department not in the traditional manner of file reference leaving little time for pre-Budget scrutiny. Soon after finalisation of the Annual Plan of the state, Secretary of each administrative department would convene a meeting with designated officers of Finance and other departments concerned, where financial details of the schemes of that department would be settled by discussion and those details would be incorporated in the Budget for presentation to the

State Legislature. Minutes of those meetings, signed by the authorised officers, were to serve as clearance for implementation of the schemes after legislative approval was accorded. Through this process we were able to do away with much avoidable movement of papers back and forth among different departments and substantially increased the time for implementation of the schemes during a financial year.

This was a radical departure from the Budget Manual. Ordinarily, such a reform would have required prior approval of the Finance Secretary, as well as the Minister. But I had gone ahead without seeking any higher approval. When the matter came to the notice of JS Baijal, who meanwhile had taken over as Finance Secretary, far from upbraiding me for exceeding authority, he encouraged me to take many more initiatives. It was a privilege for me to work under such a person who carried his enviable competence lightly on his shoulder and gave opportunity to younger colleagues to grow.

The reform not only made more time available for the implementation of schemes but also brought about another desirable change. The pre-Budget meetings, chaired by Secretaries of different administrative departments gave them opportunity to better appraise and appreciate the schemes of their own departments which, in the usual process of paper work which often amounted to quibbling over inanities, had the tendency to escape broader view.

Shortly, afterwards, I was appointed concurrently Joint Secretary in the Planning Department as well. That enabled me to secure better coordination and streamlining in the working of both departments, where there was a practice of each repeating the same exercise already done by the other in the process of giving clearance for implementation of Plan schemes.

While I was glad to work in both departments, one day I was surprised by the Chief Secretary showing me a telegram from the Government of India asking for my services to be placed with the Centre. The state government had not offered me for Central deputation. I was therefore not prepared mentally to shift to Delhi at that stage. However, on learning from the Chief Secretary that the telegram had come at the instance of the Cabinet Secretary my hesitation disappeared. I felt happy that Sivaraman, my mentor and ex-Chief Secretary who was now the Cabinet Secretary, had got me posted as Deputy Secretary (Economic Coordination) in the Department of Cabinet Affairs, directly under him. That gave me a wonderful opportunity to grasp the working of the vast machinery of the Government of India, particularly in the growing field of economic administration.

Chapter 5

At Cabinet Secretariat

Those were the early days, following Bank Nationalisation, when Prime Minister Indira Gandhi had embarked on a host of economic measures to assert her brand of socialism after splitting the Congress Party in 1969. PN Haksar had joined as Secretary to the Prime Minister and had also brought PN Dhar as Officer on Special Duty to the Prime Minister's Secretariat but the PM's Office (PMO) had not yet become all-important at that time, as it turned out to be in course of time. Haksar initially leaned on the Cabinet Secretary, perhaps in deference to the enormous administrative experience of the latter.

The Cabinet Secretariat, a small and rather sleepy organisation earlier, started buzzing with activity. My job was to serve the Committee of Economic Secretaries where all important issues relating to economic policies and their implementation were thrashed out. Unlike the states, where Chief Secretaries have supervisory control over Secretaries, the Cabinet Secretary, Government of India, was considered first among equals. Secretaries to Government approached him only when they needed help or guidance. With increased emphasis on economic issues, the Committee of Secretaries became a major device to enable the Cabinet Secretary co-ordinate activities of different Departments and agencies of the Government.

In the matter of coordination, I am tempted to recall here an anecdote concerning Sir Raghavan Pillai, ICS, whom Jawaharlal Nehru had sent to London shortly after independence to study the working of the Cabinet Office there. This was a part of the preparatory exercise in the setting up of a Cabinet Office in Delhi where the colonial administration had not set-up an equivalent office for us to inherit. At the conclusion of his study, Sir Raghavan had a meeting with the British Cabinet Secretary whose name, if I remember correctly, was Lord Hankey, who had served with distinction as Cabinet Secretary for many years. Sir Raghavan, referring to the complexities and vastness of the far flung British Empire of that time, enquired of Lord Hankey how he managed to cope with the problem of co-ordination, which must have been most challenging. In reply, Lord Hankey said with a hearty laugh that far from being challenging, co-ordination was the easiest part of his work because matters, when they reached him, came already well co-ordinated. On return to India, when Prime Minister Nehru was told about this, he too had a laugh but agreed with Sir Raghavan that in Indian conditions it was necessary to institute a system for co-ordination at the highest level, since co-ordinated action could not be taken for granted. The Committee of Secretaries was the answer provided by Sir Raghavan when he set-up the Cabinet Secretariat.

Sivaraman, was able to secure inter-Ministry co-ordination by energising the Committee system with extra-ordinary effectiveness. His grasp of development administration, anticipation of long-range implications of measures advocated by busy bodies to please the PM and candid expression of views were greatly valued. He was also a stickler for enforcement of routine. I remember how, on finding laxity in the recording of papers, he took enormous pains to activate all Ministries to ensure meticulous observance of the Records

Manual and laid great emphasis on preserving the 'memory of Government'—an expression he often used. Had the established practice not been neglected in later years, the country could have been saved the regrettable experience, not so long ago, of Prime Minister Manmohan Singh conceding responsibility in the Parliament for wrongly appointing a tainted officer as Chief Vigilance Commissioner. The officer, it may be recalled, needed to be removed by the Supreme Court because crucial papers concerning the allegation against him were missing from the dossier placed before the appointing authority.

During my four year tenure (1970-74) in the Department of Cabinet Affairs at the Central Government I served two more Cabinet Secretaries: T. Swaminathan (ICS) and BD Pande (ICS). They too had exceptional qualities and each one of them contributed to the shaping of my character and personality. During my tenure as Deputy Secretary I was also witness to the gradual decline in the pre-eminence of the Cabinet Secretariat. Haksar, the redoubtable Secretary to PM, had a towering personality with a prodigious mind. He was an ardent advocate not only of socialistic policies but also of committed bureaucracy. Above all he was close to the PM; senior officers preferred to toe his line. Under him, and thereafter, the PMO became the focal point of administration; the Cabinet Secretariat was overshadowed.

This concept of committed bureaucracy marked the beginning of an imperceptible trend of ambitious officials cultivating political elements perceived to be close to the fountainhead of power. Young officers, keen on career prospects, started looking for closer association with those who could commend them for positions of trust and power on the basis of personal loyalty rather than competence and integrity. Adherence to norms and established procedures came to be derided when seen as impediments to accomplishing tasks that were neither welfare-oriented nor in the public interest. The salutary principle of civil service neutrality was getting eroded slowly but surely. As if to reinforce these trends and weaken the higher civil service, the report of the Administrative Reforms Commission headed by Hanumanthaiah was released around that time, severely limiting the role of the IAS in the system of governance. Not that it was promptly put into operation, but it did exacerbate the sense of insecurity among officers who believed in the principle of rule of law rather than loyalty to a personality cult. On looking back, it appears that the breakdown of governance that we now see, had its origin in the pernicious concept of committed bureaucracy which, was promoted those days and perfected during the black days of Emergency Rule.

Chapter 6

In Newly Liberated Bangladesh

An unforgettable experience of my days in the Cabinet Secretariat was the war of liberation culminating in the creation of Bangladesh. Soon after the war started and blackout was observed in Delhi owing to bombing by the Pakistan Air Force in the western sector, I was speculating one day, along with a batch-mate of mine who also worked in the Cabinet Secretariat, how exciting it would be to work as District Magistrate in a border district rather than pushing papers in the Secretariat! Soon thereafter, a message came that the Cabinet Secretary wanted me to see him immediately. I thought he might ask me to write a paper on economic co-ordination to strengthen war efforts but that was not the purpose. On my entering his room he first put me at ease and started explaining to me how our army on the eastern front had entered Pakistani territory faster than expected, liberated substantial areas of erstwhile East Pakistan and urgently needed civilian officers to restore normal administration in the liberated areas. He then went on to say that since working conditions there would be both challenging and risky, choosing officers for the purpose was left to random selection through the computer based on laid down criteria, and my name had come up in the process. He added that a few more officers would also be sent but he anticipated resistance on the ground that some of them were already engaged in war efforts in their respective departments and could not therefore be spared. He went on to say that he would like to forestall resistance by demonstrating that if the Cabinet Secretariat could spare its officer no one else would have any justifiable reason for foot-dragging and enquired how much time I needed to move. I offered to proceed any time I was required to do so.

He rang up the Defence Secretary, ascertained the departure time of the next courier flight of the Air Force to Kolkata and asked me to be at the airport by 1 p.m. or so, leaving me hardly two hours to pack and get ready for a mission of indefinite duration. I rushed home, picked up a few clothes and proceeded to the airport without having had time even to assemble a bed-roll, which I procured in Kolkata.

After elaborate briefing at the Eastern Command Headquarters in Kolkata I joined an army convoy, carrying an identity card which said that in the event of being taken prisoner, I was entitled to be treated as a Prisoner of War under the Geneva Convention. Some consolation indeed! The convoy deposited me late in the afternoon at a place called Kushtia, headquarters of the district of the same name in erstwhile East Pakistan, now Bangladesh. The Fourth Division of the Indian Army, to which I stood attached, had liberated the district of Kushtia, adjacent to West Bengal, the previous day after a decisive battle. I stayed in the Circuit House which had been converted into the Officers' Mess of my Brigade Headquarters but worked from the District Office which I found deserted, except by a few junior officials. The District Jail was empty and the police practically nonexistent. All the senior officers of the district, including the District Magistrate and Superintendent of Police, had gone into hiding, not knowing what our attitude towards them would be. Armed groups were roaming around looking for reprisal against collaborators of the previous regime, avoiding contact with Indian Army. Fortunately, we had the overwhelming support of the local population of East Pakistan.

My first priority was to get back the DM and the SP, assuring them, through different channels, of their reinstallation with dignity. They were both Bengalis, known to have covertly nursed sympathy for the liberation movement. I was therefore keen to have them resume duty and help in the early restoration of normalcy. But it took them a few days to surface after gaining sufficient confidence. Meanwhile, I learnt that about two hundred Bihari Muslims had taken shelter in a mosque fearing reprisal by members of the Mukti Bahini, the local militia that led the movement of liberation from Pakistan.

The apprehension of the Bihari Muslims, who had never identified themselves with the local population, much less participated in the liberation struggle, was understandable. They had migrated to East Pakistan from Bihar without any affinity to the local population, were in the habit of looking down upon the local Muslims and had actively collaborated with the Pakistan Army in their ruthless repression of Bengali Muslims. The local population was naturally seething with anger against the Biharis. Our intervention was imperative to prevent their massacre. With a small Army contingent I entered the mosque, led the Biharis into the vacant District Jail and kept them there in the protective custody of the Army. Sometime later, they were transferred to centralised camps specifically created for rehabilitation of Biharis.

The next major task was to disarm the gun-toting groups of Mukti Bahini volunteers roaming around on streets. By making use of our army personnel we could have tackled them effectively but we did not wish to expose our soldiers to any operation against the civilian population. My effort to have them disarmed picked up momentum and succeeded after the DM and the SP resumed duty, following the surrender by the Pakistan Army. Shortly thereafter, Shaikh Mujibur Rehman, the towering leader of the liberation movement, returned from incarceration in West Pakistan and took charge of his newly created country amid tumultuous welcome by the people. There were extensive celebrations and great jubilation all around in East Pakistan.

An experience of mine, just when the war of liberation ended with jubilation all around needs to be told. On fall of Dhaka and announcement of cease fire, we in Kushtia learnt that while the main body of the Pakistan Army would formally surrender at a function in Dhaka, there would also be a ceremonial surrender at Faridpur (Divisional Headquarter of Pakistan Army facing us) to the General Officer Commanding of my Division. The Colonel attached to me suggested that I should also proceed to Faridpur, which was at a distance of about 100 miles, to witness the surrender and both of us proceeded there. We had timed our departure expecting to reach Faridpur shortly after our infantry men arrived there to disarm Pakistani soldiers. As we approached the outskirts of the town, we noticed from a distance fully armed personnel gathered in large number in an open space on both sides of the road. We took them to be our men but as we came closer we discovered that they were khaki clad soldiers of the Pakistan Army. The Colonel, who was driving our vehicle, instinctively stopped and alerted me of the possible danger of our driving into a large body of defeated soldiers fully armed, who were fighting against us bitterly until less than 12 hours before.

The alternatives before us were either to make an about turn or proceed ahead to link up with our army personnel who might have come by a different route. We opted for the latter. The 15 minute drive through dour looking, six feet tall soldiers of the Pakistani Baloch Regiment in full battle gear, angrily staring at us, was a chilling experience. The road took us straight to the Pakistani Divisional Headquarters where the officers received us as advance party of the Indian Division, which we clearly were not. On contacting our Divisional Headquarters we had been informed that there had been a change of plan. We decided to return but only after savouring the delectable snacks and coffee served to us in great style. The service was in shining silver set served by smartly dressed bearers in sparkling white. As we drove back, I reflected how compared with the luxurious life style of officers of the Pakistan Army even in battlefront, the facilities available to our officers were plain and simple at Kushtia and even at the Divisional Headquarters; and that perhaps was among the factors which gave our army an edge over their adversary.

After the war ended we embarked in full steam on restoration of law and order. Getting back the administration on its feet, however, was quite a job. Once normalcy was restored, it was no longer necessary for me to actively participate in general administration, which the district officials were competent to handle. But there was acute shortage of essential commodities, causing intense suffering to the people. Supplies had to be brought in from India. I restricted myself to ensuring that distribution of the available supplies was fair and equitable. This entailed extensive touring of rural areas and I availed of the opportunity to interact closely with the common people. An interesting incident of those tours is worth a mention.

While discussing with a group of villagers during one of my visits, I noticed a few persons huddled together at a short distance, engaged in animated discussion. Curious to know what engaged them, I asked an accompanying district official to find out. He reported, after our return to the district headquarters, that the subject of the discussion had been whether I could really be the CSP-level officer that I was said to be. The Civil Service of Pakistan (CSP) was the Pakistani equivalent of the IAS. The CSP officers, drawn mostly from West Pakistan, whom these simple folk had seen earlier, hardly ever descended to the level of common villagers. They had maintained the image of the old colonial masters and were seen in East Pakistan as instruments of oppression.

The officer accompanying me went on to add that even they (the local officers at the District Office) were struck by the informal and friendly manner in which IAS officers like me and others, assigned to neighbouring districts, could so comfortably interact with the common people, unlike the overbearing and condescending CSP officers. My response to him was that only a vibrant democracy under enlightened leadership could have a sobering influence on officials and we had been fortunate in having tall leaders like Nehru and Patel, whose influence in shaping the higher civil services had not worn out entirely. During the three months which I spent in Bangladesh there were many other interesting experiences, some of them risky and exciting. But the memory I cherish above all is the sense of pride I felt, as an Indian, on winning the esteem and affection of the emotional people of a newly liberated nation.

Only after my return to Delhi I could be able to find out how I came to be in the zone of consideration for the Bangladesh assignment. The laid down criteria were: Bengali-knowing officers, in the seniority range of Deputy Secretary, with prior experience of serving as District Magistrate, not belonging to West Bengal cadre of the IAS (which was already over stretched). The criteria laid down were no doubt appropriate. The procedure of picking up individual officers was also salutary—computerised random selection. How I wish this method, adopted forty years ago when computerisation was in its infancy, for an assignment which was unattractive and patently risky, was also subsequently used extensively for the placement of officers in general and particularly for jobs that were sought after!

While I was working in the Cabinet Secretariat, I was selected for a short course of two months or so at the Economic Development Institute of the World Bank in Washington DC. The course was to commence towards the conclusion of my tenure in the Government of India and it had been agreed that I would revert to my state after completing the course in the USA. I had planned my journey accordingly and was waiting for the air ticket. At that stage I was informed by the Department of Economic Affairs that my candidature was withdrawn at the last moment to enable someone else to join the course. This came to me as a big surprise and disappointment too, but I was quickly reconciled to it as there was nothing I could do about it.

A few days later, at a party to bid me farewell at the end of my tenure, the Cabinet Secretary enquired when I would get back to my state after completing the course in Washington DC. I replied that I would report at Bhubaneswar within a week or so after my relief from the Cabinet Secretariat. He was visibly surprised as he did not know of the last minute cancellation of my selection for the course. He asked me how it had happened but I was not in a position to clarify; I was so disgusted with the last minute withdrawal of my name, for no ostensible reason, that I had not bothered to find out how the mischief was done.

Chapter 7

Back to State: Planning Department

I went back to Orissa and joined the Secretariat as Additional Secretary (Planning). Having already worked in that department as a Joint Secretary, prior to my deputation to the Centre, I did not have much difficulty in picking up the threads again. But hardly a fortnight had passed when I was informed, by a phone call from Delhi, that I should keep myself in readiness to proceed to Washington DC, to join a course at the IMF Institute, this time of a longer duration. The caller was the same officer who had informed me about my earlier selection and its subsequent cancellation for the course at the World Bank. When I enquired if I was again going to be tossed around and embarrassed at the last moment, he assured me that there was no such possibility as the Cabinet Secretary himself had intervened. He had found out that the shabby treatment given to me was done under pressure on behalf of the officer who replaced me at the World Bank course. The Cabinet Secretary, BD Pande, saw to it that I was selected for the next course at the IMF Institute which was decidedly more attractive, particularly because the IMF paid for my wife's travel as well. I marvelled at the interest which the senior most civil servant in the country (BD Pande) took in setting right a wrong done earlier, that too without my pleading. It served as a valuable lesson that guided me later in the life.

Chapter 8

At IMF Institute

The course at the IMF Institute was on Financial Analysis and Policy. The participants, some of them very senior officials, were drawn from both developed and developing countries. The Faculty was composed of professionals of high intellectual calibre. I benefited greatly from them as well as from interactions, we had with some experts of international repute who were invited as guest speakers. An issue that came up at one of these sessions may be of an interest even now. A participant from a country just liberated from a colonial power, questioned a guest-speaker on the impact of unfettered international trade on less-developed countries and made scathing remarks against the practices of multinational companies. The guest-speaker, an American, was unable to appreciate the sentiment of the participant or understand the soundness of his logic. He sought intervention from other participants. Instead of entering into the economic merits of laissez-faire, I interjected by mentioning how multinational companies that had, in the past, come to trade had stayed on to rule, taking advantage of the political situation. I gave the example of the East India Company.

The speaker dismissed my remarks by stating that colonialism was a thing of the past and had no relevance to the modern world. I promptly rebutted him by explaining that although colonialism in the classical sense was no longer prevalent, economic disparity among countries continued to give rise to the dominance of some countries by others. The Bangladesh war of liberation was still in my mind and I recalled how the US Seventh Fleet had been ordered to move to the Bay of Bengal to prop up a repressive regime by pressurising India to desist from participating in the war to liberate East Pakistan. I said that if the Indian Army had not moved fast to secure surrender by the repressive regime, the people of Bangladesh would have continued to suffer repression under the regime of Pakistan similar to colonial exploitation. I got strong support from several others, including participants from Bangladesh as well as some European countries. The participant from Pakistan, however, quietly withdrew from the seminar room. It was agreed, in conclusion, that free trade was beneficial only when disparity among the trading nations was minimal.

Apart from class room lectures, seminars and freewheeling discussions, we had many field visits and much useful exposure to the working of many of the US federal institutions in different fields of economic administration. We also had the benefit of enjoying orchestras, plays and operas featuring internationally admired artistes. Rejuvenated by a highly useful six-month-course at the IMF Institute I returned to my state cadre.

Chapter 9

Back to Planning

On my return to Orissa in February 1975 I resumed work on my earlier position as Additional Secretary (Planning); the post was lying vacant since my departure. Several officers junior to me were now holding full charge as Secretary in other departments and an impression gained ground that I had been bypassed. Even my immediate boss, the Secretary of the Department, thought that the Chief Minister (Nandini Satpathy) was perhaps not pleased with me. But that was not my perception. As the posts of Secretary and Additional Secretary carried the same scale of pay, I genuinely felt that there was no cause for grievance.

The period spent in the Planning Department was, however, brief for me. After a couple of months I was posted as a Secretary (Labour), to head the smallest department of the Government. Even that was interpreted to mean that I was not in the good books of the Government. My friends and well-wishers, including some very senior officers, commiserated with me. I was touched by their sympathy but there was really no need for it as I had no feeling of neglect. I firmly believed that officers, particularly at higher levels, should work with equal vigour irrespective of the relative importance of posts. Treating placements with a measure of indifference, irrespective of the perceived importance of any position, would provide, apart from peace of mind, the possibility of enjoying the work assigned to them.

Chapter 10

As Labour Secretary

As Labour Secretary (1975-76) my tenure was also brief. When I looked back, I felt that a couple of incidents of that period contributed greatly to my will to withstand high level pressure. Strange as it may appear, the very first provocation came from the judiciary, the Orissa High Court in particular. About a week after my joining the Labour Department, a decision of the High Court came quashing an order issued by my predecessor that an industrial dispute between the Orissa State Electricity Board and its labour union did not merit reference to adjudication by Labour Court under the Industrial Disputes Act. On ascertaining the facts I found that the impugned order was in fact most appropriate in the given circumstances, though it had been clumsily drafted and did not appear to have been properly reasoned out.

I also found that while the High Court was competent to set aside any order of the Government, it had no jurisdiction to direct the Government to decide the substantive issue involved one way or another—that is to say, whether or not a dispute needed to be referred to adjudication was a matter which the Government alone was competent to decide, but the decision had to be given in the form of a reasoned order. Therefore, I felt that all that was required was a fresh application of mind and issue of a cogently reasoned order in support of whatever decision was to be conveyed. I did exactly that; drafted the order myself, got it vetted by the Law Secretary and issued the order, again refusing reference to adjudication as done earlier.

Some days later, I got a phone call from the Advocate General anxiously asking why I had not responded to a notice of contempt issued by the High Court. As I had no idea of any such notice, I promised to call back after ascertaining facts. Soon thereafter, he called me again to say that meanwhile he himself had found out that I could not have given reply to any notice because no notice was issued; the Court had initiated contempt proceedings against me without even asking me to explain why action should not be taken against me. I was advised that the only course left for me was to prepare to answer the charge. The Advocate General and the Government Counsel (my friend GB Patnaik, who many years later became Chief Justice of India) both assured me that I had done nothing wrong nor did I do anything that could even remotely attract the charge of contempt of court. I was informed that the party aggrieved by our order had also filed a petition, perhaps a writ petition, challenging the order that I had issued.

On appearing personally before the Court I learnt from the Government Advocate that the Court adjourned the case and rejected his request to dispense with my personal appearance on future dates. Strange as it might appear, the case was never heard; only adjournments came one after another. Meanwhile, lobbying started at the political level. First it was my Minister, a decent man, who one day casually enquired how the case was progressing and after explaining by me that there was no progress, he suggested that I might consider referring the dispute in question to adjudication and be done with the entire matter. He did not press me hard that day and asked me to get back to him after giving serious consideration to his suggestion. On the next meeting, when I met him, I explained the legal position and told him that reversing our decision while the matter was *sub judice* would only strengthen the charge of contempt, but he was unimpressed. He let out, perhaps unwittingly, that the opposite party had assured him withdrawal of their petition in the event that we reversed our order and that it would be followed by the contempt charge being dropped. This time the Minister was insistent but I held my ground.

After a few days it was the Chief Minister Nandini Satpathy, who enquired about the case. She too would have been glad if the matter was amicably settled but did not pursue it when, after explaining the legal aspect, I politely submitted that it would not be desirable to amicably settle with an attacker brandishing a dagger in the form of a case slapped against a formal order of the Government when we were on firm grounds. I was fortunate that the Chief Minister was open to reason. Even so, pressure on me continued through informal channels; but I stood firm.

My personal appearance in the Court continued until a new Chief Justice came to the Orissa High Court on transfer, perhaps from Delhi. After the Government Advocate presented a gist of the matter, the new Chief Justice promptly ruled that the contempt proceedings need not be considered until the substantive matter contained in the writ petition on the same issue was decided; he also exempted my personal appearance in the court. In due course the writ petition was dismissed and the contempt matter dropped. Since then I have a healthy contempt for 'contempt proceedings'.

The shadow over the higher judiciary of unhealthy liaison between lawyers and judges, which a distinguished judge of our Supreme Court bemoaned many years later, is by no means of recent origin. The real cause of the contempt proceeding against me, as I came to understand, was not any infirmity in the order that I had issued nor even any remote expression of disrespect for the Court. There was no way the order I had issued could be overturned by the judiciary; the only way open was to pressure the Government into submission for which no effort was spared. Those were the black days of Emergency, notorious for emergency excesses, when one could have looked up to the Judiciary for protection of one's rights but here was a case of high-handedness by the Judiciary itself under the garb of contempt of court, a clear case of judicial excess terminated only when a new Chief Justice came to the Orissa High Court on transfer.

Another incident which helped to shape my attitude and strengthened my ability to withstand undue pressure was related to a serious unrest of workers at a major industrial establishment. The grievance against the management was genuine and the conciliation machinery was unable to rein in the management. A person close to the Chief Minister, working through my Minister, was able to persuade me that nothing short of intervention at my level would normalise the situation which was deteriorating fast. I got myself fully briefed by the Labour Commissioner and advised him to get the senior management to me; union representatives were in any case available on call. The negotiations were protracted as the management was proving intransigent but ultimately they climbed down. However, a totally unexpected development occurred just when a settlement was in sight.

The same person at whose instance my Minister had asked me to intervene, requested that I may soften the terms to the management's advantage. What led to this change of heart is best left to imagination. I explained that the terms of settlement had been thrashed out after protracted negotiations and it was not desirable to reopen settled issues. The Minister sent for me and employed his ample persuasive talent. On my expressing inability to reopen the negotiation he cautioned me that I might be displeasing the Chief Minister too. As it happened, I was summoned to the CM's presence where the person who had got me into the negotiation was also present. I explained the position for the third time that day. On answering the CM's question if nothing more could be done I replied that I should be happy if she herself sent for the labour leaders, whom she knew personally, and ascertained if anything less was acceptable to them. I must give the credit to the CM that far from showing any sign of unhappiness or impatience, she promptly asked me to go ahead with the settlement as negotiated by me. She was known to be a strong-willed person keeping the bureaucracy on a short leash. Her letting me proceed with what I had proposed in this case gave me strength.

Being the smallest department of the Government, in Labour, my workload was considered light. Whenever a Secretary proceeded on long leave, the charge of his department was added to mine and I thus had the opportunity of gaining experience of many more departments than is ordinarily possible for an officer. One such additional charge was of the Education Department. This department, like the Health Department of which too I had earlier held additional charge, was beset with problems of transfer and posting. The Director of Public Instruction (DPI), a highly respected Professor of admirably mild manners, one day dropped in, with a worried look on his face, and told me that due to his preoccupation with transfer and posting of college professors and school teachers he had not been able to devote himself to the work of introducing the newly evolved 10+2 system of school education due for implementation. Neither new text books were ready nor were teachers recruited, although the Chief Minister had announced in the Assembly a year earlier that the new system would be adopted from the next session which was about to commence. He said that he had requested the Minister to permit deferment by a year but he declined because of the commitment made by the CM and suggested that I should be approached for advice.

The only expertise I could remotely claim to educational planning was a sliver of teaching experience I had acquired as a Lecturer for one season, awaiting entry into the IAS. That was hardly of any use for the work in hand. But putting on my thinking cap I came up with a solution, quite comical but the only one I could think of in the given situation. The solution I suggested was the following: Class XI, which was the final year of the Matriculation system that was prevalent, should be renamed Class XII of the new 10+2 system, the old Class X re-designated Class XI and likewise the old Class II made the new Class I. In the same sequence, the old Class I would have become Class 0 – but as that would appear odd, it could be called Class IA. Text books for all classes would be prescribed by separate orders. All this would be couched in a verbose Gazette Notification conveying the decision of the Government to introduce the new system, with the usual pompous preamble: "after careful consideration of all aspects of the matter".

I was surprised to find that this comical suggestion was entirely acceptable to the DPI, desperate as he was for a solution to meet the approaching deadline. He also agreed to first seek the Minister's approval and thereafter both of them would meet the CM to apprise her before going ahead. The Minister, anticipating the CM's annoyance, wanted me to join them. In the CM's room I had to broach the subject with profuse apology and said that in the circumstances of the situation the alternative being presented was the only course available unless she agreed to defer implementation of the 10+2 system by a year. Peremptorily ruling out any deferment, she asked the Minister to go ahead with the introduction of the new system as proposed and be ready for brick-bats. The new system was notified accordingly but there was hardly any reaction. Public awareness of issues of education was of course seldom articulated those days but I was surprised by the muted response of educationists!!!

Shortly thereafter, the Education Secretary, who had gone on leave, returned. I was preparing to hand over charge to him the next day when the Chief Secretary told me that I should continue to hold charge of both Labour and Education Departments as desired by the CM. I was taken by surprise and requested his permission to seek reconsideration by CM. With the Chief Secretary's permission I met the CM and told her that I was seeking a favour. She looked pleased that at long last I had approached her for a favour. The subsequent conversation was somewhat as follows:

I prefaced my request by explaining that I was happy with my appointment as a Labour Secretary, had also enjoyed the additional responsibilities of other departments given to me for short periods from time to time and could assure her that I would be glad to continue serving in that arrangement. Then I added that the Chief Secretary had sprung a surprise by announcing that Government wished to saddle me with the Education Department on a regular basis. I pleaded for reconsideration, as I clearly visualised that I would prove extremely inconvenient to the Minister who had to manage numerous requests for transfers and postings of a large number of teachers of schools and colleges.

The CM interjected by responding that the Education Minister too wanted me to continue as his Secretary. I replied that it might be so for the time being but if I continued as the Education Secretary on a long-term basis I would insist on transfers and postings following clearly spelt out norms, which could come in the way of the Minister's exercise of unfettered discretion. The CM responded by asking me sternly what I intended to do if Government did not accede to my request for reconsideration of my proposed posting. I blurted out that I would apply for a long leave. She immediately asked me, again with a stern look, what I would do if my request for leave was turned down. My impulsive reply was that even though I had about twenty years of service left, I might submit my resignation.

Having blurted out words to that effect, I felt sorry that I might have offended the CM and was apprehensive that I could be thrown out of the room. But I saw a sudden change of expression on her face which turned distinctly benign and what she said to me became a source of great strength and encouragement. The gist of what she said was that many of my colleagues approached her, through different channels, seeking bigger charge and greener pastures; it was a pleasant surprise to see someone declining a much larger department which Government was offering. She added that she was also glad that I did not enjoy dispensing favours of transfer and posting.

I mumbled some words of both gratitude and apology and came back with a sense of relief. Shortly thereafter, I was posted as Secretary, Finance Department; the largest Department then and perhaps now too. Incidentally, the same Chief Minister had posted me as Labour Secretary, to the smallest of the departments. The same friends and well-wishers who had earlier commiserated with me now came to offer congratulations. One of them, a good friend, enquired what miracle I had performed to get into the good books of the Chief Minister. I replied that while I never felt that I was in her bad books, there were just about two occasions when she had evinced interest in matters concerning my Labour Department functions and on both occasions (described above) I had been unable to deliver.

I also apprised him of my conversation with the CM in the matter of posting as Education Secretary. After an intimate discussion he conceded that many of our problems arose because some of us willingly departed from norms in pursuit of petty privileges and political leaders took advantage of that weakness. But a well-intentioned Minister or CM also needed officers of integrity and ability; it was for the civil servant to choose the category to which he wished to belong. The huge deficit in governance that we are experiencing now is due to two sets of facts: not only has the number of officers willing to compromise increased but there is also a dearth of political leaders genuinely committed to good governance.

Chapter 11

As Finance Secretary

The Finance Department was by no means unfamiliar to me. I had already worked there as a Under Secretary, Deputy Secretary and Joint Secretary. I therefore joined as Finance Secretary with a degree of self-confidence that enabled me to address immediately issues of streamlining the department's work and procedures. According to earlier practice, the Budget Division of the department used to be busy mostly at the Budget preparation stage and thereafter financial control was exercised through the Expenditure Division where schemes and expenditure proposals were sanctioned individually. I was convinced that this not only led to divided responsibility but also uneven workload. Likewise, the work of certain other Divisions needed to be rationalised. A comprehensive reorganisation of the department was therefore, carried out in the first few weeks of a longish tenure (1976-81).

My next important mission was to put an end to the practice of bunching of withdrawals from Government Treasuries towards the end of March, which marked the close of the financial year. Much of the year used to be lost in the movement of papers back and forth, leaving less time for the actual implementation of schemes. As a result, field officers found it difficult to utilise the money provided in the Budget. To prevent the consequent lapsing of funds, a pernicious practice had evolved of authorising withdrawal of unutilised money from the Treasury towards the fag end of the financial year for incurring expenditure later. The rush of withdrawal not only put enormous pressure on the staff engaged in disbursement at the Treasury, but more importantly provided ample opportunity for mistakes and misappropriations.

The Finance Department was not blameless in the chain of events. Although circulars were issued ritualistically from time to time, sanctimoniously deprecating this practice, no firm action was taken to put a stop to it. The root cause of the malady was avoidable delays in the issue of sanction orders, starting with another avoidable practice of making budget provision for schemes "subject to scrutiny at the time of sanction", to which the Finance Department was a party. Delays were thus built into the wasteful practice that inevitably led to leisurely issue of sanction orders, in most cases in the second half of the year, with a large number being bunched together at the very end.

In my previous tenure in the Finance Department, the old process of making budgetary provisions subject to further scrutiny at the time of sanction had been substituted by interactive sessions of pre-Budget scrutiny, where the Finance Department's concurrence was recorded in the minutes of meetings taken by Secretaries of administrative departments. Budget provisions were made accordingly and further scrutiny was made redundant to avoid delays. There was hardly any justifiable reason for administrative agencies to issue expenditure sanction on the closing days of the year, but the practice had regrettably continued.

After joining as Secretary in the finance department I had seen a startling report that on the preceding 31st day of March, Rs. 5 crore (a sum much larger than then and now) were drawn in cash from the Treasury at Bhubaneswar, late at night, for disbursement by an improvised channel because the disbursing staff had got exhausted and could not work longer. An equally disturbing part of the report said that accounts for the questionable disbursements which continued well beyond midnight, had not been squared up even after several months. As the Finance Secretary I made a firm resolve to prevent any such thing happening during my tenure. Strict instructions were issued, and repeated several times, right from the month of January that, except in emergent cases, no sanction order should be issued in the last week of March; further, Treasuries were instructed not to accept bills for encashment beyond normal hours on the 31st of March.

The experience of that fateful 31st of March remains permanently etched in my mind. At about 9 p.m. that night, when I was about to sit for dinner, a group of messengers descended at my house. They were the 'Treasury Sarkar', whose job was to present bills at the Treasury and collect money for utilisation by their respective government agencies. Their grievance was that they could not draw large amounts of money as disbursal at the local treasury had just been closed. I was surprised that disbursement had continued that long despite instructions to the contrary. But the more surprising part for me was their demand for special arrangements for resumption of disbursement as done in the previous year. I ruled that out and tried to reason with them that no one could fault them if funds lapsed because they had done their duty as messengers and had even represented to me. But my words fell on deaf ears as they had a keen interest in getting cash in their hands. However, they left when they realised that I would not relent. The matter was far from over though.

A short while later, I was summoned to the Chief Minister's residence. There had been a change of Government and Nandini Satpathy had been replaced by her Finance Minister Binayak Acharya, who continued to hold the Finance portfolio. On entering the sitting room I found the CM sitting on a large sofa, flanked on either side by two prominent

Ministers. A fine gentleman and polite to core as the CM was, I was softly asked by him if something could be done to alleviate the problem of massive lapse of funds if further disbursements were not allowed. I explained the entire background, emphasised the serious charge that could be made of our abetting in misappropriation of public funds and cautioned against relaxing firmness to put an end to the pernicious practice of taking liberties with the exchequer. I assured him that I would reallocate the lapsed funds out of next year's budget and augment it suitably by seeking supplementary grants in due course to prevent any loss to ultimate beneficiaries.

The CM seemed inclined to accept my view but the two of his Ministers kept egging him on. Just at that time a phone call came from the Editor of a widely circulated Oriya daily to the Chief Minister. The Editor was also a former Finance Minister of the State. He was anxious about the grant-in-aid to a college which would lapse if disbursement was not resumed. The CM had a few words with him and then passed on the phone to me. I struggled hard to convince the Editor that he had nothing to worry about as I would ensure that his college got the amount the very next day out of the sanctioned Budget for the new financial year but he appeared unconvinced. The two Ministers present renewed their charge against me and did not refrain from warning the CM that Government would have to face stinging news reports and editorials in the widely read daily whose Editor had just spoken to me.

While the conversation continued, I slipped into the ante-room, rang up my Joint Secretary looking after Treasury matters, asked him to stand by for an important instruction from me and returned soon to the room where the CM was still being pressurised by his colleagues. Addressing the CM with utmost respect I told him that I could appreciate his predicament and had therefore asked my Joint Secretary to stand-by to organise disbursement at that late hour. The Ministers immediately sprung to their feet and shook my hand expressing immense happiness. The anticlimax followed soon as I told the CM that the following morning he would have to find a new Finance Secretary as I would be unable to function effectively any more.

The CM's response was magnanimous and statesman-like. He got up, placed both his hands on my shoulders, and said in his usual measured tone that he had not yet permitted me to take any action whatsoever and was not going to ask me to resume disbursement. Thereafter, addressing his colleagues, he spoke kind words about me and advised the two Ministers never to pressurise their officers. The pressure was really on him and he bore it admirably. How I wish there was such enlightened leadership now!

But, the Binayak Acharya ministry was short-lived as President's rule was imposed in all Congress ruled states including Orissa, soon after the Emergency regime at the Centre was replaced by the Janata Party Government led by Prime Minister Morarji Desai. A fresh election was held in the state and the Janata Party came to power with Nilamani Rautray as CM; the Finance portfolio went to Ramprasad Mishra who, in course of time, became a pillar of strength to me. Several officers were reshuffled at the senior level but I was left undisturbed. After a brief pause I resumed work at full steam.

There used to be a practice under which the Accountant General (AG) was required to issue fresh authorisation, called 'Pay Slips', to officers for payment of their salary and other entitlements every time after transfer. This was creating avoidable hardship to field officers owing to delays involved in the process of issue of the Pay Slip. Lower level employees were exempt from this. Their entitlements were determined in accordance with rules and settled by their office locally. I saw no reason why officers at higher levels could not be brought under the same discipline and the AG left to concentrate on a more vital function of audit. To change a practice sanctified by long usage was not easy; here I wanted to take away a function from the AG's office and decentralise it, to be handled by the existing staff in respective state government offices! One had to overcome too many obstacles. Fortunately, the incumbent Accountant General was a forward-looking person who extended full co-operation, much against resistance from his own office. The exercise that eliminated avoidable delay, removed much hardship and put an end to wasteful paper work, was accomplished in record time.

Another purposeless practice that generated a huge amount of paper work each year was the system of creating temporary posts, that continued endlessly year after year but required extension of tenure each year. The number of such posts had multiplied enormously with the advent of Five Year Plans. Since expenditure on staff had to be kept in check, the concurrence of the Finance Department was mandatory before a temporary post could be allowed to continue beyond a year. All that happened in practice was the back-and-forth movement of papers between offices and there were delays of several months before an order could be issued allowing a temporary post to continue.

This was not only purposeless work, generated in practically all Government offices but a large army of temporary staff was put to avoidable hardship, as their salaries were disbursed months after the commencement of a new financial year. An exercise which I had undertaken during my previous spell in the Finance Department had shown that not a single temporary post had been abolished as redundant in the preceding three years; on the other hand, there was an average loss of over 100 days in the issue of orders from Secretariat departments permitting a post to continue. The delay often extended to six months for those at the lowest formation to get their first salary of the year. Thus, large numbers of employees remained without salary for almost half the year for no fault of theirs or any gain to Government. On the other hand there was colossal wastage of stationery and man-hours.

Initially my idea was to declare all the posts permanent,

but that would attract too many rules in force and create an opportunity for adverse comment by uninformed critics in other departments whose views had to be sought. While deliberating various options, it occurred to me that the simplest course of action was to remove, by an executive order within exclusive jurisdictions of my own department, the distinction between temporary and permanent posts for the purpose of their continuance. After all, government rules provided for abolition of permanent posts as well; there was no need to limit the tenure of any temporary post to one year on the assumption that it would not be required next year. After a thorough discussion with my colleagues we instituted a new system. It envisaged that all temporary posts would continue to remain *until abolished*. The new system also required the Head of each office to review his staff requirements at the commencement of a year and record a certificate that the sanctioned posts continued to be needed. All employees were entitled to receive their salary on the strength of this certificate alone, and a copy of the review was required to be sent to the next higher formation for information. It was also stipulated that no Head of any office, be it a Tehsil office or a Secretariat department, would draw his own salary until he had carried out the review for his own office. No reference to Finance Department was necessary in this matter. Where any post was found redundant, the competent administrative authority was free to abolish it.

After issue of these instructions, in the following year I found that the number of references received in the Finance Department alone fell by close to 1.5 lakhs. Since each case used to come to us from the administrative department concerned and was filtered through Heads of departments and their subordinate offices, there used to be at least three additional references for each case that came to us. It could therefore safely be assumed that a single administrative measure (reform is too pompous an expression for it) led to saving of Government stationery and man-hours of 6 lakhs cases annually.

An archaic institution within the Finance Department that called for reorganisation was the Accounts Section, which was almost as large in size as the rest of the Department. It handled drawing and disbursement functions for the entire Secretariat and had a large work-force, larger than several departments of government. The work was entirely of a routine nature and therefore only a couple of junior officers supervised a huge staff. Every now and then there were complaints, particularly from low paid employees, of harassment and delay in disbursement of salaries and other entitlements. My placing a senior officer to strengthen supervision did not help. It occurred to me that a lasting remedy could be found in decentralising the organisation so that each Department could handle its own Accounts work and the staff would be answerable to the Secretary concerned, instead of a remote Finance Secretary.

While details of the decentralisation plan were being worked out, one of my trusted officers cautioned me that the proposed move would be strongly resisted by a small group with vested interests. I had been informed that the amount of cash handled by the Accounts Section was so large that it always had undisbursed money, in the range of around Rs. 20 lakh (a much larger amount in those days). These funds were being used for usurious activities by a few unscrupulous persons, who were advancing money to small traders. As decentralisation would hit these people hard, they were bound to incite, on some false pretext, the rest of the staff to protest.

To meet this possibility, I held several rounds of meeting with the staff. I explained to them that since there was a common gradation list for the entire Secretariat, the proposed decentralisation would not hurt their career prospects at all; on the other hand it would provide them the opportunity to handle different types of work in their respective departments by getting integrated into those departments rather than remaining chained to the drudgery of routine work in the Accounts Section all their life.

The younger sections of the staff were easily won over by

this but a hard core of opponents remained. I was going ahead somewhat slowly with the scheme so as to wear down the opposition, when objection came from entirely unexpected quarters. Two Secretaries, one very senior and the other less so, tried to convince me that the status quo should continue as they felt that the Accounts Section was quite efficient and it served them and their departments well. It was obvious that they had been briefed by the group with vested interests, of which I had been cautioned. After some discussion I told them bluntly that if they appeared satisfied it was because they themselves did not experience the problems frequently faced by the low-paid staff of the departments.

My resolve to decentralise became stronger after that. I apprised the Chief Secretary and my Minister because I anticipated some overt protest by a small section of the staff. Both of them supported me and I went ahead with the scheme of decentralisation. The anticipated protest did happen but it fizzled out in no time because the majority of people welcomed decentralisation. With the Accounts staff thus made accountable to their respective departments, where they were also physically relocated, there was satisfaction all round, barring a few hard core opponents. There was also another unintended benefit. With the shifting of the staff to the respective departments, a large chunk of space vacated by them in the Finance Department, became available to the rest of the department, where officials were badly cramped for want of space. Thus a small step towards decentralisation resulted in multiple benefits. But a major step was still to come.

The colonial system had vested practically all financial powers of the Government for centralised control through the Finance Department, leaving very little financial autonomy to implementing agencies. This did not suit the radically different situation which had been brought about by planned development and adoption of the principles of a welfare state. Financial powers remained concentrated under a false notion that only centralised control over expenditure could prevent waste. What it did in effect was precisely the opposite. By remote micro-management of development schemes it generated among administrative agencies a measure of disinterest in critical financial appraisal of schemes under the impression that it was best left to the Finance Department, although in reality they themselves were in a better position to secure economy as details were best known to them. To justify its role, the Finance Department developed a practice of raising queries which, in most cases, only contributed to massive delays in the process of sanction.

Administrative Departments and Directorates had all been provided Financial Advisers and supporting staff but they were not authorised to exercise adequate power, which remained concentrated in the Finance Department. There was an urgent need for decentralisation of financial approval by delegating powers extensively to administrative agencies. This we achieved by promulgating the Delegation of Financial Powers Rules 1978. By these Rules powers were delegated not only to Administrative Departments but also to Directorates and Heads of Offices below them. Furthermore, all Departments were empowered to delegate their powers to subordinate formations down to the lowest level as required.

The extensive delegation of financial powers, far from leading to profligacy in public expenditure, the main fear that inhibited delegation earlier, actually promoted greater purpose and better discipline in exercise of financial control. Prior to such delegation, Orissa had a long history of revenue deficit in the past; revenues of the state used to fall far short of the expenditure incurred leading to large overdrafts. The delegation of powers, coupled with purposeful budgetary control by the Finance Department, marked a complete reversal of this unhappy trend. Not only did overdrafts were negligible, if at all, but the curse of revenue deficits occurring year after year since almost the inception of the state became a thing of the past. The more striking aspect was that this happened despite substantial increase in developmental outlays and their utilisation, leaving behind the pernicious practice of last minute rush of withdrawals from the Treasury. I hope it continued after I left the Department.

The important event of yet another Finance Commission also occurred again when I was Finance Secretary: the Seventh Finance Commission. They were naturally happy to see that the finances of the state had been put on an even keel. I was of course familiar with the process of preparation of the state's case for presentation to the Finance Commission, having handled this twice before in my earlier assignments in the department. This time, however, the setting of our interaction with the Finance Commission in Bhubaneswar became particularly memorable for me. In a large conference hall the Commission was given the opportunity to interact with the entire higher bureaucracy, along with the full Cabinet headed by Chief Minister Nilamani Rautray.

To avoid mutual contradiction I had taken advance action to brief my colleagues; they were advised to reply only when specifically identified to do so. They were also given their lines to speak in response to possible questions and advised to pause thereafter, allowing me to take over. I had learnt this trick from Sivaraman, my mentor, who had led us to face the Fourth Finance Commission as Chief Secretary. This arrangement worked beautifully. We had a long discussion with the Seventh Finance Commission, who rewarded us handsomely in their recommendations. The Chief Minister and the Finance Minister, who were present throughout, were very happy. The Finance Commission also made no secret of their appreciation.

Sales Tax being by far the major source of revenue of the state, I was naturally keeping a close watch over its collection. At a review of Sales Tax assessments I was astonished to find a huge pendency, far exceeding what could be imagined for a state like ours. It was clarified that about 90% of the pending assessments related not to Sales Tax but Agricultural Income Tax, whose yield was negligible (in the range of just about a couple of lakhs of rupees). The piling up of assessments therefore appeared even more baffling. It transpired that some years earlier, an over-enthusiastic Commissioner of the combined department responsible for administration of Sales Tax, Agricultural Income Tax and a few other minor taxes, had ordered that all those who owned land in excess of ten acres or so should be deemed liable to pay Agricultural Income Tax.

Accordingly, assessment proceedings were initiated on the basis of land records. The field officials knew that it was an exercise in futility but carried on with the assessments. They thankfully took no coercive action and thereby saved the unsuspecting farmers from totally avoidable harassment. But a lot of wasteful paper work continued to be done. I advised the officials to close the assessments that were unnecessarily clogging the departmental machinery and recorded this in the minutes of my meeting. But the assessing officers dragged their feet. The incumbent Commissioner supported them saying that they might be faulted later by Vigilance, which would attribute motives to them. I found that we in the Secretariat had no power to issue formal direction in the matter. Nevertheless I resolved to put an end to the wasteful churning of paper that had been going on for years.

The Commissioner and I together went to the Law Secretary. The latter advised that the best course in the circumstances was to have the Orissa Agricultural Income Tax Act repealed having regard to the fact that the tax was not yielding revenue adequate to meet even the collection cost. I was not too sure of the likely political response to the idea of repeal and hesitantly approached the Minister. He agreed with the purpose but said that since the matter would need to go to the Cabinet, where some Ministers were in the habit of advancing pseudo-socialist principles, he would like to sound the CM before sending up the proposal formally. Meanwhile, he suggested that I should brief one senior Minister, Pradipta Kumar Das who was then the Education Minister, and convince him of the merits of the proposal as he, with his impeccable credentials of a Socialist, would be in a position to silence any possible opposition in the Cabinet on ideological grounds. I had no hesitation as I held him in high esteem for his unimpeachable integrity. After giving me a patient hearing he questioned me bluntly if I was convinced that the proposal was in the genuine interest of the State. On my giving him an unequivocal confirmation, he assured me of his support.

The Repeal Bill had a smooth passage not only through the Cabinet but also in the Assembly. With the enactment of the Repeal Bill all those superfluous assessment proceedings that consumed, year after year, huge quantities of stationery and man-hours were closed and Sales Tax officers could devote more time and attention to productive cases that yielded revenue.

The measures indicated above and many more that were taken, which contributed greatly to better financial management in the State could not have come through if I had not been fortunate in having as the Finance Minister a bold, seasoned and far-sighted person like Ramprasad Mishra who gave me a free hand, provided unstinted support and defended me against unwarranted criticism. He never asked me to do anything against my conscience. I wish there were many more Ministers like him in the country. As a political administrator of long standing he too believed in the streamlining of procedures and delegation of power as important tools for promotion of development and good governance. Encouraged by him and ably supported by my colleagues, I initiated several measures and together we were able to achieve a lot of success. I was fortunate in having with me a number of exceedingly talented officers without whose wholehearted support and commitment it would have been impossible to achieve the level of success that was attained in bringing about financial reform. Two of the officers to whom I remain particularly indebted are MP Purohit and VK Samantaray. The reform measures were many and varied. Narrating them all would be excessively burdensome. I would therefore like to switch to other events.

Public enterprises of the state, like those at the Centre, were generally running at a loss. While many of them were potentially viable, the Orissa Lift Irrigation Corporation did not offer any hope of viability. The Finance Department was therefore, reluctant to meet its ever growing requirement of funds without a proper revival plan. The then Chief Secretary, personally a man of impeccable integrity, had a soft corner for the Lift Irrigation Corporation and was ever willing to support its recurrent demand for funds irrespective of performance. In deference to him I provided substantial amounts but made a firm stipulation that no further amount would be given without a credible revival plan. Even so, a proposal came for fresh release without any plan, which I returned, reiterating the earlier advice.

While I was on an official visit to Delhi the request for funds was referred back, without a revival plan as before, and my Joint Secretary was pressurised into releasing the money. He had of course done this after obtaining approval of the Chief Secretary, placing on record the fact that the latter had asked him to release the funds. I was informed of this on my return from Delhi and I submitted the case to the Finance Minister for his information, as he too was keen on a revival plan as a condition for release of funds. The file did not return to me for a long time but when it did, I was taken aback after reading its contents. The Finance Minister had recorded a terse minute in his own hand mentioning how wrong the Chief Secretary was and emphasising that in future he must not take any decision on behalf of the Finance Department without prior approval of the Finance Minister. He had sent the file to CM who endorsed it to the Chief Secretary for comments and after perusing his comments (which were not recorded in that file) agreed with the Finance Minister.

The Chief Secretary was understandably upset; he also failed in his efforts to have the decision reversed. Unwittingly and for no fault of mine I became the butt of his frustration. A few months later the Chief Secretary was replaced though it had nothing to do with the matter mentioned above. Much later, I came to know that he had made a serious attempt to damage my career. Far from succeeding, however, he had only harmed his own image. But I was lucky not to know anything while my goose was being cooked.

Throughout my service career I never bothered about my Confidential Character Roll (CCR) nor did I ever record an adverse remark on any officer. The Chief Secretary could not find anything wrong in my work or integrity but chose to hit where it would hurt me most. He recorded that he did not have my loyalty, an adverse remark in the worst possible form for a senior officer. In normal course that remark would have been conveyed to me, giving me an opportunity to rebut. But how on earth could I have rebutted a subjective feeling and proved my loyalty? I could have attributed his action to bias but he never gave me to understand that he was biased against me, such was the camouflage! He knew that it was precisely the time for my batch of officers to be assessed for Joint Secretary level empanelment in the Government of India. With the blot of disloyalty stamped in my CCR, it was certain that I would have been left behind. But Providence intervened. The Deputy Secretary dealing with CCR matters under the Chief Secretary happened to be a person who had worked with me years back in Talcher. Having studied me well in those days and watched me later in the Secretariat, he could not be a mere witness to the malice of the Chief Secretary. This relatively junior officer, AN Das, had the courage to take the initiative personally in righting the wrong that was going to be perpetrated. Taking an enormous risk, he confided the matter to two of his colleagues and together they saw to it that the damaging sentence was removed under the orders of the Finance Minister and the Chief Minister, without my knowledge.

They came to me after accomplishing the task which they had cast upon themselves and gave me a detailed account of how they did it. They perhaps succeeded in enlisting the support of the Secretary to the Chief Minister (Mr. Biswal) but never disclosed it to me. I was deeply moved. For me they were the visible instruments of the invisible Lord who guides the destiny of all. This incident, more than anything else, strengthened my belief that if one acts scrupulously according to the dictates of his conscience no real harm can come to him in the long run and in case it does, it should be treated as an accident of life that must not deter one from doing one's duty.

The new Chief Secretary, who succeeded the one who tried to harm me, was not vengeful like his predecessor, but was prone to trying to please where one might expect him to resist undue demands. Soon after assuming office, he asked me to find a solution to a financial crisis facing the Orissa Textile Mill, the first major industry set-up in the state after independence by a private promoter. Since there was no proposal pending with us, I could not figure out what assistance was expected from the Government and told the Chief Secretary so. After a couple of days the Finance Minister called me and on arrival in his room I found the Chief Secretary there, pleading the case of the Textile Mill. It transpired that the Mill had secured a hefty unsecured loan by influencing the CMD of a nationalised bank, thanks to the resourcefulness of the industrialist who had not only promoted and managed the Mill but also rendered it sick by siphoning off funds over a long period.

Inevitably the loan remained un-serviced and came to be questioned by the Reserve Bank of India. The CMD was held accountable for the large Non Performing Asset of the bank and it had come in the way of his appointment by the Government of India to a high position in the Reserve Bank itself. The CMD and the industrialist together had convinced the Chief Secretary, that the problem could easily be solved by the State, providing a Government guarantee for the unsecured loan which the Mill had availed but not serviced for years. The stigma attaching to the CMD would then no longer stand against his appointment in the Reserve Bank. The Finance Minister was given to understand that since it did not involve any outgo of funds from the Government, we could give the guarantee without any strain on the Budget. When this was put to me as a simple proposition, my blood boiled and I blurted out that the State Government's business did not include baling out undeserving CMDs of nationalised banks working in collusion with unscrupulous industrialists. However, I managed to restrain myself soon thereafter and politely explained that while it was true that a guarantee entailed no cash outgo immediately, it constituted a contingent liability which, in the circumstances of the case under consideration, would certainly need to be discharged soon by the State as the bank would invoke the guarantee immediately after the CMD left for greener pastures. I also added that the Government had already lost its own investment in the equity capital of the Mill owing to mismanagement and should not undertake further liability. The Minister agreed with me as the Chief Secretary had nothing more to add. I thought the matter ended there, but I was wrong.

Shortly thereafter, the Union Finance Minister (HM Patel) accompanied by Dr. Manmohan Singh, then Secretary Department of Economic Affairs, came to Bhubaneswar to preside over a conference. During the lunch break, I was asked to join the table where they and the industrialist concerned were already seated. HM Patel began by enquiring about the Mill and expected me to answer. I explained the exact position and added that while it was difficult for the state with its slender resources to rescue the Mill, if the Central Government wished to do so, the problem was a minor matter for them to solve. I felt relieved that the Minister left it at that. Some months later the CMD in question was appointed Deputy Governor of the Reserve Bank of India. I have no idea how the stigma against him was whitewashed.

I would like to recall one other incident that came as a big challenge and helped me to stand firm against unethical pressure by the high and mighty. The state Budget for the year to follow had just been approved by the Cabinet and I was feeling relaxed after a strenuous spell of work. One of those days, perhaps that was a Sunday, on my return from a friend's house my wife told me that several phone calls had come from the Chief Secretary who wanted to speak to me urgently. Before I could call him back, a brief hand written note by him was delivered to me. The note was a direction to me to incorporate in the just approved Budget a provision for introduction of Crop Insurance in the state, as desired by Biju Patnaik who was the then Union Steel Minister and supreme leader of the state Janata Party whose Government I was serving. This came as a surprise because no scheme on Crop Insurance had ever come from any Department, nor was any such idea ventilated by anyone in the Cabinet. The Chief Secretary rang up again, this time to make sure that I had seen the note. I took the opportunity to express my surprise and reservation in the matter to which his peremptory response was that I should carry out orders. I thought there was no point pursuing the matter over the phone.

Next morning when I reached office, I recorded a well reasoned note why I was unable to incorporate in the approved Budget any provision, even a token amount, for a nebulous idea which had neither been formulated into a scheme with any financial estimate nor sponsored by any Department of the Government. I pleaded that the sanctity of the Budget needed protection and ended up mentioning that I would be guided by nothing short of a direction by the Cabinet which could be summoned only by the Chief Minister; even the Prime Minister, not to speak of any Union Minister, had any authority in the matter. I submitted the note through the Chief Secretary for consideration and orders of the Finance Minister and Chief Minister. I did not know what transpired thereafter but next morning Biju Patnaik spoke to me from Delhi. In his characteristic way he tickled my ego and asked how a 'brilliant' officer like me was unable to smuggle in a token provision for an eminently beneficial scheme like Crop Insurance. I explained to him why, with all the humility at my command. When he found me unwilling, he gave up, adding a snide remark on the Chief Minister's inability to conjure up impressive schemes for the benefit of the people. The irony is that even over a decade later when Biju Patnaik himself became Chief Minister of the state again (1990-95), he did not provide crop insurance which he had tried to foist on the state in 1977 keeping an eye on the imminent election which his party lost. That however did not diminish, in my esteem, the enormous contribution he made to the development of Orissa in his first spell as Chief Minister in a brief period of two years (1961-63).

With growing dissension in the Janata Party, a mid-term election to the Lok Sabha became inevitable and Indira Gandhi returned to power at the Centre in early 1980. Soon after that Orissa, along with other Janata Party ruled states, was placed under President's rule and fresh Assembly elections were ordered. With the return of the Congress party to power at the Centre, the Chief Secretary (SMH Burney) was called back and appointed Union Home Secretary. Before leaving the state he gave me a pleasant surprise by issuing a formal letter conveying the Government's appreciation of my steadfast adherence to propriety and unremitting efforts to protect the finances while promoting development of the state. Unlike his predecessor who, placing personal loyalty to him above my loyalty to the state, had unsuccessfully tried to harm me, the departing Chief Secretary did not find any personal affront in my unwillingness to go by his instructions in a few cases where I was convinced that a contrary approach was more appropriate. I salute officers like him.

The Congress Party returned back in the state assembly with a comfortable majority and JB Patnaik, a Minister in the Union Cabinet, came to the state as Chief Minister. I was deeply impressed by the keen interest and driving energy with which he embarked on the state's development. He made quite a few changes in the senior bureaucracy but I continued as Finance Secretary even though I had already been there for four years. Like his predecessor, he too did not retain the Finance portfolio and appointed one of his colleagues in the Cabinet as Finance Minister. The new Minister, a well educated and highly courteous person, addressed officers of the Department at a meeting specially convened for the purpose, soon after assuming office. In course of his speech he laid great emphasis on the need to cut down red tape, delegate financial powers and decentralise administration to accelerate the State's development. I felt happy but when I shared this with a friend, his response was rather cynical. He soon proved right.

In my usual enthusiasm for simplifying financial rules and streamlining procedures I had set for myself a target of at least one such measure a week. One of the earliest cases I sent for the Minister's approval was for deletion of a Rule in the Treasury Code which stipulated that anyone wishing to deposit into the government account an amount exceeding Rs. 500 had necessarily to get the prior approval of the Treasury Officer. This was an ancient provision that had been rendered wholly redundant over time. Deletion of that rule was overdue. Even the Accountant General readily agreed to its deletion when I took up the matter. More important changes in various spheres had been introduced under my orders, but this particular case file had to be submitted for the Minister's approval as it involved amendment of a statutory Code. I was taken by surprise to see the file marked back to me for discussion. The matter was simple and had been explained briefly in a lucid note which was there on the file. I wondered what could be the aspect that had escaped my attention. The surprise that awaited me turned stunning when I met the Minister for discussion.

As I had just started to explain the justification for the proposal, the Minister intervened saying he had no objection to it and signed in token of approval. Thereafter, pushing the file aside, he pulled himself closer to me and spoke to me as if he was sharing a secret. His words were to the effect that if we continued to give up powers we might regret it later, for no one would come to us seeking favours. I was stunned, and wondered if this was the same person who had given us the call, just a few days before, to decentralise, delegate and cut down red tape! The message I got was clear; his words of exhortation at the meeting of officers were not intended to be taken seriously. My friend's cynical response, referred to earlier, proved correct. But that did not deter me from pursuing my pet project of delegation and decentralisation as long as I could do so without involving the Minister. In fairness to him, however, it must be said that he never came in my way and, barring a case or two, supported me when my proposals on important financial issues faced rough weather.

A case that came from the Forest Department soon after installation of the new Government was in respect of revision of royalty on bamboo procured by paper mills. Orissa had extensive bamboo forests which, in those days, were an important source of revenue for the state. If I remember correctly, the practice was to revise the royalty once in twelve years. Renewal had become due while the previous Janata Party government was in power in the state. The Forest department, after protracted negotiations with representatives of paper mills, had referred to us a proposal suggesting a revised rate of Rs. 69 per ton.

In the Finance Department we came to the conclusion that the rate should be around Rs. 100 and suggested, leaving a small margin of error, a rate of Rs. 96 per ton. The figures are still fresh in my memory even after forty years, for the striking reversal of digits in the two rates. The Forest Department disputed the rate suggested by us and asked for reconsideration. Meanwhile there was hectic lobbying, as generally happens in all such cases with large financial implications, and a strategy was worked out essentially to keep officials of the Finance Department out. It was decided that as the matter was important, a Committee comprising the Chief Minister, Finance Minister and Forest Minister would decide the revised rate of royalty, to be serviced by the Secretary, Forest Department.

Expectedly, the Committee approved the rate of Rs. 69 proposed by the Forest Department; the paper mills rejoiced. But unfortunately, the Government fell and the President's rule was imposed before the new rate could be notified. The lobby on behalf of the mills being strong, the proposal was revived during President's rule. It was about to be cleared by the Governor when someone brought to his notice that the draft order put up for his approval did not record the mandatory concurrence of the Finance Department. The case therefore came to us again and I had the opportunity to reiterate once more our earlier view. The Governor did not approve the lower rate. It got stuck the second time.

When the same proposal was revived once more soon after the new Government assumed office, I decided to do some plain speaking before putting up the file. I explained the entire background to both the Finance Minister and the Chief Minister and told them that while I recognised the influence of the paper mills, the State did not deserve to be orphaned. I further added, that even the higher rate suggested by the Finance Department left a substantial margin and, pressed a little hard, the paper mills might well accept it. On the other hand the State would suffer a massive loss (estimated at Rs. 26 crore per year for twelve years or so as indicated in our note) if the lower rate proposed by the Forest Department was to be approved. I pleaded that too much should not be given up for too little. My pleading had its effect. The Finance Minister gave strong support and the Chief Minister was able to hammer out a good rate, perhaps what we had suggested, or close to it.

The new Chief Minister, in his enthusiasm to accelerate development of the state, launched a number of programmes including a new Industrial Policy and found that the Finance Department was not an obstacle. On the other hand, its suggestions often contributed to improving the quality of the schemes under formulation. Perhaps because of that I was instructed by the Chief Secretary to be present at all Cabinet meetings although the established practice was that only the Chief Secretary attended its meetings as Secretary to the Cabinet and other Secretaries were called in as and when necessary.

A major policy decision of the Government which I heartily

supported at that time, but came to regret later, as I became aware of its abuse, was on private practice by government doctors. Private practice had assumed such notoriety that the common man did not get the benefit of treatment offered by Government. At the same time, genuine practice could not flourish when self-employed doctors wished to set-up private clinics. When the new Government came up with the idea of abolishing private practice, there was stiff opposition from the Government doctors. Their Association, while demanding high Non-Practising Allowance (NPA) as compensation, expected the Finance Department to have the Government's move nipped in the bud on the ground that the state did not have sufficient funds to bear the heavy burden of NPA.

This apparently was the reason why the move, mooted in the past as well, had been given up. I was perhaps naïve enough to believe that the abolition of private practice would actually improve the quality of health care services. With that hope I caused some surprise by assuring the Government that it would be possible to provide the funds to meet the cost of NPA. The Government abolished private practice but the objective was not fulfilled. A few unscrupulous doctors managed to continue their private practice, stealthily to start with but openly and with impunity later; others followed. The purpose of the measure was completely defeated but the State continued to remain burdened with the NPA as Government refused to withdraw the scheme and acknowledge its failure.

A major testing time for me came after a few months. The Orissa Mining Corporation, a state government enterprise, came up with an ambitious proposal for establishment of a Charge Chrome Plant for processing of chrome ore, involving an outlay that might appear small now but was large in those days. The proposal envisaged import of plant and equipment along with processing technology, all to be procured from Austria on a turnkey basis. On examination in the Finance Department, many infirmities were found in the project proposal. But time lines had already been set for establishment of the Plant, assuming prompt approval of the investment.

The Minister concerned was known to be a person very close to the Chief Minister, with enormous influence over him, so much that even as a Minister of State he used to be referred to as 'Super Chief Minister'. He could not countenance any adverse comment on his pet project and asked the Secretary of his Department to have it cleared immediately by the Project Approval Committee of the Government so that Cabinet approval could follow as a matter of course and a delegation could proceed to Austria for finalisation of the deal, which he had taken as done already. What he failed to factor in, was the presence of the Finance Secretary as a member of the Project Approval Committee chaired by the Chief Secretary; other members of the committee were the Additional Chief Secretary, Secretary (Mines Department) and Chief Executive of the Mining Corporation.

All of us were aware of the urgency and also the importance of the Minister behind the project. Secretary (Mines) was anxious to have the project proposal cleared without delving deep. Nevertheless I brought out the points that required a fresh look at some of the important parameters of the project for which the meeting had to be adjourned. If I remember correctly, there was no satisfactory response even after two adjournments, particularly on the vital issue of project cost. According to the analysis done in the Finance Department, a realistic estimate of cost was turning out to be close to three times the estimate in the project proposal and therefore the viability of the project was seriously threatened. No convincing reply was forthcoming but I was repeatedly advised to join the consensus and approve the project. I refused to do so. The Chief Secretary (SM Patnaik) was good enough to permit me append my dissenting note.

I knew that the Cabinet would approve the project notwithstanding my note. I also knew that the Mines Minister would not forgive me for my dissent. What I did not expect was the Government's desire that I should be a part of the delegation that would proceed to Austria to finalise the agreement for setting up the project. That was too much for me to swallow. I declined to go. The Chief Secretary, keen to prevent me getting into serious trouble, advised me not to disobey Government orders conveyed to me in writing. But I refused to budge. Those who knew about it feared that I might immediately be suspended for challenging the all-powerful Mines Minister. But nothing of the sort happened. By the grace of God, and perhaps tolerance of the Chief Minister, no harm came to me. The project cost ultimately turned out to what we had anticipated in the Finance Department. The Plant incurred heavy losses and had to be sold off many years later as Government could not revitalise it. I was told that the sale of the Plant came up before the Orissa High Court where my Note of Dissent was produced to substantiate the point that the project was unviable to start with.

Another incident worth narrating was of purchase of an aircraft. The state Government already owned two aircrafts but the Transport Department all of a sudden proposed to purchase one more. There was hardly any credible justification and the Finance Department sent back the file with some queries. Without giving any satisfactory reply to the queries the proposal was referred back to us again for concurrence, evincing great urgency. This time I recorded a strongly worded note declining concurrence and emphasising that finances of a state like Orissa could not be burdened by purchase of one more aircraft, that too without specific budget provision for the purpose. I had been informed later that a well known Yoga Guru of Delhi, considered close to Prime Minister Indira Gandhi, was the person through whose mediation such planes were being forced not only on Orissa but several other states.

As expected, I was overruled under orders of my Minister and CM. But the file came to us yet again for sanction of an advance from the Contingency Fund because the Budget did not provide for purchase of a plane. This time I sharply pointed out that the proposed purchase could be considered neither emergent nor unforeseen. Since those preconditions, laid down for taking recourse to the Contingency Fund, were not fulfilled, no advance from that Fund was admissible and therefore I pleaded that the purchase of the aircraft be deferred. I was again overruled by my Minister and the CM endorsed the proposal to the Governor who alone could sanction money from the Contingency Fund.

On the following day, while I was in a meeting in the Additional Chief Secretary's room, a phone call came for me from the Governor who sought my advice on the proposal which had reached him in the meantime. I merely said that my opinion was already recorded in the file which his Secretary may please be asked to bring to his notice. I was somewhat surprised when the Governor said that he had read the two notes of mine and was speaking to me thereafter. When I told him that I had nothing more to add he congratulated me for the principled stand I took, and proceeded to ask me what he should do. With all humility I said: "Sir, that's your privilege". He repeated twice and both the times my response was the same. He thanked me and hung up after giving a few more encouraging words.

The Additional Chief Secretary, though a highly knowledgeable person, was by nature timid before higher authorities. He was aghast. As a well-wisher of mine he asked me in disapproval why I repeated thrice the words quoted above to the effect that it was the Governor's privilege to do what he wished to do. He felt visibly relaxed when I explained that the Governor did not seem to take offence and on the other hand he had closed the phone call with nice words for me.

Governor CM Poonacha was an extremely decent person with a rich fund of experience in public life and administration. He came as Governor of Orissa after serving as Union Minister. I had developed deep respect for him after interacting closely during a spell of President's rule when he conducted the administration of the state with great dignity. In the matter under consideration, I could have suggested him to return the file without according sanction but the CM would certainly have asserted himself again and in a matter like this the Governor was bound to be guided by the CM's advice. I had consciously refrained from playing the Governor against the Chief Minister, to no purpose. The Governor was too good a person to be egged on to a constitutional crisis in which ultimately he would have been forced to resign to preserve his dignity.

I had already served as Finance Secretary for five years, with three Finance Ministers, four Chief Ministers and two Governors during President's rule. Although happy working as a Finance Secretary despite occasional tension and disappointments, I was looking forward to avail of a fresh tenure of deputation at the Centre where I had been empanelled for appointment as Joint Secretary. SP Bagla, a close friend of mine from our student days in Delhi School of Economics before we both joined the IAS, was Establishment Officer to the Government of India. It was through him that I received the offer of the Central Government for appointment as Joint Secretary (Heavy Industry). The Chief Minister, after some reluctance, allowed me to go as I was also keen to do so.

Soon after my joining in Delhi, a popular news magazine published a story bringing out the matter of the aircraft purchase mentioned above. It carried extracts of the two notes I had recorded in the file, adversely commented on the profligacy of the State Government and concluded with the remark that I was transferred from the state because I had opposed the purchase. Though my moving away to Delhi might have been good riddance for some in the state government, the news story was entirely wrong in linking my Central deputation to my objection to the aircraft purchase.

I felt embarrassed because I had come to the Centre of my own volition. My objection to the aircraft purchase or even the Charge Chrome deal had not soured the Chief Minister's attitude towards me, for which my regard for him was high. I disliked the insinuation made in the news story that I had been sent away to the Centre because of my stand on the aircraft purchase but could do nothing to dispute it publicly as that would have made my situation clumsy.

Chapter 12

To Centre again in Ministry of Industry

The Government of India was not new to me, nor was Udyog Bhavan, where I came to work as a Joint Secretary (Heavy Industry), was unfamiliar. What came as a new experience to me was having a boss, who was not an IAS officer. The Secretary in the Department of Heavy Industry, who joined the Department soon after I reported there, was DV Kapur, a Power Engineer with an outstanding record as Chairman, National Thermal Power Corporation (NTPC). Those were the days of industrial licensing and the Department was entrusted with the development and regulation of the entire range of heavy industries: Machine Tools, Heavy Electricals, Automobiles, Heavy Machine Building etc. In addition, we were responsible for administering related public sector enterprises such as HMT, BHEL, HEC, MAMC, BEML, BHPV, Maruti Udyog and a host of engineering industries, mostly in the Calcutta region, which had been taken over by the government after they were rendered sick by their previous owners in the private sector. Soon after taking charge, the

Secretary redistributed the work among officers to remove unevenness and promote efficiency. I was placed in charge of Machine Tools, Heavy Electricals and the Structural Fabrication industry, along with HMT, BHEL, BHPV and the Calcutta group of companies taken over by the Government, besides administration of the Department. Apart from me there were three other Joint Secretaries, and a large number of other officers. I was deeply impressed by the method and orderliness with which the Secretary managed the Department, giving Joint Secretaries ample autonomy in managing their respective divisions. He also inculcated in us a culture of non-interference in the management of public enterprises within our charge while enforcing performance and accountability. By far the major part of my five year tenure (1981-86) in the Department of Heavy Industry was spent while he was my Secretary. I learnt a lot from him.

Conservation of foreign exchange and promotion of self-reliance were among the principal goals of national policy those days. Dealing as we did in machine-building industries, our mandate was to prevent avoidable import of machinery and equipment and promote domestic manufacture. In this we often had to encounter the demands of user Ministries such as Power, Fertilizers, Petroleum, Steel, Coal, apart from Defence, who usually displayed a distinct preference for import, citing cases of delays by domestic suppliers as well as quality problems. In some cases the complaints against domestic manufacturers were genuine but in many other cases demands for imports were pressed on extraneous considerations propelled by high-pressure marketing by foreign suppliers.

My biggest problem was to fend off the import of power plants that were within BHEL's manufacturing capability. Thanks to dedicated efforts of a succession of competent technocrats, BHEL had established indigenous capability of international standard in the design, manufacture and supply of power plants. With complementary systems of marketing and finance, the organisation was capable of participating effectively in international competitive bidding. The problem was its inability to offer soft-financing terms which foreign competitors often provided with the assistance of their respective governments and export promotion agencies. To make matters worse for BHEL, foreign governments used their aid packages, meant for the benefit of the common man in this country, to sweeten the commercial offers of their suppliers. In a period of prolonged slump in the demand for power plants in developed countries, India offered an attractive market to giant multinational companies to execute their power play in which BHEL often became the victim even in the home country.

As the Joint Secretary in-charge of this wholly-owned government company it was my responsibility to protect it from unfair competition by utilising various forums in the government. I had taken my responsibility seriously; perhaps too seriously at times to induce a Cabinet Secretary of the time to give me the epithet of 'BHEL's Vakil' (Advocate for BHEL). Hardly a month passed without my having to struggle hard at inter-Ministry meetings to argue against the import of power plants that could be supplied by BHEL. In most cases my efforts were not wasted. In one case where I failed to stop import but the country almost got the imported plant free is worth recalling.

A public sector fertilizers company had invited global bids for the establishment of a captive power plant and BHEL's offer was the lowest. The next higher offer was from a British company that managed to bring in some softening in the financing terms and induced the fertilizer company to strongly support its offer. The inter-Ministry Committee empowered to clear such imports deliberated over the matter at length and accepted my view that the modification offered by the British company, subsequent to the evaluation of the bids was inadmissible and the order should go to BHEL, the lowest bidder. But the matter did not ended there. A couple of weeks later, Prime Minister Margaret Thatcher of the UK came on an official visit to Delhi. At a preparatory meeting to work out the agenda I found a proposal for procurement of the same power plant from Britain. My objection was brushed aside on diplomatic considerations of strengthening bilateral relations.

Shortly before Mrs. Thatcher was due to arrive for the meeting, our PM was being briefed by a few of the Secretaries concerned. I was representing my Secretary, who was on tour, abroad. Being the junior most among those present, my turn came last. Just as I started to speak, someone announced that Mrs. Thatcher had arrived. Indira Gandhi got up and left the room to receive her, telling me to explain at the meeting whatever I had been trying to say. I was not sure if it would be proper for me to oppose the import in the exalted presence of two Heads of Government and might not have opened my mouth, but as soon as that particular item came up, the PM looked at me and asked me to complete what I had started to say earlier. I summoned all my courage and put across the case within a couple of minutes.

The PM, who was well aware of BHEL's attainments and was proud of her policy of self-reliance, was quick to nod her support. She put the matter before Mrs. Thatcher in a broad canvas of national pride and development so convincingly that the latter chose not to pursue the British company's case to sell the power plant to India. She did some quick consultation with accompanying officials and said that she had asked them to examine if the power plant could be given by Britain to the people of India as a gift. I do not recollect what ultimately happened but I was certainly thrilled over what transpired at that meeting.

One could not, however, always be sure of political support, even from quarters ordinarily expected to be supportive. One such case related to a power project in Uttar Pradesh. Here again BHEL should have been the obvious choice in competitive bidding but strenuous efforts were made to scuttle that process in order to favour a foreign company. A mighty multinational company tried, by every conceivable means, and almost succeeded in securing the support of both its home government and the Government of India at the Centre. In this case my difficulty was compounded because not only the

Government of Uttar Pradesh and the Power Ministry at the Centre but also the Ministry of Finance supported the import.

As a matter of fact the Union Finance Secretary became the principal proponent of import in considerations of availing of foreign aid. He himself organised several rounds of meetings to evolve a consensus. The first of these was adjourned to allow more time for reflection on all relevant issues though the pressure for import was clear. Since the Minister of Industry, ND Tiwari, was from Uttar Pradesh, I went straight from the meeting to brief him. I was surprised that the Finance Secretary had already given him a detailed account over the phone, particularly of my opposition to import. I was left in no doubt that the Minister too was in favour of import but in fairness to him it must be said that he did not utter a word to influence my opinion. He was perhaps confident that the Finance Secretary would be able to sort out the matter. The Finance Secretary on the other hand was keen to secure concurrence of my Ministry but I continued to resist—so much so that when he made a final attempt to evolve a consensus at a meeting (where, incidentally, an order appointing him Cabinet Secretary was delivered in the midst of much rejoicing) I kept on pleading that no decision should be taken to clear the import without competitive bidding. It was after this meeting that the new Cabinet Secretary started referring to me as BHEL's Vakil. I have no idea if the import was eventually cleared in the manner proposed, and if so, by whom.

Apart from the fight against unjustifiable import proposals, another source of strain, though it was of a different type, was the unhappy condition of the Calcutta group of enterprises which all became sick. These—to name a few: Jessop, Burns, Braithwaite, Standard Wagon—were all blue chip companies at one time. While under private management, they became sick and had to be taken over by the Government of India in the interest of large numbers of workers as also for maintaining vital supplies, particularly to the Railways. Years of mismanagement by the former employers had not only taken a heavy toll on morale in those companies but also left them utterly primitive in terms of technology.

Productivity was low and finances were invariably over stretched. I found that while large multi-unit enterprises like BHEL and HMT, with excellent organisational capability, technological strength and financial stability were able to forge ahead, the taken-over units preferred to lean on the Government for guidance and financial support. After studying them closely I concluded that many of their problems could be addressed effectively by reorganising them to get the benefit of scale and synergy rather than remaining fragmented and engaged in mutual undercutting. The reorganisation was not easy but I got the full support of my Secretary. The taken-over units were brought under two Holding Companies, both with their headquarters in Calcutta. I have no idea of their present condition but the Holding Companies started off well but close integration in the working of the constituent units took time.

An experience, though completely unrelated to the work of the Department, caused deep anguish and shock to the nation. The news of Prime Minister Indira Gandhi's assassination was given to me while I was appearing before a Parliamentary Committee reviewing the performance of BHEL. That news was shocking but the attacks on innocent Sikhs that followed were barbaric, shameful and unforgivable. Sporadic to start with, the attacks soon became widespread. Marauding hordes moved around freely on the streets of Delhi for the next three days and indulged in targeted attacks inflicting mindless violence, plunder and arson, murdering thousands of innocent Sikhs. While the law and order machinery in Delhi had completely collapsed, it was puzzling why the Army was not called in. Whispers were heard that the Congress Party wanted a free run for the marauders but I found it difficult to believe at first. Things started unfolding gradually. On the evening of the third day an urgent summon was received by me to be presented at the Cabinet Secretariat.

On reaching the Cabinet Secretariat I found a dozen of my friends—Joint Secretaries in other Ministries—already assembled. The Cabinet Secretary told us in a grim and subdued voice that the local administration of Delhi having become utterly dysfunctional, he had found it necessary to call upon us to proceed to our assigned areas to oversee work at the ground level to provide relief to the thousands of Sikh families that had been rendered homeless. I was asked to go to the camp set-up at Farash Bazar Police Station but no one could tell me its location. The only place I knew by a name resembling it was Farashkhana near Chandni Chowk where I proceeded immediately. I was told that the Thana (police station) I was looking for was far away, across the Yamuna, in a newly developed area of East Delhi. By the time I reached there, after some exploration, it was late night.

The camp was in a large newly built high school building next to the Police Station, now known by a different name, perhaps Vivek Vihar. An army unit under the command of a Major had just arrived. About two hundred persons who were brought to the camp had been given loaves of bread and milk for dinner and most of them were asleep. The Thana Officer told me that a number of victims in need of assistance were still huddled together some distance away in a Gurdwara, reluctant to move out as they were not sure if they would be safe outside.

Next morning I met the people in the Gurdwara and they moved to the camp only after I assured them that the Army had been deployed to protect them—such was their belief in the Army, or rather lack of faith in civil administration of Delhi! As I made a detailed inspection of the camp I was struck by a total absence of any male adult except officials. I was told that all adult male members of the families of the victims had been murdered; the camp had only women and children. Later in the day I visited the site of what was left of their dwellings. It was a colony of utterly poor Sikhs who lived in mud huts built on a piece of waste land. The entire colony was burnt down by the marauders. The place was Trilokpuri which became infamous for the dastardly crime of mass murder committed on helpless victims by criminal elements unrestrained by an uncaring society and a callous administration.

Public memory being proverbially short, the present generation may only be vaguely aware of the carnage but the survivors and family members of the victims can never forgive those who organised the killing. While watching that ghastly scene where some of the burnt-down huts were still smouldering, I wondered if there was a conscious design behind the governance paralysis that led to this inhuman tragedy. If Police proved inadequate to control the situation that erupted after the late Prime Minister's assassination, why did it take three days to call in the Army? However, I managed to push away those thoughts and got busy with my job of ensuring care of the inmates of the camp. Perhaps my grounding in the basic values of governance made me disbelieve allegations, earlier heard in whispers but openly narrated by the victims, that the Congress party had deliberately allowed the carnage to continue. A clinching evidence of the anger against the governing political class came a few days later.

All those in the adjoining area who needed relief were brought over to the camp and within a couple of days the camp got well-provisioned and organised. Those who had left their houses fearing possible attack that did not materialise took the earliest opportunity to return home as normalcy was restored. The seething anger that prevailed in the camp was gradually subsiding. But I did not see a single political worker of the ruling party visiting the camp although social workers were closely interacting with the victims, trying to soothe their frayed nerves. The area was believed to be a stronghold of the Congress. I was told that no Congressman of any consequence had the courage to face the victims who believed that the marauders in whose hands they suffered had the support and encouragement of those very political elements.

About a week or so later when the camp was entirely

peaceful and I was discussing some matter, late in the afternoon, with the Major in-charge of the Army unit and the Station House Officer (SHO) of the Police Station, massive roars of the challenging slogan—*Jo Bole So Nihal*—erupted all of a sudden from the direction of the camp. We were taken aback. Fearing an attack on the camp, the Major ran to alert his Unit and I rushed to the camp along with the SHO. The sight at the camp was unbelievable. Over a dozen hefty women inmates of the camp had pounced upon someone lying on the ground and being kicked and boxed relentlessly; the rest of the camp swearing bitterly. The victim, rescued by the SHO, turned out to be Late HKL Bhagat, a Minister in the Union Cabinet. We were shocked but he was resilient enough to assure us that nothing much had happened and we should ignore the incident. He was the unchallenged leader of the trans-Yamuna area, repeatedly returned to the Parliament from the East Delhi constituency. The virulence of the attack on him and the sharp invectives hurled at him left no doubt in my mind that the victims of the carnage saw in him the perpetrator of the dastardly crime of mass murder. Decades later and after several more enquiries, HKL Bhagat was ultimately identified, along with Jagdish Tytler and Sajjan Kumar (both Members of Parliament at the time of the carnage) for probe into their highly questionable role in the Sikh riots.

While Bhagat escaped accountability because death rescued him, the other two powerful Congress leaders managed to have the course of criminal justice derailed repeatedly. Even so, curse of the surviving victims dogged them relentlessly and their misdeeds kept resurfacing. Tytler with his clout as Minister in successive Central Cabinets of Rajiv Gandhi and Narasimha Rao, has yet not escaped criminal investigation. We must thank to the judiciary, CBI's repeated attempts at exonerating him have not succeeded so far; latest in April 2013 when the Court rejected an obliging CBI's plea for closure of investigation against Tytler. Sajjan Kumar got the benefit of doubt by the trial court on account of shoddy investigation led to virulent public protest on Delhi roads. His culpability is far from over.

Complete breakdown of law and order in the national capital that resulted in the killing of three thousand innocent Sikhs and many more subjected to lifelong hurt and suffering was a harrowing experience. It was worse to watch the criminal neglect of governance in the national Capital. While ultimate responsibility to provide security lay with the political executive, the civil service was even more blameworthy. After all, the Criminal Procedure Code empowers Magistrates to call upon the Army to aid civil authorities in such times to quell violent activities by unlawful mobs. And in Delhi the carnage was allowed to continue for three days!!! Why was it that the Police Commissioner, not to speak of the Lt. Governor (a civil servant), failed to call in the Army? No credible explanation has been given to my knowledge. Mere visibility of the Army was enough to restore peace in the Capital. But it was called in only on the third day of the carnage, for reasons best known to the administration.

The Lt. Governor and his administration having miserably failed to protect the Sikhs and even ensure adequate supervision over relief work in the camps, making it necessary for a dozen Joint Secretaries like me to be deputed for the purpose, was keen to expedite closure of the camps and early return of the inmates to their homes to show that things were normal. The message to this effect was clear at meetings he took with us, almost daily. While all of us were equally interested in early restoration of normalcy and my colleagues were giving short dates for closure of their respective camps, I was in no position to do so. The inmates of my camp were almost entirely widows and children who had no homes to return to, their dwellings having been burnt and razed to the ground by marauders.

My repeated assertions of the ground situation did not please the Lt. Governor. As he kept pressing, I told him in no uncertain terms that though my short-term assignment of relief work may end soon, the inmates of the camp would need to be there for months or more as they genuinely needed long-term relief. I had nothing to do with the camp after a fortnight or so when we the Joint Secretaries returned to our normal work in Ministries but I remained in Delhi for two more years to learn that inmates of the Farash Bazar camp were far from rehabilitated.

Official work used to take me abroad quite often to countries with which India had standing arrangements for economic cooperation. During one such visit I had a unique experience in Tripoli (Libya) where we had a joint project with the Libyan Government. Since the work was not progressing owing to some bottlenecks that needed intervention at the highest level, the Libyan side suggested that they would seek an appointment for me to take up the matter. I was not hopeful of getting access to Col. Gaddafi but the Libyan side was optimistic. The very next day they gave me the news of the appointment granted to meet him after three days. Hence, I had to extend my stay by a day but it was well worthwhile. In those days Col. Gaddafi was like Lord almighty to the Libyans. Protocol-wise I was way below. Even so, I was given the opportunity to meet him; such was the esteem in which he held India. Although the meeting was short and all that was to be said on our behalf was said in Arabic by a Libyan Minister present, there was an instant solution. The effectiveness of dictators, for good as well as evil, is well-known; I was a witness to its better side.

Another dictator in whose country our enterprises had ample opportunity to execute large construction projects was Saddam Hussein of Iraq. I did not have the opportunity to meet him but his Minister whom I met in Baghdad was all praise for the excellent cooperation they received from India and conveyed Saddam Hussein's appreciation.

In pursuance of our policy of international economic cooperation, Joint Commissions had been set-up with a number of countries for regular interaction. The Department of Heavy

Industry was the nodal Department for many of these Joint Commissions. Their meetings used to be held every year, alternately in Delhi and the other country. These meetings provided excellent opportunities to Ministers and officials to visit the host countries and I personally visited in this connection many fine cities such as Algiers, Budapest, Belgrade, Berlin, Sofia, Teheran, Warsaw and many others. But looking back, I wonder if any real benefit accrued either to us or to them, except promoting mutual goodwill in a general way. Western countries on the other hand believed in sending their Ministers to promote bids of their companies for major projects in India.

One such visit was to my Minister (ND Tiwari) by his Canadian counterpart. He was pressing hard to persuade us to support a massive sale of machine tools by a Canadian company for a Defence project where HMT was well poised to get the contract. The Canadian Minister was articulate and persuasive. After some polite conversation it occurred to me that we could raise with him a matter of our interest in Canada. I referred to a power project there, added that BHEL had offered to supply the plant and requested his support. I had barely finished when the Canadian Minister exclaimed how disastrous it would be for his electoral interests to allow an import with adverse impact on employment in his own constituency which produced power plants. I got an opportunity that I did not expect.

With humility I submitted that my Minister too had a constituency to nurse and import of Machine Tools would adversely affect HMT which was setting up a new plant there. After a moment of stunned embarrassment both sides indulged in humorous exchanges and the meeting came to a happy end. The point to be noted however is that while high dignitaries from foreign governments invariably and unabashedly promoted the interests of their companies, I found, to my disappointment, that our Ministers often felt it was beneath their dignity to project the interests of even our public enterprises in course of their interaction with counterparts of other countries. This attitude had its inevitable impact on our career diplomats as well.

While relentlessly pursuing the goal of preventing avoidable import, particularly of capital goods, I was convinced of the futility of industrial licensing which was also a part of my responsibility. I had realised that the capital goods sector had to be given all possible assistance to expand and strengthen rather than remain ham-strung by obsolete licensing regulations. I did not succeed in my effort to de-license the Machine Tools industry. But I was able to work out an arrangement, with the co-operation of other colleagues, to accord automatic approval to applications for expansion or establishment of facilities to manufacture machine tools, thereby rendering industrial licensing irrelevant in the case of the Machine Tools industry. In the case of other sectors of capital goods such as heavy electrical and heavy machine building, investment requirements were so large and technology was so sophisticated that applications were few and far between.

Having failed to influence the policy to abolish industrial licensing in the capital goods sector, I took recourse to a Committee set-up by Prime Minister Indira Gandhi to recommend measures to reform economic administration. The Committee, headed by LK Jha, had invited suggestions for consideration. In response to the Committee's invitation I sent a reasoned note advocating complete abolition of the industrial licensing system. My Minister, to whom I marked a copy of the note for perusal, was surprised to see that a Joint Secretary in his Ministry had taken the liberty of expressing such a radical view on a policy issue. I had to clarify to him that the Ministry was in no way committed to what I had suggested as the LK Jha Committee, while inviting suggestions, had assured everyone that the views expressed would be treated as personal. My Minister, a firm believer in the licensing system, may not have been fully put at ease by the clarification, but he left me unharmed.

A serious threat came from a different Minister and on a separate issue. A fertilizer plant in the public sector had floated a global tender for the setting up of a captive power plant and BHEL would have bagged the order in any normal evaluation. But a Japanese offer found favour with the project authorities and the matter of import clearance came up before an Empowered Committee which found fault with the reasoning in support of the import and decided in favour of BHEL. True, I tried hard to convince them but the committee, chaired by none other than the Secretary, Department of Fertilizers and the decision of the committee was unanimous. Even so, the Minister of Fertilizers chose to write a letter to my Minister accusing me personally of sabotaging what according to him was a fully justified import proposal.

Holding me responsible for the imaginery setback which would be caused to agriculture owing to shortfall in fertilizer production, he requested my Minister to accord import clearance at his level. On receipt of that vicious letter, I recorded a note explaining how the proposed import was completely unjustified and how wrong the Minister of Fertilizers was in making a personal attack on me. It was a well reasoned note that clearly brought out the hollowness of the Fertilizer Minister's charge. The closing sentence of my note, which I remember even today was: "had the letter come from an officer, I would have extracted from him an unqualified apology, but here it happens to be a Minister; I suppose he was not well briefed". While the strong note remained on our file, a polite reply went from my Minister explaining why he was unable to clear the import.

Ordinarily the matter might have rested there but a few days later I was surprised to see a news story by an investigative journalist (a well-known commentator now) who had obviously gained access to my note. He gave an account of the undue pressure the Minister of Fertilizers had exerted and how it was successfully resisted. The report contained extracts from my note and ended up by saying that the sting was 'in its tail' (the last sentence of my note, quoted above).

The story carried the caption "Yes Minister, you are wrong", alluding to the popular BBC serial which was being telecast those days by Doordarshan. The Minister of Fertilizers was already disappointed that he did not succeed in his import bid; the exposure in the news story might have added insult to injury. Instead of trying to regain composure and maintain dignity, the Minister of Fertilizers descended to a level far below his status. He wrote to my Minister making the entirely baseless allegation that I had leaked the contents of my note for publication. He demanded that formal proceedings should be instituted to account for the leakage of an official secret.

By that time I had already worked through almost my entire tenure with my Minister who had a fair idea of my character and integrity. He showed me the letter he had received and decided not to take the allegation seriously. After a couple of months I went back to my state on completion of my tenure and forgot all about this matter. The Minister of Fertilizers was persisting in his effort to punish me for something for which I was not responsible at all. I was lucky not to know what was going on in Delhi as that would have bothered me unnecessarily. I came to know about it only on my return to the Government of India as Additional Secretary after a year.

I learnt that having found my Minister lukewarm to the demand for proceeding against me, the Minister of Fertilizers got an enquiry instituted by an Intelligence agency who ultimately gave me a clean chit. This was the second time my career was sought to be spiked at a crucial stage by the vindictive action of people in authority because I gave priority to public interest over their personal agenda. The earlier case was in Orissa where a severe setback to my career would have been inflicted had the Chief Minister not set aside the sinister design of a Chief Secretary, referred to earlier. Both the incidents reinforced my belief that where action is guided by good intention, the higher power that guides the destiny of men protects one against vindictive action.

Chapter 13

Back to State: Industrial Development Corporation

On my return to Orissa towards the end of 1986, I was first posted as Chairman, Industrial Development Corporation, a state government enterprise owning and operating industrial units manufacturing a range of products such as pig iron, ferrochrome, cement, power cables and transmission towers. I happily settled down in the new job when I was suddenly transferred, within less than a month. But even during that short period I had to face a piquant situation. A meeting of the Board of Directors had been convened by my predecessor to consider modernisation of one of the plants that had become derelict and was a drag on the Corporation. Preparatory action had been taken for placement of an order on the equipment supplier who had perhaps come to collect the order. Approval of the Board had been taken for granted.

In course of my discussion prior to the Board meeting I did not get a convincing reply to some of my queries. Since members of the Board had arrived, I started the meeting and continued to seek clarification on the points that had not been answered satisfactorily. Though most of other Members were ready to approve the proposal under the impression that it was well formulated, they realised that further evaluation of the techno-economic aspect was necessary before a large outlay could be approved. We agreed to consider the matter at a later date after certain aspects were further examined.

As I left the Corporation to join as Home Secretary, I had no idea of the form in which the project was finally approved. But it came to my knowledge much later that the investment made did not yield the expected result and a few years later the entire plant had to be scrapped; an enquiry was also instituted to examine the entire matter and fix responsibility. In retrospect I wondered if my sudden posting elsewhere, hardly a month after I took over as Chairman of the Industrial Development Corporation, was intended to get rid of the questions I had raised on the viability of the investment which went waste!

Chapter 14

As Home Secretary

Immediately after joining the Home Department I was surprised to receive a call from the Governor desperately looking for a report which he was not getting from his Government. The report he had called for was on what used to be referred to as the issue of 'Church Burning' in present-day Kandhamal district. Before my return to Orissa I had seen news reports about the matter involving burning down of a number of churches which had generated intense anger all over the country against the vandalism. It had even caused deep concern to the Pope who shared it with the President of India. There were allegations that the state Government was down-playing the incident.

The President called for a report from the Governor who, in turn, had sought a report from the Home Department. On checking up papers in the Department, I found that adequate material was not available for me to send a meaningful report. I therefore called back, explained the situation to the Governor and requested him to give me a couple of days time, so that I could get the District Magistrate and the Superintendent of

Police to Bhubaneswar, have the matter discussed in detail and then send him the report rather than spend time in exchange of letters. The Governor readily consented. Soon thereafter, I held the meeting where initially I found a measure of reluctance on the part of the District Officials to open up but it did not take long to get from them a comprehensive idea of the situation as it developed. I don't wish to recount the details, all of which I gave in my report to the Governor. Suffice to say that the administration failed to deal with the situation firmly. Had there been firm action against vandalism at the initial stage and politicians refrained from playing up communal sentiments in this predominantly tribal area, the burning down of a large number of churches could have been easily avoided. Incidentally it was the same district of Kandhamal which suffered communal violence of unprecedented ferocity directed against Christians that shook the conscience of the nation years later in 2010.

It is often forgotten that the party in power at the centre in 1984 when Sikhs were killed in Delhi and at the state level in 1986 where churches were burnt down in Kandhamal, was the Congress. The BJP's culpability was believed to be no less in the mob violence against Muslims in Gujarat in 2002, and it was the failure of yet another party—the BJD of Orissa—that compelled thousands of Christian families of Kandhamal to flee to escape targeted violence in 2010. While the record of both the national parties (not to speak of a regional party like the BJD) in the matter of exploiting communal sentiments for narrow political interests is equally suspect, the conduct of the civil administrations in all these cases is no less blameworthy.

Under the mandate of law it is the duty of Police and District Administration to put down mob violence and maintain peace and law and order. In carrying out this mandate those who are in charge of Districts have no business to look to their political bosses for instruction. Doing so and refraining from the discharge of duty by taking refuge in political protection is not only morally degrading but also legally indefensible. Officials, particularly those at senior levels, should realise that they are bound by their oath to the Constitution and laws framed under it; they are not to carry out orders that are contrary to law, howsoever exalted be the source of the authority. This was precisely the ground for which I refused to carry out an order given at the highest level as it was not in conformity with the statutorily promulgated Transaction of Business Rules of the Government of India. That matter shall be explained later on in these pages.

In this connection it may be of interest to recall another matter in which financial relief granted to a Company was withdrawn by us citing, among other grounds, infirmity of the order giving the relief. The order in question, giving a patently undeserving relief at the cost of the exchequer, was issued not in accordance with the Rules of Business of the State Government. I had taken the view that it was invalid and hence inoperable. The facts of the case were briefly the following. While Orissa was under President's Rule, a financial relief of substantial amount was granted to a private company. The order granting the relief, issued under the signature of the Adviser to the Governor, was subsequently reviewed by the state Government and the financial relief was withdrawn.

The Company in question challenged the withdrawal of the relief in Court. Among the grounds we gave for withdrawing the relief was that the Adviser to the Governor, under whose signature the relief was given, was not competent to authenticate that order as he was not an authorised signatory under the Rules for transaction of government business; the impugned order was therefore invalid. A curious situation indeed! An Adviser to the Governor during President's Rule ordinarily exercises the powers of a Minister, or at times Chief Minister. But irrespective of whether or not a state is under President's Rule, orders formally conveying decisions of the Government are required to be authenticated under the signature of such officials as are listed in the Rules. Neither the Adviser to the Governor nor Minister or Chief Minister features in the list. They may pass orders on file, but the authority to issue Government Orders is vested in specific officials whose job it is to ensure that the order in question is issued after observing due process such as mandatory consultation with Finance and/or Law departments where necessary. The Adviser in this case was obviously in a great hurry to sacrifice revenue and please someone at the cost of the State. Our stand withdrawing the benefit given by the Adviser stood judicial scrutiny and the mischief did not succeed.

My induction into the work of the Home Department had started even before I joined the Department. I was called to a meeting in Delhi where the Chief Minister (JB Patnaik) was already present along with Chief Secretary, Home Secretary and a few other officers. I was still Chairman, Industrial Development Corporation and was wondering why I had been called there. The mystery was cleared by the Chief Secretary who told me that I would need to attend an important meeting the following day in the Ministry of Defence as the incoming Home Secretary. The meeting was convened to review the progress of land acquisition for a major expansion of a pre-existing Artillery Range of the Defence R&D Organisation (DRDO) to make it capable of test-firing new generation heavy artillery ammunition and missiles.

The project required massive acquisition of fertile land on the Balasore coast of the Bay of Bengal, involving eviction and relocation of thousands of families. The Chief Minister had assured Prime Minister Rajiv Gandhi, who also held the Defence portfolio at that time, that land would be made available for the project but there was severe resistance to land acquisition and the project was getting delayed. An account was given at the meeting of the steps taken by the State Government in pursuance of statutory provisions of the Land Acquisition Act but there was deep concern over the delay. On my return to Bhubaneswar, when I reviewed the ground situation, I was stunned. Massive police force was deployed around the designated project area within which residents had formed themselves into strong resistance groups.

No Government officials, not even extension workers, were permitted to entre into that area by the villagers. They had declared the entire area virtually self-governing and brought the acquisition process to a standstill. In the meantime, a year had passed.

After several rounds of discussion I found that while some of the officials having access to the CM were giving him optimistic reports, sober elements with a feel of the bitter popular resistance felt diffident. My own assessment was that the proposed acquisition on a massive scale was no longer feasible without strong police action that would provoke violent protest and lead to a situation unacceptable in a democracy. My discussion with the CM left me in no doubt that he remained promise-bound to acquire the land in view of the commitment he had given to the PM. Fully aware of the explosive potential of the ground situation, the CM was in a Catch-22 state. In those circumstances there was no point in either trying to persuade him to relax pressure for land acquisition or to beat down the resistance against acquisition. I decided to interact quietly with DRDO to explore the possibility of reducing the area for acquisition to the minimum and eliminate, if possible, relocation of families.

To my pleasant surprise, the response of the DRDO officials was positive. They saw the reality of the situation on the ground and were not willing to suffer indefinite delay in project implementation. We held several rounds of discussion which were very fruitful. Ultimately DRDO was able to manage with very little extra land beyond what they already had in their possession. There was no cause left for resistance to the project nor was there any need for further police deployment. The Test Range became fully functional in due course. A major problem with potentially explosive implications was diffused. We now see news reports frequently of newer versions of missiles test fired from the site and the nearby Wheeler Island.

My tenure as Home Secretary, and also my stay in the state, was short but eventful. Early in my tenure a delegation of the State Pensioners Association met me to present their charter of demands because the Home Secretary was the nodal officer of the Government for this purpose. The delegation, led by a former Director of Health Services, included among others a retired officer known as 'brains trust of financial rules' with whom I had worked for long years in the Finance Department. He was the spokesman of the delegation. Right from my early days in service I had a keen interest in simplifying and liberalising rules; my sympathy was always with the pensioners. I gave the delegation plenty of time to present their case.

While the spokesman was making his presentation I was briefly noting down my comments on each point. At the end of the presentation I questioned the spokesman, whom I held in high esteem for his mastery of details and dedication to duty, to recall if out of the twelve demands they had just presented, we had not discussed nine at different stages while he and I had worked together in the Finance Department. He gave no reply but I saw tears rolling down his eyes. I closed the meeting soon thereafter, promising early announcement of the Government's decisions. It did not take me much time to have those nine demands accepted by the Government as I was fully convinced of the merits and it was not difficult to get the concurrence of the Finance Department. After the issue of orders, the President of the Pensioners Association, accompanied by the Spokesman, came and thanked me. The latter not only thanked me but went on to express regret that he had argued against the grant of the same relief while he had been the dealing officer in the Finance Department. The facts are briefly the following:

Back in late 1960s, when I was Joint Secretary in the Finance Department and the Spokesman referred to above was the Branch Officer dealing with Pension matters, not under me. Even in those early days of my career I used to take an interest in Pension Rules which had remained archaic and unreformed for years, all over the country. Though my official duties did not relate to Pension matters even remotely,

I used to dabble in discussing those matters with him. His knowledge of rules was formidable and his integrity unimpeachable. But he had a mind firmly set against the slightest change of status quo. Let me add that perhaps a majority of the bureaucracy, barring the corrupt and the lazy, has these attributes. In their mistaken notion of carrying the entire burden of judging what is in the best interest of the State they seldom realise that some day they themselves may be at the receiving end of a rule or practice rendered redundant or unjust over time.

That precisely was the mindset of the officer when he held charge of the Pension Branch. It became his habit to politely turn down suggestions given by me to make benefits admissible as a matter of course, rather than leave a clause allowing exercise of discretion to relax those rules selectively. He had even asked me those days why I should at all evince interest in Pension matters far away as I was from my own retirement! He did not realise how time passed and made him a pensioner. Ironically, the very benefits that he had gone on denying others were the ones he was now pleading for. That was the reason why he could not hold back his tears.

Let me mention another incident which took place at about this time. One day I had a surprise visit by the Engineer-in-Chief of the Irrigation Department who approached me in a highly agitated state. His grievance was that a Junior Engineer posted at Cuttack had been stabbed by a known criminal, against whom the Police was not taking any action under the impression that he was close to the CM. I was aware that the Engineer-in-Chief was also close to the CM, told him so, and asked why he had not approached the CM, who held the Home portfolio, directly instead of coming to me.

Unable to conceal his closeness to the CM, he pleaded for my intervention explaining that he was facing a threat of imminent strike by Junior Engineers and it would be embarrassing for him to approach the CM in this matter. In his presence I spoke first to the Superintendent of Police, Cuttack. Not satisfied with his response, I spoke to the District

Magistrate who corroborated what the Engineer-in-Chief had told me. When I asked what action he was taking to discharge his duty he assured me of immediate intervention. His assurance resulted in a prompt arrest of the culprit. He called me back, perhaps the next day, to say that he was sending me a detailed report.

On receipt of his report I found that the arrest had been made under the National Security Act (NSA) and required approval of the Chief Minister (as Home Minister) within a certain period, perhaps 12 days, failing which the detainee would have to be released. I recommended the case for the CM's approval and submitted the file immediately. It took a few days for the file to come back, during which time there was some speculation whether the Home Secretary would regret his intervention. However, the approval of the CM was obtained well in time, giving the right signal to the District Administration. Years of interference in routine administration had rendered it so ineffective that even senior officers found it best not to act lest someone higher up was displeased. I was later asked by a friend who had been following this matter closely if I had had a prior discussion with the CM before sending up the case for his approval. I told him that no discussion was necessary as the case did not involve any controversial issue of public policy on which I needed his guidance.

Another incident of police inaction against culprits allegedly close to the CM came to my notice from news reports. It was reported in local dailies that two well-identified anti-social youths had publicly molested a girl in broad daylight, in full view of onlookers. The incident reportedly occurred in the outskirts of Bhubaneswar and it was alleged that police was taking no action against the culprits who lived nearby because they were believed to be close to the CM. On my enquiring about the incident from a top police officer who was with me when the news report came in, his reply was that there was hardly any need for me to bother as the girl was of questionable morals. I retorted by telling him that even a prostitute had full right to her privacy and the Police was duty bound to act against violators.

Immediately thereafter, I said in a reflective mood that neither I nor he would always remain in positions of power in the Government and in all probability both of us would settle down after our retirement in the very state for which we were working; would we be happy in a society where anyone could take liberties with the dignity of women? I then moved away from the subject. But the officer's conscience was perhaps aroused. On the next day or the day following, he informed me that the culprits had been arrested. My faith in administration was at least partly restored for the time being.

Policing in Orissa, as in most other states, was far from reassuring. Complaints of excesses by the police as well as inaction against criminals were common. There were serious allegations of misuse of the police to secure political gain. The Chief Minister was repeatedly giving assurance that lawlessness would be curbed but public perception was otherwise. I used to initiate action whenever a serious lapse came to my notice from news reports, particularly on custodial deaths. In the first such case, I ensured immediate suspension of the Officer-in-Charge of the Thana pending investigation. The Chief Minister, while speaking approvingly of the action taken, expressed his confidence that the police would no longer be found wanting. I remember telling him at the time that the malady was so deep-rooted that it called for firm action repeatedly for several years, not just once or twice, to bring governance back on rails. In my brief tenure I repeated this to the CM several times more on different occasions.

Public perception of the Government's sincerity about improving the law and order situation did not change. Charges of criminalisation of the society and complicity of the police in it became more and more virulent. There were several incidents of murder and grievous hurt having political overtones. Political leaders from opposition parties whom I had known personally when they were Ministers in earlier Governments, started coming to me with serious grievances and allegations. Clear evidence was noticeable of the Government losing popular support and there was little that I could do to improve matters. Meanwhile, my batch mates in Delhi were promoted and I was expecting my posting there as Additional Secretary at any time. When the offer finally came, the Chief Minister was reluctant to release me—a repeat of his unwillingness to do so seven years earlier, when I had gone from the post of Finance Secretary to join the Central Government as Joint Secretary. But when I persisted in pleading with him to release me, he was good enough to do so.

JB Patnaik, the then Chief Minister, had led the Congress Party to power for a second term of five years and was successfully implementing many schemes of development and welfare. But he was gradually becoming controversial and had started losing popular support. Dissidence within his party also grew and led to a change of leadership, forcing him to give up the office of Chief Minister before his second term came to a close. I had left the state long before that but felt sad. I had worked rather closely with him early in his first term as his Finance Secretary and mid-way in his second term as Home Secretary. Negative qualities apart, I admired him for his energy and dedication to the cause of the state's development. I was deeply impressed by his vision and ability to mobilise the administration to attain developmental goals. His was arguably the only regime, with the exception of the two year stint (1961-63) of Biju Patnaik, when the state recorded really impressive development.

Of course there were serious charges of corruption against both regimes. I was too junior and inconsequential in the earlier regime but not so in 1980s under JB Patnaik. With all sincerity I can only say that not even once I was asked, directly or indirectly, to do anything that went against my conscience. True, I was overruled on a couple of occasions but that was Government's privilege. Fortunately, the Chief Minister not only did not ever pressurise me but also shielded me from those of his colleagues who were known for their proclivity to pressurise officials. I was also struck, as many others were, by his great erudition. In my entire career, much of which was spent in the Secretariat in noting on files and drafting of letters and speeches, the only occasion I felt glad over my draft being modified was when it was done by JB Patnaik as it enhanced the quality.

When I left the state in spite of his reluctance to relieve me from the post of Home Secretary there were false allegations that I was unwilling to serve because the CM had no desire to curb criminal activities. Prior to that, while working as Finance Secretary in his first administration, I had stubbornly opposed, though unsuccessfully, two of his Government's favourite projects: the Charge Chrome plant and the purchase of a state plane. These had nothing to do with my leaving the state to join the Government of India. As mentioned in an earlier chapter, a popular news magazine published a story, along with my photograph, alleging that I had been shunted out of the state because I opposed those proposals. But the CM did not hold it against me. What a refreshing contrast compared with the vindictive attitude of the Union Minister of Fertilizers who relentlessly pursued me in the matter of publication of a news story (Yes Minister; you were wrong) in which I had no hand at all!

Chapter 15

To Centre once again at Ministry of Water Resources

On return to the Government of India in late 1987 I joined as Additional Secretary in the Ministry of Water Resources, a Ministry not exactly sought after by an IAS officers. But I was glad as the job offered me the opportunity to explore areas of work with which I was not very familiar. Besides, Naresh Chandra, the Secretary of the Department, was a fine person to work with; I knew him well, having succeeded him some years earlier as Joint Secretary (Heavy Industry). The Minister, B Shankaranand, moved away soon after I joined the Ministry to take up a crucial appointment as Chairman of the Joint Parliamentary Committee probing the notorious Bofors bribery case.

No one was appointed as his successor and the Ministry came under the direct charge of the Prime Minister Rajiv Gandhi. It was during his stewardship of the Ministry that a landmark event took place: adoption of the National Water Policy whose formulation provided me a comprehensive understanding of major issues concerning management of the nation's water resources. It also gave me the opportunity to interact with Rajiv Gandhi as the Minister. He was being widely discussed for having publicly ticked off the Foreign Secretary, leading to his resignation. I was therefore, quite apprehensive at first but soon found him pleasant and extremely polite.

The work of the Joint Parliamentary Committee continued longer than expected and a whole-time Minister of Water Resources was therefore appointed. He was Dinesh Singh, a seasoned political administrator, possessing enormous old world grace. Soon after he assumed office a curious situation arose concerning senior level promotion of engineers in the Central Water Commission. Over a dozen of serving Superintending Engineers were due for promotion to the level of Chief Engineer. A select list of senior Superintending Engineers was drawn up, in consultation with the Union Public Service Commission (UPSC) and sent to the Establishment Officer in the Department of Personnel for obtaining approval of the Appointments Committee of the Cabinet (ACC) composed of the Prime Minister, Home Minister and Minister of Water Resources.

In accordance with usual practice I had sent the proposal after obtaining prior approval of my Minister. When ACC's approval came to me I was surprised to see that, barring the top two, the rest of the list had been rearranged thereby upsetting the gradation of the officers. On checking with the Establishment Officer, I was informed that the list had been reordered by the Minister of State in the Department of Personnel (P Chidambaram) who, though not a member of the ACC, had access to those papers. I notified promotion of only the first two, both clear cases, and submitted the case to my Minister, pointing out the anomaly involved in the rest of the list approved by the ACC as notifying the rest would result in superseding some officers without giving any reason. The Minister agreed with me that we should re-submit the case reiterating our recommendation. This was done also pointing out that implementing the list as rearranged by ACC would amount to disagreement with the UPSC.

After a few days I was called for a discussion with the Minister of State (Personnel) whose first question to me was why could we not differ from the UPSC? I replied that Government did have the right to differ but there must be a cogent reason to do so and I saw no such reason in the case under consideration. With a sense of unmistakable annoyance, the Minister pulled out a bundle of Character Rolls of the officers and a sheet of comparative evaluation made by him or on his behalf justifying the revised ranking and asked me what was wrong with it. I told him politely that a comparative evaluation by yet another person could yield a different result as it was essentially a subjective exercise and the process could well become interminable; that was the reason why the procedure laid down was to go by the informed judgement of not a single individual but a group of persons comprising a Promotion Committee headed, in this case by, the Chairman UPSC.

My reply might have caused further annoyance as the question that was shot at me this time was whether or not the ACC had any role other than approving a given list. I replied that the ACC certainly had an important role as it had a much wider span of information (such as intelligence reports not available to administrative departments or the UPSC) and could bring it to bear on the decision process, but not relative merit already judged by a competent body unless there was any patent mistake—which was by no means visible in this case. My concluding remark was that if the ACC were still to adhere to the earlier position conveyed to us then the right course would be to obtain prior concurrence of the Minister of Water Resources, preferably by discussing the matter with him. This obviously did not please the Minister of State (Personnel). But better sense prevailed and a few days later we received the approval of the ACC to our original list.

The purpose of narrating this seemingly minor incident is only to illustrate unnecessary interference of Ministers in established procedures, rarely done earlier but now rampant, leading to avoidable lobbying for posting and promotion in Government. Had the Minister of Water Resources not been a strong pillar of support to me in the matter mentioned above, the select list, unjustifiably reordered, and approved by ACC in the first instance, would have been implemented and a much junior person would have bypassed his seniors to become not only Chief Engineer out of turn but eventually Chairman of the Central Water Commission without any overriding merit or creditable attainment. By maintaining the list certified by the UPSC one could notice a visible relief among senior officers in the matter of fairness in promotions which is vital for the morale of civil services.

My tenure in the Ministry of Water Resources was very short—less than a year, as I was quite unexpectedly transferred laterally to the Department of Economic Affairs in the Ministry of Finance. During this brief tenure I had to deal with a petition which I was instrumental in bringing to a happy conclusion, leaving me with one of the better memories of my service career. The petitioner was the widow of a former lowly official in a remote field establishment of the Central Water Commission. Being illiterate, she had affixed her thumb impression and penury might have prevented her from availing the services of an English knowing petition writer.

The petition was hand written in Oriya, my mother tongue. All that she was desperately seeking was a Family Pension which had not been sanctioned for years. The relevant file showed that several earlier petitions from her had been forwarded to the Central Water Commission without any action being taken. When I insisted on a report and the matter was examined, the claim was found to be legitimate. The admissible benefit was sanctioned at long last, from the due date. I have mentioned it briefly but it involved a lot of back and forth movement of papers to overcome reluctance to interpret rules constructively. Once the realisation came that I was pursuing the matter with some knowledge of the rules on the subject, not only was the sanction communicated with retrospective effect but the arrear amount was hand delivered at her place of stay. A few weeks thereafter I received a letter, again written in Oriya, expressing her gratitude and favouring me with a shower of blessings. I never met her or any one on her behalf but greatly cherish the memory and value her blessings to this day.

Chapter 16

At Union Ministry of Finance

My posting as Additional Secretary, Department of Economic Affairs (DEA) dealing with external finance, generally coveted in civil service circles those days, which came to me as a surprise. The post was formally referred to in the Ministry of Finance as AS(EF). Since the earlier incumbent of the post had gone on promotion, another Additional Secretary in the Ministry was managing the work in addition to his own. This combination of assignments had continued for several months, giving the impression that it might become a regular arrangement. Be that as it may, orders were conveyed to me, telephonically at first, followed up in writing, asking me to report for duty immediately. I held that post for close to three years, until my appointment as Secretary. Those three years (1987-90) were among the most critical in the management of the external finances of free India. The foreign exchange reserves of the country were seldom plentiful but never as critically low as in those three years.

SB Chavan was the Finance Minister when I joined as AS(EF). I had not worked with him till then except as a member of a delegation led by him to one of the many Joint Commissions for Economic Co-operation. He had a laid back style of working, in contrast to the hands-on practice of younger Ministers of the Rajiv Gandhi era. The Secretary was S Venkitaramanan, who retired a few months later and was succeeded by Gopi Arora. With a change of Government, following the defeat of Rajiv Gandhi's Congress Party in the election, VP Singh took over as Prime Minister and Madhu Dandavate as Finance Minister. Bimal Jalan, who was Chief Economic Advisor at the time when I joined the Ministry and later became the Executive Director of IMF, became Finance Secretary. They all had differing approaches and attitudes to economic management but each of them gave me full liberty to express my views, ample space to exercise my discretion and unqualified support when needed.

Of the several posts of Additional Secretary in a large Ministry like Finance it was AS(EF) that had the widest mandate, as the AS(EF) usually deputised for the Finance Secretary at numerous Standing Committees and other meetings. One had also to handle matters concerning foreign aid and bilateral economic co-operation with all countries along with the critical task, on a day to day basis, of foreign exchange release.

In a situation of extreme paucity of foreign exchange our problem was further compounded by a near total drift in policy on whether or not India should approach the IMF to avail of its structural adjustment facility. The management of foreign exchange in those days was nightmarish, leading ultimately to the ignominy of a part of the country's gold reserve being shipped out to prevent default in meeting international obligations. Our foreign exchange reserves were being supported by NRI deposits carrying not only high interest liabilities but also the danger of uncertain reliability. The deposits were essentially of the nature of 'hot money' that could vanish any time on fear of economic uncertainty. External borrowing was another source of funding that inevitably mortgaged the future of the nation.

During VP Singh's tenure as the Prime Minister, when I felt very uneasy about the growing helplessness on the foreign exchange front, I pleaded with Madhu Dandavate, the Finance Minister that the unsustainable situation could lead to a disaster and needed urgent attention of the government. He was a decent person of unimpeachable integrity. But without slightest clue to the solution of the problem, he assured me that the Prime Minister, who was knowledgeable in matters of high finance, was fully conscious of the dangers ahead and he undoubtedly had worked out the requisite strategy. Since the Minister did not share any details with me, I decided that I had nothing more to do except to wait for the grand strategy to unfold.

The strategy the government had decided upon was never revealed. It became increasingly clear that soon there would be no option left with the government except taking the help of the International Monetary Fund. As a matter of fact this option had always been there and IMF was only too willing to take India under its wings. But there was strong feeling against this course because of stiff conditions of austerity, fiscal correction and the opening up of the external sector which IMF usually imposed. Some of these measures were no doubt necessary in our own national interest but their adoption under duress was opposed as surrender of economic sovereignty.

About ten years earlier India had obtained a loan from IMF under its Structural Adjustment Facility to tide over the balance of payments problem, but when Prime Minister Indira Gandhi found some of the conditions the IMF imposed unacceptable, she repaid the loan ahead of the due date and got rid of the conditions. She was a patriot of great courage and iron will. I wish she had willingly ushered in economic reform best suited to Indian conditions as that would have strengthened the economy and saved the nation from the ignominy of having to mortgage its gold reserve to avoid default in 1991. But that never happened.

By the time I joined as AS(EF), the bribery scandal

concerning procurement of artillery guns from Bofors that engulfed the Rajiv Gandhi government, had assumed serious political dimensions. Though the matter related essentially to the Ministry of Defence, the Department of Economic Affairs (DEA) too was inevitably associated at the stage of initial evaluation of offers made by competing firms, and one of our Joint Secretaries at that time was on the Evaluating Committee. He had reverted to his state cadre when the scandal broke out and later a Joint Parliamentary Committee took up examination of the matter. Investigating agencies were also engaged in tracing the money trail. News reports were appearing thick and fast. In the light of all this the officer referred to above met me and made anxious enquiry if there had been any fault on his part. He had never worked with me but I knew his reputation as a fine officer. Since I had already made a thorough scrutiny of the papers in DEA on the Bofors gun procurement, I was satisfied that his conduct was blameless. He was visibly relieved when I told him so. The purpose of my referring to this is only to bring out how innocent officers who had diligently discharged their duty were made to feel apprehensive owing to the wrong doing of others, while the deal-fixer who was later found to be the conduit for the bribe and also its beneficiary masqueraded as the representative of a multinational company, claiming close links with the Prime Minister's family.

The reference is to Ottavio Quattrocchi who straddled the corridors of power with enormous clout because of his known proximity to Prime Minister Rajiv Gandhi's family. I first became aware of this name soon after my arrival in the Ministry of Industry in early 1980s, and that too from none other than my Minister who wanted me to consult Quattrocchi on some issue concerning BHEL. On my enquiring foolishly who Quattrocchi was, the Minister must have wondered how I would survive in the Government without knowing that man's clout. I got no reply and the Minister switched to some other subject. It took little effort on my part to learn about the massive clout of this man in swinging deals of large value in practically all major imports.

I had no contact with him till I went back to my State and came to Economic Affairs much later. He could not avoid me there. We met several times, mostly on import projects in the oil sector. Those were all high value imports where he was getting the full co-operation of the Petroleum Ministry; DEA was the only stumbling block. His persuasive skill and cultivated practice of name dropping were adequate to push through the Petroleum Ministry a proposal to import a particular high value project. But we in DEA were of the view that the import was avoidable as we believed that there was proven indigenous capability to meet the requirement locally.

The file on the subject was therefore returned by us more than once, with the advice to place the order indigenously. This clearly was not acceptable to those who looked forward to attractive benefits from import. Quattrocchi was livid with anger at the temerity of DEA officials to come in his way. He resorted to bullying which might have worked for him elsewhere but not with my Joint Secretary, who was warned by Quattrocchi that in case the file was returned again without our concurrence, the Joint Secretary and the Additional Secretary would suffer bitter consequences. The Joint Secretary, a clean image officer of the Indian Foreign Service, naturally felt offended. He rushed into my room in a state of great agitation and wondered how the mere agent of a foreign commercial firm could muster courage to hold out such unconcealed threats to the senior officials of a sovereign nation.

In a lighter vein, I told him that if we were shunted out of the DEA he, as a senior IFS officer, could look forward to a more agreeable destination in the West while I would be perfectly glad to revert to my home state of Orissa. The file did come back with remarkable speed and this time the denial of our concurrence was equally prompt and more clinching. Yet no harm came to me or my Joint Secretary. I have had the benefit of working with several officers at the Centre and in the State who were as competent and straightforward as my colleague but unfortunately a few over-enthusiastic climbers, ever willing to sacrifice public interest, permit operators like Quattrocchi to subvert the system.

It was the same Quattrocchi who was the principal conduit in the Bofors bribery case, which shook the Rajiv Gandhi Government and became the cause of the Congress party's defeat in the general election of 1989. He remained under investigation for years bringing disrepute to the Central Bureau of Investigation (CBI) for its readiness to be manipulated by the Government of the day, and ended two decades later in Quattrocchi being let off with the loot despite overwhelming evidence against him. It marks a shameful chapter in the vulnerability of the criminal justice system in our country. It is also an amazing saga of an international crook successfully manipulating the entire system over such a long period of time owing to corrupt politicians, venal bureaucrats, spineless investigators, malleable prosecutors and even judges who erred.

My days in DEA were marked as much by the sad spectacle of the nation's economic sovereignty being compromised by the foreign exchange crisis as of a series of questionable procurement deals by the Government; though with a silver lining of some of these not fructifying. A typical case of the high and mighty in the government actively promoting wrongful gain at the cost of public funds and governance ethics is given below.

Of all commodities, sugar arguably has the distinction of providing maximum opportunity to unscrupulous politicians to manipulate trade policy in our country so as to derive wrongful gain. I had to grapple with one such occurrence. An entirely manipulated shortage of sugar created in the domestic market in 1988 was sought to be met by resorting to large scale import—that too without following any transparent procedure for going to the international market in time, but deliberately delaying the import proposal. The intention was to purchase sugar at exorbitant rates from speculators holding stocks in ships floating on the high seas.

The Food Minister in those days was Sukh Ram and he was responsible for Sugar. He was convicted years later for amassing ill-gotten wealth. Having found it attractive for himself to import sugar from the high seas, he personally directed the move to procure sugar at prohibitive prices evincing grave urgency. When the case came to DEA for release of foreign exchange we obviously could not agree. At the Finance Secretary's suggestion an inter-departmental committee was set-up by the Food Department, with me representing DEA, to decide the Government's stand.

The Committee, chaired by the Food Secretary, had several rounds of discussion where I reiterated our view which essentially was the following: consumers in India had already suffered enormous rise in the domestic price of sugar because Government did not take timely action to increase availability. There would be fresh arrival of sugar from the new crop that would provide relief within weeks. The timing and method of procuring sugar from the high seas were inappropriate and the exorbitant price proposed was utterly unacceptable as the sale of imported sugar at that price, together with handling charges, would further push up prices in the domestic market instead of cooling it down.

The Minister was so determined to have his pet idea pushed through that he himself chaired a meeting of the Committee to have me bulldozed on the grounds of public policy to meet essential requirements of the people. When I found that my reasoning was having no impact on him I emphasised that my dissenting note should be recorded in the minutes of the Committee's report. The Minister, clearly in a huff, asked his officers to do so and closed the meeting. On cooler reflection he may have realised that with my recorded dissenting note it would be difficult for him to go ahead with his pet project. On the following day, which was a holiday, I got a message that the Minister wished to discuss the matter further and I should join a meeting in his room immediately. I declined to do so informing that I was busy otherwise and there was nothing more for me to add except what I mentioned already. Thereafter, no further development took place to my knowledge for a couple of weeks and I thought that the preposterous move had been given up. But that was not to be.

The Food Minister had roped in other powerful persons who could hijack the system and hand down a peremptory order asking me to release the requisite foreign exchange. A letter, signed by the Cabinet Secretary, conveyed to me the Prime Minister's order to release the foreign exchange. I do not know who benefited but domestic price of sugar certainly did not soften. And later, with change of government, the CBI was asked to investigate the matter. I do not recollect how it concluded but what I do remember is that I was asked to confirm the objection to the procurement that I had insisted upon. When I did so the investigators asked me how foreign exchange was released in the face of my recorded dissent. Once they came to know that the decision to release foreign exchange for the import was taken at the level of the Prime Minister, they were amazed; what they did thereafter was best known to them.

While corrupt Ministers often milked the Government, a major issue came up of fake currency notes flooding the market. Reports of large scale smuggling of high value notes into the country, particularly of the denomination of Rs. 500, were coming thick and fast. The establishment of additional capacity for printing currency notes had been planned but the new facilities at two green field projects made slow progress. As I was trying to have the projects expedited, we received reports of industrial unrest in the government's existing note printing press on the issue of overtime payments to workers for production of notes of Rs. 500 denomination.

The demand for these high denomination notes far exceeded the normal printing capacity for which workers were being paid overtime wages. More was being demanded under threat to stop overtime work and payment of higher overtime wages was recommended to Government on the ground that the challenge of smuggling of fake notes into the country had to be met urgently. I wondered if the demand for the high value notes was at all genuine or whether it was generated for clandestine purposes of stacking black money. I had just returned from an official visit from USA where the highest denomination currency was of $ 100. There was no need, I thought, for a country like ours with far lower income levels to have currency notes of denomination higher than Rs. 100. Comparative prices also did not justify circulation of higher denomination notes in India.

My discussions with senior officials revealed that while they accepted the logic, they were skeptical about the possibility of its acceptance by the Government. The view expressed on behalf of Reserve Bank of India was that in the absence of higher denomination notes the demand for notes of Rs. 100 would go up, further accentuating the gap in domestic availability. I also learnt that they were formulating a proposal to have currency notes printed abroad to meet domestic shortage.

I discussed the matter with Finance Minister Madhu Dandavate and found his response encouraging. A man of unimpeachable integrity, he had a deep aversion for black money. He promptly approved the idea to do away with the printing of higher denomination notes and import sufficient quantities of currency notes of Rs. 100 and lower denominations to meet our domestic need. This measure by itself may not have put an end to the problem of black money but it certainly made its stacking less convenient. Besides, smuggling of fake high value notes into the country declined for some time. I do not know the circumstances in which high value notes were reintroduced some years later but I feel that even now, despite the sharp increase in prices, the pernicious role of high denomination notes in our economy outweighs the value of their contribution to legitimate monetary circulation. Now that banking services are vastly enlarged and are expanding further with rapid increase in the use of plastic money, I firmly believe that high denomination nctes can be withdrawn from circulation to curb the menace of black money.

In the midst of the drudgery of day to day work and the strain of enforcing stringent control of foreign exchange, there used to be interludes of foreign visits to negotiate bilateral economic aid. While people generally believed that foreign jaunts offered plenty of opportunity for rest and recreation, I seldom found them restful because we were niggardly in letting ourselves have the luxury of longer stay abroad than what was absolutely necessary. Besides, being usually the leader of a recipient country's delegation, I nursed a feeling of sadness at my country's economic situation which made us look for aid.

Foreign trips, which were plentiful, did not constitute any great attraction. In my earlier assignments, particularly in the Ministry of Industry, I had gone on plenty of foreign visits; the longing for such visits was just not there. However, one country to which my visit was always enjoyable was the erstwhile Soviet Union. They gave India plenty of support in her development efforts right from the early days of independence. Furthermore, the economic cooperation between our two countries was not based on aid, as handed out by western democracies, but on the basis of what was called Rupee Payment. The goods and services we imported from the Soviet Union—plenty of plant and equipment and technical know-how—were all paid for in Indian Rupees and the Rupee earnings thus made by the Soviets were used by them over a period of time to finance imports from India. The trade and economic relations between our two countries were thus based on mutual trust and equality. There were of course critics of the Rupee Payment system but all that has become history with the collapse of the Soviet Union.

My experience in matters concerning economic aid by multi lateral agencies such as the United Nations Development Programme (UNDP) was also generally pleasant. However, there was one unpleasant incident of our own creation which I regret even to this day. It needs to be narrated only to highlight how inadequate communication between our Foreign Office and our Mission in a neighbouring country pushed us into a situation where India stood isolated in an international forum. The entirely avoidable embarrassment to India happened in our immediate neighbourhood in Dhaka where the UNDP was holding an important inter-Governmental meet. An agenda item sponsored by Bangladesh had proposed a study to be undertaken by UNDP of the environmental aspects of rivers flowing into Bangladesh.

Before leaving for Dhaka, as head of the Indian delegation, I had a detailed briefing in Delhi where the Ministries of Water Resources and External Affairs had advised us that we may not support the proposed study as it would internationalise the issue which was essentially a matter of bilateral concern to our two countries. On arrival in Dhaka I was briefed by our High Commissioner who also stressed the need for us to prevent endorsement of that particular agenda item. Having worked in the Ministry of Water Resources earlier I too felt that the proposed study under the aegis of UNDP was best avoided but could not fathom why the High Commissioner, whose job it was to promote good relations with the country of accreditation, was so hung up on the issue.

After a widely appreciated statement that I made at the plenary session, when the particular item came up for consideration at a subsequent sitting, I explained why it was not necessary for a multilateral agency like the UNDP to intervene in a matter like this where bilateral co-operation would provide better and quicker results. I could see that although Bangladesh representatives were unhappy, UNDP officials seemed to go along with us and no other delegation appeared interested. At a reception later that evening I was approached by a member of the Bangladesh delegation, whom I knew well from the days of their liberation struggle. He pleaded for our support to their proposal which they intended to bring up again the following day. I also observed discrete lobbying by them with other delegations.

It was clear that Bangladesh was keen on pushing ahead

with the proposal despite our position on it. I therefore, asked my colleague in the delegation, a Counsellor in our High Commission, to apprise the High Commissioner and let me have feedback in consultation with Delhi on what should be our approach in the developing situation. It was not clear to me whether any consultation took place with Delhi but next morning I was advised that we should continue to oppose. When the meeting resumed Bangladesh brought up the matter again as expected and resumed hectic lobbying on the side lines; they also made sincere efforts to take us on board. Personally, I felt unhappy to keep opposing and genuinely felt that we could moderate our stand but that was not to be.

Soon, I noticed that unlike the previous day when hardly any country other than Bangladesh took interest in the subject, delegation after delegation took the floor in support of the Bangladesh proposal. Ambassadors and High Commissioners of all our neighbouring countries came in to join their respective delegations to express solidarity with Bangladesh. It was made to appear as if a country repeatedly ravaged by devastating floods and cyclones was being denied a just and fair treatment by the stubborn opposition of a bullying neighbour. I could clearly see that the issue had become highly politicised and we were getting isolated. From the conference hall I sent a message to our High Commissioner (the only one of those of the entire sub-continent who chose not to be present) to apprise Delhi of the clear possibility of India being in single minority in the event that we persisted in opposing the move. I got no response. Our isolation became self evident.

We succeeded in blocking the proposal, taking advantage of the practice that decisions could be taken only by consensus, not by vote. In the midst of our utter isolation in an important multilateral forum, I could hardly interpret that as success. On return to Delhi I saw to it that the entire matter was considered at a meeting taken by the Cabinet Secretary where the Ministry of External Affairs conceded that our Mission in Dhaka could have reassessed the situation as it developed and sought instructions from Delhi to enable our delegation to have greater flexibility.

Soon thereafter, I learnt that the empanelment of our batch for appointment as Secretary to Government of India had been done and I could expect my promotion any day. Having been assured of my place in the panel I relaxed, awaiting my orders and continued with my work. However, perhaps out of goodwill towards me, my Secretary kept enquiring about my choice of Ministry. His equation with the Cabinet Secretary and the Prime Minister was known to be excellent. I thought he wished to assist them in deciding the posting of Secretaries. My consistent response was that any Ministry was good enough for me. I had developed this attitude towards posting not just as a matter of form but because I had learnt from my experience since early days in service that every post offered enough work opportunity and satisfaction. Be that as it may, for want of vacancies the progress of posting was slow.

Meanwhile, the political situation took a drastic turn and the fall of VP Singh government appeared imminent. Just a day before the Ministry actually fell, the Establishment Officer in the Department of Personnel, a batch-mate of mine, rang up to say that he was sending a Government order promoting me as Special Secretary in DEA itself. This came as a big surprise for me, because my Secretary had never mentioned this possibility.

The order soon arrived and my Secretary passed it on to me for implementation. Just then the Establishment Officer called again and advised me not to do anything. He had been asked by the Secretary to the Prime Minister to hold up the implementation of the order because the President of India wished to stay the outgoing PM's order. This was quite a surprise as a civil service posting of this nature was neither a matter of high policy nor controversial. Nevertheless, I refrained from joining as Special Secretary, went home in the evening as usual and did not even bother to mention the matter at home.

Within a couple of days a new Ministry was installed,

headed by Prime Minister Chandra Shekhar. Yashwant Sinha, a friend and batch-mate of mine who had resigned from the IAS in early 1980s, became the Finance Minister. Immediately thereafter, my Secretary sprang a surprise by suggesting to me that he and I could share his work in DEA, with me functioning as Secretary (Banking) under the new Finance Minister. He had never suggested this earlier though the Banking Division of DEA had often functioned under a different Secretary in the past. For several months I was waiting for appointment as Secretary. It was easy for him to have had me appointed Secretary (Banking) long before Yashwant Sinha was made Finance Minister because it was well known that the Secretary was a confidant of Prime Minister VP Singh and was also close to Cabinet Secretary VC Pande.

The VP Singh Government had presided over an administration under which the country was progressively pushed into an economic crisis. I was certain that the new Finance Minister would like to bring a new Finance Secretary, an option he did exercise soon enough. The question of my persuading him to retain the previous Secretary appeared to me totally out of place. I also realised that if I stayed on in the Department, it would be difficult for me to suppress my pent-up feelings against the insidious manner in which the country was pushed into helplessness, rather than taking timely action to approach the IMF with some negotiating strength, however feeble. That would have embarrassed some friends with whom I had worked in the Department.

After giving some thought, I came to the conclusion that the best course was for me to move away. I therefore, took an early opportunity to meet the new Minister alone and requested him to do me the favour of having me transferred elsewhere. He looked surprised but was good enough not to be intrusive. He could have thought, as some colleagues told me, that as a former batch-mate I wished to avoid working under him but that consideration did not weigh with me at all nor did he ever breathe a word about it to my knowledge. I am glad he took the matter in good spirit and we continue to be friends.

I was soon posted as Special Secretary in the Ministry of Commerce where my tenure was short but eventful. More about it later—but let me now get back to the putting on hold my promotion and posting as Special Secretary DEA, referred to earlier. The reason given to me then was that the outgoing Prime Minister's Secretary desired it citing the President's wish. I thought it was unlikely that the President of India should be bothered by an innocuous civil service posting ordered in accordance with established procedure. On making enquiries through a friend I was informed that the Secretary to the President was not aware of any such instruction having been given by the President.

President Venkataraman was known to me personally. Out of sheer curiosity I took the liberty of meeting the President a few days after assuming office as Special Secretary (Commerce). He confirmed my belief that a civil service posting or promotion was by no means a matter of major policy over which an outgoing Prime Minister's order would need to be put on hold. He was clearly unhappy that his name had been dragged in. However, since I had moved out of DEA on my own request the matter was left at that.

Why the Prime Minister's Secretary put the order on hold was best known to him. He was always nice to me. Earlier, as Cabinet Secretary he had gone beyond the call of duty to help me get out of my State and come on promotion as Additional Secretary at the Centre; again, he was the one who had posted me as AS(EF) in DEA. It was therefore, quite puzzling for me to figure out why he spiked my appointment. My friends speculated that I might have become the unintended victim of an ego clash between the Secretary (BG Deshmukh) to PM and the Cabinet Secretary (VC Pande).

It was widely known in bureaucratic circles that the Cabinet Secretary was a close confidant of Prime Minister VP Singh, with far greater influence than the former Cabinet Secretary who became Secretary to PM. I was told that since the Cabinet Secretary had got my posting as Special Secretary DEA cleared by the Prime Minister without prior consultation with the Secretary to PM the latter got an opportunity to spite the Cabinet Secretary, taking advantage of the fall of the VP Singh government. This no doubt was a credible explanation but it was of little consequence to me as I preferred to move away from DEA of my own volition.

Chapter 17

In Commerce Ministry

In the Ministry of Commerce, where I joined as Special Secretary in 1991, Subramanian Swamy was the Minister. The post of Special Secretary and Secretary carry the same pay scale and they generally function independently of each other except that the Secretary holds overall charge of the Ministry or the Department concerned. My charge included matters concerning Export Promotion and related organisations such as International Trade Promotion Organisation which conducts trade fairs, Agricultural Produce Export Development Authority, Marine Products Export Development Authority and various other Export Promotion councils; plantation industries like Tea, Coffee, Rubber, and Spices; also state trading organisations like STC and MMTC. Montek Singh Ahluwalia was the Secretary. Those were the days of canalised trading under which massive sales and purchase transactions were being undertaken in minerals, metals, fertilizers, edible oils, sugar etc. STC and MMTC were the two principal trading houses carrying out these operations. To bring closer co-ordination and secure greater synergy, the two organisations had just been brought under a single Holding Company of which I became the Chairman.

STC and MMTC had their own chief executives (Chairmen) and ample operational freedom. While the Chairman of MMTC apparently responded well to the wishes of the Minister, the Chairman of STC, who belonged to the IAS, was perhaps less responsive. The Minister decided to have him replaced. That may not have posed any serious problem had he not desired to bring in a rank outsider of his choice as the substitute. To enlist my support he even arranged a meeting of the person of his choice with me. The bio-data he gave me contained the name of a large company in which he had served, whose Chief Executive Officer was well known to me. On checking up with him I found that the company had eased this person out on the ground of questionable integrity, which made me reluctant to go ahead.

I explained to the Minister the laid down procedure for the appointment of chief executives of public undertakings and added that neither could the incumbent Chairman be relieved of his appointment summarily nor a substitute appointed by the Ministry without prior approval of the Appointments Committee of the Cabinet (ACC). I thought that the idea would be dropped, but that was not to be. The shock came a few days later when the Minister gave me a note-sheet containing his proposal, approved by the Prime Minister and the Deputy Prime Minister (the three of them constituting the ACC in this case) appointing that particular individual as Chairman STC.

The Minister desired that the order should be implemented forthwith. I did feel unnerved for a moment but managed to collect my wits and made it clear that I would have the matter processed for issue of a formal order by the Department of Personnel to enable implementation. The Minister offered to speak with the Cabinet Secretary to have it expedited and I left with the note he had given me. On returning to my room I found the incumbent Chairman of the STC waiting for me anxiously. The Minister had already informed him to vacate the post immediately. He sought my guidance on what he should do, having regard to the fact that a meeting of the Company's Board of Directors convened earlier, was scheduled to meet in half an hour.

I advised him to go ahead with his work until he received a formal order which had not yet issued. Soon thereafter, I started dialling the Cabinet Secretary but stopped midway as I feared that in case he asked me to go ahead I would still be left in an uneasy position as the person to be appointed was clearly not suitable but nothing had formally been ascertained about his antecedents. I therefore, decided to refer the case to the Cabinet Secretary in writing and did so forthwith.

Days and weeks passed but no response came from anywhere. STC continued to function under the incumbent Chairman. The Minister was clearly not pleased but remained unruffled. He was also decent enough not to raise the matter with me any more. I thought he had realised that I was guided only by the call of my duty. But I was wrong. The extent of his wrath was revealed on the day Prime Minister Chandra Shekhar tendered the resignation of his government. Towards the close of office hours that day, the Secretary to PM rang me up and reassuringly told me that I had nothing to worry as the Prime Minister had overruled, in my matter, his Commerce Minister. Since I had no inkling of any potential danger that had hovered over me, I naturally enquired what the matter was all about.

The PM's Secretary was amused at this innocent (or perhaps stupid) query of mine and advised me to ascertain the details from the Cabinet Secretary Naresh Chandra. The latter, making light of his own role in having the wrong righted, told me what it was. The Commerce Minister had apparently given a damaging report on me following the failed attempt to have that particular person appointed Chairman STC. I have no idea till date what exactly the content of the report was but it surely had serious implications for me. I felt relieved that the Prime Minister had ensured that justice was done.

This was by no means the first or the only occasion when God rescued me from malicious damage to my career while I was blissfully unaware of either the intended harm or its neutralisation by well-meaning colleagues. There were other occasions earlier but this time an otherwise unblemished career was intended to be irretrievably damaged at the very top. That I escaped unharmed yet again further strengthened my belief that a divine force protects those who do their duty with sincerity and without fear or favour.

The General Elections that followed the fall of Chandra Shekhar government again failed to provide a decisive mandate for any party but the Congress managed to form government with PV Narasimha Rao as Prime Minister. The Commerce Ministry came to be headed by P Chidambaram, holding independent charge as a Minister of State. Pursuant to negotiations with the International Monetary Fund, action had already been initiated to dismantle, in stages, the rigid system of industrial licensing and trade control built over long years. The Commerce Ministry had taken up in right earnest the work of progressive liberalisation of import and export trade control. The vice like grip over foreign trade, exercised by the Chief Controller of Imports and Exports (CCI&E) under the Ministry, was substituted by a system where most commodities were permitted to be freely traded and the CCI&E was re-designated as DGFT (Director General Foreign Trade).

Import duties which were prohibitive under the pre-reform regime were scaled down and rationalised. The neighbouring Ministry of Industry also took major strides by liberalising the restrictive regime of industrial licensing which had become an instrument of coercion and obstacle to industrialisation. Udyog Bhavan, the home of both the Ministry of Commerce and the Ministry of Industry, shed its earlier character of being the hub of the License Permit Raj.

My tenure in the Commerce Ministry was very short, not even a complete year. While the atmosphere in the Ministry was generally one of doing away with all avoidable controls, there were queer situations in which even intrepid liberalisers eloquently defended canalised trade, a system that provided incredible powers of patronage. At the other end of the spectrum was the case of an Additional Secretary not particularly known to be a reform enthusiast, deputed to ensure clearance of accumulated export cargo at ports, coming up with the extraordinary solution of privatisation of Indian ports as the immediate solution. Just as the earlier cited defence of canalised trade was intended to please the powers that did not wish to part with privilege, the latter case illustrated the truth how some officials were in a hurry to ride the bandwagon of reform, for which privatisation was the buzzword. I recollect having recorded my comment that privatisation was not the panacea for all ills; certainly not for clearance of cargo that had piled up and needed early clearance.

The purpose of mentioning this story now is only to illustrate how calibrated economic reform, which was the need of the hour, became the occasion for mistaken and over-enthusiastic officials to demonstrate in bizarre ways their willingness to ride the bandwagon. On the flip side, even intrepid liberalisers were found too willing to defend counter-productive status quo in several cases to please persons in high office. One of many such instances that come to my mind is worth narrating. Those were still the days of canalised trading in many commodities where imports and exports were routed through one of the state organisations.

A lot of malpractice was being alleged in the export of rice to the erstwhile Soviet Union under the arrangement of canalization. Since there was no longer any need to regulate rice export at that time, I felt that canalisation had become an avoidable restriction and the time had come for its removal. This did not suit the interest of those who benefited from exercising patronage under the prevailing system. I faced resistance but the Minister found it difficult to overrule me on file. He invited me for discussion at a meeting to have a wider exchange of views. At the meeting I was glad to see a senior officer known for his vociferous advocacy of economic liberalisation, as I thought he would support my proposal for de-canalisation. To my surprise, this high priest of liberalisation argued the opposite, only to please the Minister.

As I had mentioned earlier, the economic reform set in motion in 1991 followed a long period of inaction by the Government to apply correctives to counterproductive policies and practices which pushed the Indian economy to the brink of collapse. The new economic policy, followed out of compulsion, was not a consciously evolved policy, born out of political conviction. The bureaucracy which takes direction from political executive of the day was therefore often caught at cross roads of conflicting views. This *ad hoc* manner of economic management is discussed further in the chapter that follows.

Towards the end of my tenure in the Commerce Ministry I dealt with a case that came to have resonance two decades later, when the Supreme Court was constrained to quash the appointment of the Central Vigilance Commissioner as the incumbent was found to have a criminal charge pending against him. When I saw news reports containing the names of the principal characters, I could recollect how persistently they pursed their proposal to import Palmolein directly instead of getting supplies from the STC, which was the authorised agency to import and supply edible oils to states for public distribution. Kerala required clearance from the Commerce Ministry to import directly, which they sought claiming that they could do so at a lower price.

As this appeared unlikely, we wanted to know the price range at which they intended to import. Instead of specifying the price range they continued to press for clearance at different levels. Until my departure from the Commerce Ministry the requisite clearance had not been given to them. I have no idea how they got the clearance, if at all. But I do remember that the sacked CVC visited the Commerce Ministry several times to plead the case but I had remained unconvinced. As news reports gave out later, the Kerala Government imported

Palmolein directly and sustained a heavy loss. Criminal charges were initiated against a number of persons, beginning with the then Chief Minister and including the officer whose appointment many years later as CVC was quashed by the Supreme Court.

Chapter 18

Economic Reforms

Looking back at the evolution of economic policy of free India, I admire the perspicacity of our founding fathers who gave a comprehensive plan of development and welfare the nation needed in its formative years. A contrast to that was the confusion seen in economic policy management in the run up to the crisis of 1991 and later. Particularly in recent years, which demonstrated utter incapacity of leaders of later days to envision a comprehensive socioeconomic policy more appropriate to meet contemporary requirements.

Jawaharlal Nehru with his deep understanding of India and her people gave us, soon after independence, the architecture of our development plan and policy. Impressed by enormous progress made by the erstwhile Soviet Union through planned economic development, he set-up the Planning Commission in India in 1950. But being a confirmed liberal and a firm believer in democracy, he hated regimentation. The planned development he envisaged for India was therefore, on the lines of indicative planning, not ruthless implementation of central planning of the Soviet kind.

He made this amply clear in course of his speeches at public meetings where he took pains to explain his economic philosophy to the people. One statement of his in Parliament where he expounded his concept of planned development for India is etched in my memory to this date, as I listened to it from the visitors' gallery as a student.

Emphasising the concept of mixed economy that he visualised as the cornerstone of economic development for the country, Nehru explained how the entire sector of Agriculture was intended to be developed through individual enterprise, why the State was required to build heavy industries because private enterprise did not have the capacity to do so in a big way, how multipurpose river valley projects needed to be developed by the State, why it was imperative to be mindful of distributive justice, how urgent was the need to build temples of higher learning in the field of science and technology and highlighted many other programmes of nation building. The first three Five Year Plans were drawn up and implemented only on that basis.

It needs to be remembered that in the early post-independence period Indian industry needed protection. Even the Bombay Plan of 1944, endorsed by leading industrialists like GD Birla and JRD Tata, had advocated a curb on foreign investment and called for a greater role for the State in industrial development. As indigenous industry lacked capital and know-how to invest adequately in sectors like steel, power, and machine-building the public sector had to undertake the development of heavy industry. Pressure developed progressively on our external payment system because of heavy import of plant and machinery to strengthen the foundation of the economy.

The trade and industrial policies of the country were therefore oriented towards regulation of imports, promotion of exports and channelisation of resources into socially desirable avenues. But Pandit Nehru never supported central planning or micro-management. Had he lived longer to see the fruits of his policy mature and the foundation of comprehensive development of the economy strengthened, he would have taken the lead himself to modulate and modify policies that became counterproductive later. Even Lal Bahadur Shastri, his successor, would have brought about the requisite mid-course correction in economic policy management had his tenure as a Prime Minister not been terminated abruptly by his tragic death.

Indira Gandhi who succeeded Lal Bahadur Shastri as Prime Minister of India, took the nation to great heights but sadly she believed in micromanaging the economy directed towards strengthening her personal supremacy. She not only tightened bureaucratic control over economic management but also introduced draconian measures to strengthen her government's stranglehold on trade, industry and even civic life. A stage came when she herself realised that the economy was becoming over-regulated. She appointed LK Jha, the redoubtable civil servant with enormous experience of economic administration, to examine the prevailing economic policies and recommend suitable changes. The Economic Administration Reforms Commission headed by Jha made several recommendations for policy change but nothing much was implemented.

After Indira Gandhi's tragic assassination and Rajiv Gandhi taking over as Prime Minister, a lot of promise was held out for modernisation of India. Not only he had the advantage of youth but also the support of the largest ever majority in the Parliament. But alas, he too did nothing much to reform the economic policies. His Finance Minister was VP Singh, who later succeeded him as Prime Minister. His contribution by way of economic reform, either as Finance Minister or as Prime Minister was nil. He allowed fiscal profligacy to continue and the balance of payments to worsen.

VP Singh in particular had a crucial role in the management of the economy, first as Rajiv's Finance Minister and later as Prime Minister at a critical stage. He did nothing to arrest the drift. One often heard, in whispers, that VP Singh lacked courage to take the political decision to seek IMF assistance even though he had no alternative plan. He deliberately allowed the situation to deteriorate until a critical stage was reached and going to IMF became inevitable. This theory of subterranean conspiracy appeared to me so insidious that I refused to believe that the Prime Minister of my country could be involved in this treacherous game! But the foreign exchange crisis precipitated and we were left with reserves that were barely adequate to meet a fortnight's import requirement. There was imminent danger of default in meeting our external commitments.

Around that time VP Singh resigned as he had lost the majority support in the Parliament. His successor, Prime Minister Chandra Shekhar and his Finance Minister Yashwant Sinha, shortly after assuming office, had the unenviable task of shipping out a part of the country's gold reserve to prevent default. Going to IMF became inevitable. Dr. Manmohan Singh whom VP Singh had chosen to be his Economic Adviser, in anticipation of our coming under the wings of the IMF, remained in Chandra Shekhar's PMO. To what extent Dr. Manmohan Singh enjoyed the new Prime Minister's confidence was a matter of speculation, but it became immaterial because Chandra Shekhar's government survived only for a brief period. After the election that followed, Narasimha Rao became Prime Minister and he appointed Manmohan Singh as his Finance Minister.

The usual drill prescribed by the IMF started in full steam and a New Economic Policy unfolded. The first step taken was the opening up of the external sector. The rigidly controlled import regime was loosened and procedures for issue of import license were streamlined. The Rupee was made partially convertible and foreign exchange control was liberalised. The highly restrictive system of industrial licensing was done away with. These were among some of the desirable measures that we ourselves should have initiated long before we were coerced into adopting them. But far from doing that Indira Gandhi had gone on tightening the License-Permit regime which became a mill stone for the nation.

Neither Rajiv Gandhi nor VP Singh had mustered enough courage to liberalise. It was left to the sagacity of Prime Minister Narasimha Rao that, while heading a Government with an unstable majority in the Parliament, he skilfully managed to rid the economy of many rigidities that impeded growth and was able to usher in the much needed economic reform. Rajiv Gandhi had at least taken some steps to modernise the economy by introducing computerisation and undertaking massive expansion of telecommunication. VP Singh did the disservice of precipitating the foreign exchange crisis by his subterranean conspiracy which brought the nation to the brink of default and ignominy.

Manmohan Singh is generally projected as the architect of economic reform in India. Nothing can be more misleading than this. The architecture of whatever reform took place was decided in Washington DC. The IMF-World Bank policy prescriptions that came to be implemented were by no means novel. Manmohan Singh was not a newcomer to the field of economic administration nor did he come with any fresh idea, as a Finance Minister. He had the unique opportunity of having held all top positions in the field of economic management for an extended period, right from 1970s. Starting his long inning in the Government as Economic Adviser, he rose successively to be Chief Economic Adviser, Secretary (Department of Economic Affairs), Member-Secretary and then Deputy Chairman (Planning Commission) and Governor, Reserve Bank of India. He occupied these positions not as a traditional bureaucrat but with the expertise of an economist with enviable academic excellence and considerable international exposure. It would be fair to expect such a person to bring a measure of freshness into economic administration of the country whose progress was being severely impeded by excessive control during all those years. An objective appraisal of Dr. Singh's role would reveal if he genuinely tried to liberalise or preferred to float with the tide. General perception supported the latter view.

The economic liberalisation introduced in 1991 was forced

by the IMF and political support for its implementation was provided by Prime Minister Narasimha Rao. It goes to his credit that severe austerity measures advocated by the IMF were avoided as that would have hurt the people and created serious resistance to reform. The country was spared much pain and agony that would have been inflicted by drastic cuts in public expenditure by way of austerity. It was the sagacity and political maturity of Narasimha Rao, in spite of all his frailties, which gave direction and content to the reform process adopted by the country.

Dr. Manmohan Singh, the then Finance Minister, no doubt presided over the Ministry of Finance which had the responsibility of co-ordinating with the IMF but to call him the architect of reform would amount to massive exaggeration. He was essentially a glorified Finance Secretary. It is ironical that the real architect of economic reform in India, Narasimha Rao, was disowned virtually by his own party, and a misleading impression was created giving more credit to Dr. Singh and not to Narasimha Rao.

If one tries to evaluate Dr. Singh's performance in his later role as the Prime Minister, one fails to see any major liberalisation or a sustained process of economic reform under his stewardship. Apologists may say that Left parties on whose support he ran his Government in his first term (2004-09) did not allow him the freedom to push any significant measure of reform. But they fail to remember that Prime Minister Narasimha Rao did not have a stable Parliamentary majority either. He actually ran a minority Government but could still carry forward economic liberalisation by skilful political management. Besides, even stiff opposition of Left parties to Dr. Singh's commitment to Indo-US Civil Nuclear Cooperation Bill did not deter him from risking his Government's survival and he was able to have it pushed through the Parliament by securing support through questionable means. Could he not have taken a few calculated steps to go ahead with major economic reforms of which the country was in dire need during that time? And what reform has Dr. Singh brought about in his second term as Prime Minister when his government did not depend on the support of Left parties at all?

It was often said that the Government's desire to speed up big ticket reform in areas of Banking, Insurance, Labour, etc. was being frustrated by forces that were not likely to support the requisite legislative measures. But has any progress been made in implementing measures that did not require legislation? Dr. Singh himself, as Finance Minister, was pushing for disinvestment in public enterprises; he gave top priority to disinvestment in Air India in 1991 even though the law in force then did not permit it. Two decades have passed since the law that came in the way was repealed but no disinvestment in the carrier took place. An announcement made in 2011, suddenly permitting foreign direct investment (FDI) in multi-brand retail and equally hastily withdrawn because of disagreement within the government, was entirely mindless. The government came to be widely seen as dithering on issues of economic reform. Whether on the issue of reform or on wider issues of governance, the government appeared paralysed.

Meanwhile, the growth rate of the economy declined to less than 5%, inflation remained unacceptably high, fiscal deficit kept mounting but government did practically nothing to contain it. On the other hand, public expenditure on populist measures kept increasing at the cost of capital outlays. Current Account Deficit remained unsustainably high and exchange value of the Rupee came under severe pressure. The government showed some recovery from the long spell of policy paralysis only when fears intensified of downgrading of India's credit rating to junk status in October 2012. The administered prices of diesel and cooking gas were raised after dithering for years and some announcements made permitting FDI in retail and aviation sectors, to send a signal to investors abroad. Can this knee-jerk action be called reform?

The Prime Minister himself justified the action as emergent measures to meet the challenge of a crisis, similar to the critical situation of 1991. But the question arises why the crisis was allowed to develop again under the watch of the reformist Prime Minister? The announcements regarding FDI and the price of diesel and cooking gas, coming as they did, after years of unforgivable mismanagement of the economy by throwing overboard fiscal responsibility that stoked structural inflation, confirmed my impression that the crisis which the PM referred to was created by his government in order to leave no option for the nation except yielding to controversial measures such as FDI in multi-brand retail. Strikingly similar, indeed, to the 'subterranean conspiracy' of the VP Singh period!!!

FDI is beneficial when it goes into manufacturing or infrastructure development; activities that produce goods, create wealth, generate employment and provide sustained well-being; not into large retail outlets with multi-brand products promoting consumerism, often at the cost of domestic industry. Multinational chains have the ability to flood the market with cheap imports of questionable quality and utility thereby causing harm to domestic production and employment. And after a firm hold as market leader, the scale of their operation enables them to indulge in various types of manipulations (well documented internationally) to the detriment of not only consumers but also their own suppliers, whether of manufactured goods or farm products. Even if the fears against FDI in this sector are exaggerated, the net benefits are uncertain at best.

In this context I would like to recall a policy blunder which Indira Gandhi made but was quick to seek a remedy soon after its deleterious effect became clear. In 1970s a proposal for nationalisation of wholesale trade in food grains came up for consideration by the Committee of Economic Secretaries in the Cabinet Secretariat, where my job as Deputy Secretary was to service the committee. The majority opinion in the committee was by far against the move, mainly on practical considerations. But PN Haksar, the left-leaning Secretary to the Prime Minister, dominated the discussion as usual and others yielded after making some pre-cautionary remarks as it became clear that the Prime Minister had made up her mind to go ahead with nationalisation. Soon thereafter, the government abolished wholesale private trade in food grains as a progressive measure to eliminate profiteering and bring down prices.

But the measure had exactly the opposite effect. Prices, far from falling, shot up more than 20% in each of the successive two years causing panic in higher echelons of government. Better sense dawned and the 'progressive measure' was withdrawn before it could cause further damage. Containment of the problem caused by the policy and its reversal were possible in this case because only domestic forces were involved. But in the case of the controversial measure of FDI in multi-brand retail, the domestic policy would have a crucial external implication. The foreign investor, with enormous multinational resources at his command together with powerful support of his home government, would pose a formidable, if not insurmountable, obstacle to a possible reversal of the policy were it to become counterproductive.

Time will be the best answer to tell whether massive amounts of foreign investments will start flowing in to rescue the Indian economy as a result of the bitterly resisted policy of allowing FDI in multi brand retail, but if it does, it is likely to impact in a big way on the prevailing structure of domestic trade. Livelihood of millions of small traders and their network of suppliers employed in a highly decentralised informal sector could be threatened. Rightly or wrongly, FDI in multi-brand retail is still perceived as a serious threat to livelihood and employment in our country, already suffering from acute problems of unemployment. It was therefore, imperative for the government of India to develop a consensus on such a major and controversial issue of reform instead of making a policy announcement, in a knee-jerk response to overcome a crisis of its own creation. Yet the Prime Minister was so fixated on this particular measure of FDI that he wished to force it down despite fierce opposition.

The entire country witnessed the parliamentary debate as the policy of FDI in multi-brand retail was approved in December 2012, by questionable political management. It became clear that by far the majority of parties, including those that rescued the government at the time of voting, bitterly opposed the policy and vowed not to allow its operation in their respective states. Even though, the government stubbornly pushed ahead and sharply divided not only in the Parliament but the entire polity on this issue. By making it appear as if this particularly contentious issue is the centre piece of his economic reform, the Prime Minister unnecessarily provoked severe resistance to genuine reform and provided opportunity to all opposition parties, transcending ideologies, to unite against it at a time when the urgent need was of consensus building on reform.

Serious charges have been levelled against the government of creating massive scams in awarding contracts, whether in holding Commonwealth Games, or allocating air waves (spectrum) for telecom development or leasing of mines for the extraction of coal. The amounts involved in these scams are mind boggling. Allegation of bribery has been made not only in Defence and other procurements but even in Railway Board postings too. Serious accusations have been levelled against Dr. Manmohan Singh of presiding over a corrupt government promoting crony capitalism.

The massive corruption and crony capitalism witnessed in recent years are not temporary aberrations but inevitable outcome of wrong policies and governance deficit which impeded growth. Like the much denounced License Permit regime of our old socialist days, corruption acts like a barrier, preventing efficient, innovative and honest entrepreneurs from entering business and contributing to growth. The country-wide demand for the institution of an effective and independent anti-corruption body has been stubbornly resisted by the government despite categorical assurances given on the floor of the Parliament. Humongous corruption in the allocation of rights to exploit precious natural resources has showered enormous wealth and power on cronies. This has not only discouraged the growth of principled enterprise but also caused frustration and anger among the people, particularly the youth of educated class.

The rate of domestic saving in India is still impressive though it has lately come under pressure owing to unabated inflation. Dearth of investible funds in the country is on account of wrong economic policies pursued by us. Genuine investors are shy of making investment as they find the outlook gloomy and credibility of the Government low. Government has rendered itself incapable of going ahead on a sustained path of calibrated reform and has failed to remove bottlenecks that have held up hundreds of projects with massive investments from being cleared. Instead of paying serious attention to the eradication of malefic forces that have severely damaged the investment climate within the country, the government seemed to believe that FDI was the single point remedy.

For a large country like ours, FDI can at best be a supplement to our own efforts to grow, unless we wish to destroy ourselves as a nation by looking upon foreign investors as saviours of our national interest. If our domestic savings are safeguarded and massive amounts of black money held outside are ploughed back into the economy by determined government action there would be no dearth of investible funds; we could be much more selective in providing avenues for foreign investment in the country. If governance issues could be addressed and corruption in high places curbed, the government would be in a much better position to revive business confidence which, in turn, would boost domestic investment and also attract foreign investment that could be channelised towards desirable lines of development. There would be no need to invite FDI indiscriminately in a desperate bid to send signals to the foreign investors that they alone can rescue the Indian economy.

As an observer of Dr. Manmohan Singh over a long

period, particularly while working at senior levels in the government during the crucial years of early 1990s, I did not expect great things to happen with him as Prime Minister. But I did have hope that he would make some contribution to tone up the administration and cleanse it of corruption. With his long experience at different levels in the government and enormous moral authority he could have exercised as a man of clean image and austere habits, one expected him to usher in an era of transparent governance, with efficiency and probity. But the outcome has been the opposite. His tenure as Prime Minister, far from being marked by any positive impact by way of administrative reform, has been a long period of directionless, slothful administration embroiled in massive corruption and crony capitalism.

From Jawaharlal Nehru's socialistic policy of mixed economy to promotion of crony capitalism under Manmohan Singh, the Congress party has come a long way. Yet the Planning Commission, which has no role in a market economy that we apparently have opted for, continues and may have grown in size. Dr. Manmohan Singh, I am sure, has not forgotten the 'bunch of jokers' remark on the Planning Commission by its youngest ever Chairman, Prime Minister Rajiv Gandhi. That was three decades ago when Dr. Singh himself was its Member-Secretary or Deputy Chairman.

Even the fig leaf of nominal planning that provided some justification for the Planning Commission's existence then has meanwhile vanished. But the jamboree of Annual Plan discussions with state governments and central Ministries continues, involving a huge wastage of time and expenditure, particularly for states which have to send large contingents every year to Yojana Bhavan in Delhi. Some years ago the Chief Minister of one of the southern states, perhaps Kerala, had refused to send the usual large contingent for the annual jamboree but was later persuaded to fall in line. That was when Planning Commission exercised unfettered discretion in doling out central assistance. The first step was taken to contain discretion and introduce norms in the allocation of central assistance under the Gadgil Formula, named after Prof. DR Gadgil, a distinguished economist who was Deputy Chairman of the Commission in 1960s. Some modifications to the formula have been made, but not always, to make it more normative, depending upon whether or not the Centre wished to leverage central assistance as an instrument of political discrimination.

The pioneering step taken under the Gadgil Formula to impart objectivity and transparency in the allocation process needed to be enlarged and entrusted to a statutory body like the Finance Commission for periodic review. A reform of this nature, eliminating the Planning Commission, is necessary in the larger interest of healthy federalism but the Centre chooses to keep the process opaque. Had Dr. Singh been genuinely reform-oriented person he could have given a big lead in this direction. Since he missed the opportunity to do so in his tenure as Deputy Chairman of the Planning Commission, he could have done it as its Chairman with all the power and authority of the Prime Minister. But far from taking any initiative to curtail the role and size of the Planning Commission which has become anachronistic under the prevailing market oriented regime, the Prime Minister has preferred to give it greater visibility. A reform oriented Prime Minister wishing to avoid wastage of money and manpower should require no prompting to abolish the Planning Commission and redeploy the resources saved for productive purposes elsewhere in the government.

Not the Planning Commission alone but several Ministries of the Government of India would also be good candidates for abolition if economic reform were to be meaningful in cutting down to size the unnecessarily big government. A large number of Ministries and Departments came to be created over the years as Government progressively entered new fields to manage industrial and business enterprises. Since disinvestment and privatisation have come to be accepted as government policy, there is no need whatsoever to retain all those Ministries and Departments. If certain enterprises are required to be retained in the public sector even in the changed circumstances they should all be given real autonomy to function, unencumbered by a whole lot of Ministry officials, presided over by a Minister, breathing down over the management.

India's large economy is governed not only by the policies of the government at the Centre but also the policies of states. There is need for plenty of reform at the state level too but precious little has been achieved yet. Nothing much can even be expected in the absence of inspiring leadership capable of galvanising the nation and leading it to greater heights by power of vision and force of statesmanship. It is therefore, not surprising that an eminently desirable measure of tax reform, debated extensively for introduction of Goods and Services Tax (GST), has remained unimplemented for years. The GST is a major instrument for removal of avoidable impediments to trade and commerce. Its adoption is also expected to raise the country's GDP by two percentage points, a massive gain for the nation. But instead of being adopted expeditiously, the issue gets remitted to committees, one after another.

Another major area of reform, again requiring effective participation by states, is the power sector. Legislations were passed long ago to facilitate reform of this major sector of infrastructure but it continues to be a huge constraint on progress of the economy. I remember in this connection my personal experience as Chairman of a Committee of Independent Persons set-up by the Government of Orissa way back in 2001 to review Power Sector Reform in Orissa which was the first state to undertake reform of its power sector. This pioneering effort was preceded by extensive studies after which the World Bank gave Orissa a loan of Rs. 1,500 crore to strengthen its Transmission and Distribution system and implement the reform which had two major components: restructuring of the State Electricity Board and privatisation of its distribution segment to step up efficiency and bring about qualitative improvement in energy supply.

It also envisaged increase in power tariff to make the

system self-sustaining. The review we undertook, almost five years after restructuring and privatisation, showed that the only difference the reform had made to the customer was repeated hike in power tariff without the slightest improvement in power supply. Transmission and Distribution losses continued to be as high as before despite massive capital investment. And overall losses remained unacceptably high even after repeated hike in tariff.

Stunning facts emerged when we went into details of the capital investments made. Massive expenditure of over Rs. 600 crore had been incurred but not even a single project had commenced on the ground; the money was spent on mere purchase of material that was lying unused. The recommendations we made apparently were unpalatable to the government who kept delaying their decision. The High Court had to intervene in that because of a PIL filed by a group of concerned citizens. Then only the government abruptly announced its decision accepting our recommendations which they could conveniently have done at least a year earlier.

It is regrettable that our record of economic reform, whether at the centre or in the states, has been one of action under duress rather than propelled by a sincere desire for reform, backed by sustained effort. The burst of economic policy measures announced in September 2012 by a politically beleaguered Central Government only conforms to that dismal pattern. After assuming office as Prime Minister in 2004, Dr. Manmohan Singh's government junked the prudential principle mandated by the Fiscal Responsibility and Budgetary Management (FRBM) Act and went on incurring unsustainable budget deficits to indulge in populism in the name of inclusive growth. Did the 'reformist' Prime Minister, who is also an economist, not realise that the fiscal imbalance which his government was creating would boomerang by stoking the fires of inflation, which lies at the root of much of the current sickness?

The growth model we have followed in recent years in the name of economic reform is a variant of the Trickle Down principle of capitalism. Undoubtedly it created many new business opportunities but it also gave rise to humongous corruption, unacceptable disparity and a bitter sense of deprivation to the vast majority that was left behind. Even the emerging middle class which the flawed policy claims to have created and those Below Poverty Line who managed to escape hunger through doles from the government, feel deprived when they see vulgar demonstration of opulence and extravagance by the few who have gained most under the Trickle Down policy.

Such a policy obviously cannot be relied upon to provide inclusive growth with social justice. Those who steered the adoption of this policy did not have the political courage to spell it out to the Indian people. They perhaps believed that success would ensure its acceptance. President Pranab Mukherjee was, I think, the first leader of stature who publicly referred to the trickle down policy; to say how unsuitable it was for a country like ours. But to do so he had to wait till he gave his inaugural address as President of India. The two-pronged policy—of promoting crony capitalism under the trickle down principle and giving doles and dispensing populist favours to please deprived classes—has produced a toxic mixture of opposites in the management of the economy: liberalisation that accentuated corruption and promoted disparity, while populist policies led to abandonment of fiscal prudence.

This deadly mixture brought the economy again to the brink of a crisis. The government tried to ascribe it to external factors and dug its head ostrich like, hoping for better time to come on its own. Scam after scam surfaced in quick succession of time and instead of taking resolute steps to tone up the economy, the government kept busy in cover up exercises. Downward spiralling of the economy was the inevitable result. Not only growth declined but in critical sectors it became negative. Inflation, more particularly food inflation, became intolerably high.

There was sharp increase in public debt, external debt in particular. Unsustainable fiscal deficit forced the government to cut down public expenditure but the axe fell not on wasteful populist measures but on defence and developmental outlays. Unemployment grew day by day, even among skilled and professionally trained persons. Non Performing Assets (NPA) of the banking sector rose alarmingly. Lack of confidence in the economy induced foreigners, ever in search of greener pasture, to pull out their investment thereby accentuating pressure on our already overstretched balance of payments.

Exchange value of the Rupee started falling. But instead of taking firm remedial measures, the government kept giving the alibi that all emerging economies were in similar position. The reality however was, that most other emerging economies were doing far better than us. August 2013 witnessed the free fall of the Rupee going down below 65 to US $ with the ominous forecast that it may go down further. Our foreign exchange reserves were no longer robust and foreign investment, whether FDI or FII, on which Government had placed all hope of revival dried up. Under pressure of Parliament and public opinion Government conceded that the situation was indeed critical. But the Prime Minister tried to downplay the criticality, telling the Press that the situation was not as critical as in 1991. He was right. The crisis this time was worse—a massive crisis of confidence.

Reform in any sphere, whether economic, social or political, requires genuine belief, firm commitment and inspiring leadership. In a large democracy like India, it cannot be forced from outside. In the dire distress in which we found ourselves in early 1990s, the economy was liberalised to some extent under IMF's pressure and Prime Minister Narasimha Rao's skilful political management. But beyond that no real reform has been taken place, except in a halting and limited way. Perhaps a leader like Indira Gandhi could have carried out major economic reform had she believed in it.

Two other Prime Ministers that I can think of—Lal Bahadur Shastri and Atal Bihari Vajpayee—had the stuff of which reformers are made. Alas, destiny took away the former too soon and the latter was let down by failing health and his over-ambitious party that pushed to a midterm election in 2004. Since then, the Congress Party-led coalitions have been ruling the country, with Dr. Manmohan Singh holding the exalted office of Prime Minister, not in his own right but as Mrs. Sonia Gandhi's nominee. As a Rajya Sabha member, he is not even directly elected by the people. Thus the Prime Minister has the mandate of neither the party nor the people, in the real sense. Is it realistic to expect such a person to be a crusader for reform in a massive democracy like ours, bristling with problems and diversities?

Those who raised him to the high pedestal of 'architect of economic reform' did so as a political strategy to sidestep Narasimha Rao. The media lapped it up. And people started believing it because of constant dinning. But those who watched Dr. Singh carefully from his early years in the government knew that he has been a careerist, performing well when guided by a leader. He obviously could not succeed in the challenging task of economic reform when he himself became the leader by proxy.

Chapter 19

In Civil Aviation Ministry

The appointment given to me next, after the assignment in the Commerce Ministry, was as Secretary in the Ministry of Civil Aviation. This also marked the last phase in my civil service career. For one recruited to the Indian Administrative Service, the peak of ambition is to attain the level of Secretary to the Government of India, which is about the highest level an officer can ordinarily attain. Very few reach the position of Cabinet Secretary, a single post in the entire Government. No one from my batch could become Cabinet Secretary owing to age constraint. Air transport was a field entirely new to me but I was confident enough to do it. I believe that a long journey in higher civil service gives adequate opportunity to grasp the essentials of higher management in any field. I did not know, however, that I was coming into Civil Aviation at a particularly turbulent time.

The origin of civil aviation in India can be traced to JRD Tata's air-mail service in 1932 but its real growth came after World War II. With war-surplus transport aircraft becoming available at throw-away prices, several business houses in India had set-up air transportation companies, resulting in a glut. At the time of our independence there were as many as nine airlines, all owned by well-known industrial houses. Each of these was also close to terminal sickness. The situation did not improve despite state patronage and subsidy. The option of voluntary merger, suggested as a way out, did not materialise. The industry continued to drift until it was nationalised in 1953. A perusal of government papers leading to nationalisation and the formation of Indian Airlines and Air India leaves a distinct impression that the financially exhausted owners of the erstwhile airline companies, having failed to rehabilitate through voluntary merger, felt relieved at the prospect of nationalisation, notwithstanding some murmur. They received assured compensation and additionally, in recognition of JRD Tata's pioneering work in the field of aviation, the Government of India retained, under his Chairmanship, Air India as a separate public sector corporation while merging the rest of the industry into the Indian Airlines Corporation.

Thereafter, for forty years, from 1953 to 1993, scheduled airlines operation remained a state monopoly by an Act of Parliament. Not only was the industry saved from imminent collapse but air services expanded progressively, covering a large number of destinations all over the country including the north-east, where Indian Airlines provided vital communication links. But a noxious combination of industrial unrest and insensitivity to passenger needs developed alongside. The international arm—Air India—functioned better for some years but deterioration set in there as well. Even Indian Airlines had several bright patches, thanks to the determined efforts of some dedicated employees, but the overall experience was one of deteriorating service quality. Strike and go-slow on the part of better paid operational staff—pilots and engineers—had a crippling effect.

The finances of both companies took a severe beating. In this unhappy scenario came the huge burden on Indian Airlines of a massive fleet acquisition of over 30 Airbus A320 aircraft.

This expansion which became highly controversial and, after the change of government in 1989, became the subject matter of a CBI case, would in any case have thrown a heavy burden on the airline, ill-prepared as it was for the induction of the new generation of aircraft on such a large scale. The problem was compounded by the grounding of the entire newly acquired fleet for over a year, following a crash at Bangalore. The grounding of the fleet was ordered by Prime Minister VP Singh on political considerations to show in a bad light his predecessor, Rajiv Gandhi who had approved the purchase. It was a blow even the best world-class airline would have found hard to recover from; it severely damaged Indian Airlines. Indiscipline among employees grew and passenger discontent turned into disgust against the state monopoly.

This prompted some enterprising people to enter the field of aviation with air-taxi services catering to the connectivity requirements of foreign tourists. The Air Corporations Act of 1953, under which Air India and Indian Airlines had been created, permitted *ad hoc,* non-scheduled service of the nature of taxi operation by private agencies but vested monopoly rights to operate scheduled air services in the state-owned corporations. The law did not permit air-taxi operators to start scheduled air-services, which they did—initially on the sly but later in full knowledge of the government. This infuriated the unionised employees of the air corporations, who were perhaps more keen to protect the monopoly rights of their corporations than to improve the quality of service to passengers.

This was the scenario when I joined as a Secretary (Civil Aviation), towards the close of 1991. The first day in my new Ministry passed off with usual courtesy calls by senior officers; Minister Madhavrao Scindia was out of station. Late that night, at around 1 a.m., I was woken up by ringing of my RAX (restricted telephone). At the other end was the Minister himself. I wondered for a moment if he was calling up at that hour to tick me off for not meeting him soon after he was scheduled to return to Delhi, early in the evening. Although that, happily, was not the purpose of his call, the reason was even more disturbing. He told me that he had just arrived in Delhi as his flight from Bombay (now Mumbai), scheduled to reach Delhi in the evening, was deliberately delayed by a 'Go Slow' launched all of a sudden by Indian Airlines pilots to protest against some management decision. From his tone and the brief conversation we had at that hour, I got the impression that he was not only enraged at this action of the pilots but also considered it as a personal affront. I spoke a few words to soothe his nerves and assured him that I would follow up early next morning. While his anger against the irresponsible act of the pilots was understandable, I wondered why he was taking it as a personal affront!

That matter became clear when I discussed next morning with the Chairman, Indian Airlines and other senior officials. The immediate provocation for the pilots was an order by the management, requiring some modification to their uniform, passed apparently without adequate prior consultation. This was such a minor issue that ordinarily the grievance could have been redressed by discussion and the matter should not have led to an agitation. The real cause was the perception that the management was riding rough shod over the Pilots' Union and Scindia, a high profile hands-on Minister, was perceived as the architect of the aggressive policy.

It appeared that the Chairman of Indian Airlines, Air Marshal (Retired) Ramdas, a fine straight-forward person, was not in a position to defuse the agitation, which had already disrupted several flights in the morning with inevitable cascading effect. My subsequent discussion with the Minister gave me the impression that though he was not averse to meeting representatives of the pilots, he expected them to seek an interview, which was unlikely. The only other way to normalise flights was for me to take the initiative of discussing with the pilots. The Minister readily accepted my offer to do so. The Director (Operations) of Indian Airlines, himself a senior pilot, agreed to get them to meet me. Air Marshal

Ramdas voluntarily stayed away lest his presence became an impediment to a frank exchange of views.

My meeting with the union representatives started late that evening, around 9 p.m. Apart from the President and half a dozen office-bearers of the Union, the only other person present was the Director (Operations) who brought them to me. I had been apprised of repeated misconduct on the part of pilots and was doubtful initially if they would at all be amenable to reason. But their courtesy and sobriety put me at ease soon after our talks started. They spoke their minds freely and I was impressed that, far from misusing their freedom, they put across their grievances cogently and politely. After an exchange of views I got the impression that the basic problem was one of bruised egos, owing to inadequate communication. The pilots felt that the management did not care to give their views due regard and consideration while the management thought that firm handling would disabuse them of their inflated ego.

Being a complete stranger to civil aviation at the time, I did some quick thinking and decided that I must first establish my sincerity as an unbiased person genuinely interested in removing obstacles to harmonious functioning of the airline. Naturally, a lot of discussion was necessary. The meeting continued till well past mid-night and the outcome was pleasant beyond expectation. The pilots agreed to resume normalcy early next morning and I undertook to have further consultation on all outstanding issues. I also obtained an assurance from the pilots that as a gesture of goodwill they would make a courtesy call on the Minister next morning, after resumption of normal flight schedule. Soon after the meeting dispersed, I rang up the Minister and delivered him the good news. He was mightily pleased and was generous in his compliments to me. Both of us were relieved (as was Air Marshal Ramdas) that the unhappy situation had been defused.

Little did I know that a plan had been launched by self-seeking elements to misuse this occasion and discredit the Air Marshal and have him replaced. Ramdas was a man of character and integrity. I was looking forward to working closely with him in sorting out problems that had weakened Indian Airlines over the years. But that was not to be. I had no idea who the principal actor was in the sinister plan; maybe someone who thought he could step into the Air Marshal's shoes. Be that as it may, the following morning, while I was delighted to find that the pilots had resumed normalcy as promised, a totally unexpected situation awaited me in the office.

Ramdas came with his letter of resignation and told me that he wished to leave with dignity. He had failed to get an appointment to meet the Minister to discuss some outstanding matters and this had confirmed his impression that he was no longer welcome as Chairman. I was utterly surprised. My efforts to dissuade him from taking the precipitous step on a mere presumption succeeded when I assured him that I would arrange his meeting with the Minister so that issues, if any, could be sorted out. He waited in my room and I went across to the Minister. I asked him plainly if he wanted Ramdas to go. He expressed no emotion but gave a reply in the negative. Capitalising on that, I requested him to allow me to send Ramdas, waiting in my room, to see him. The Minister replied that he would send for him after a while. I came back and gave Ramdas what I thought was good news. We chatted for quite some time but no call came from the Minister. I sent a reminder, without effect. I had no idea if he consulted anyone else but since no call came until about 1 p.m., Ramdas left, leaving his letter of resignation with me. He was in no doubt that the Minister wanted him to make room for a favourite. Had he not insisted on tendering his resignation, I would have tried my best to bridge the gap between the Minister and the Chairman. In any case, it would not have been possible for any 'favourite' to just walk in and take his position.

When I met the Minister later in the day with Ramdas's resignation letter, he expressed no surprise or regret. It became obvious that he had wanted him to go. But in fairness I must record that he did not give even the slightest hint that he wanted anyone in particular to succeed Ramdas. He suggested that I should act as the Chairman until a regular appointment was made, but I explained that a better alternative would be to give interim charge to a Joint Secretary, leaving the Secretary to remain as a buffer between the airline and the government. He agreed with me. An excellent opportunity of addressing some nagging problems of Indian Airlines pilots, with goodwill and cooperation of the pilots themselves, was lost. A Ministry official, howsoever competent, holding charge as Chairman on *ad hoc* basis in addition to his normal duties could not be anything other than a mere holding operation. This continued for a long time until the Public Enterprises Selection Board found a successor to Ramdas.

There was another unexpected development within a day or two. The Minister called up early one morning seeking my view on a note for consideration of the Cabinet. As no such note was given to me the previous day until I left office late in the evening, I was somewhat surprised. When I informed the Minister that I would get back to him after going through the papers in the office, he replied that the Cabinet was going to meet in a short while and offered to send his car to me so that we could drive together to the Prime Minister's house for the Cabinet meeting and I could brief him on the way. That suited me fine although I had no inkling of the matter that was coming up for consideration. The 'Note for the Cabinet' which the Minister gave me, as he got into the car on my reaching his house, had been sponsored by the Ministry of Finance; the subject was Disinvestment in Public Sector Undertakings (PSUs). It was a brief note with an annexure listing twenty or so PSUs, for which the Cabinet was requested to approve disinvestment of 20% of the share capital. On top of the list was Air India.

As a very short time was available to me, I refrained from going into the desirability or otherwise of the proposal and merely said that the proposal, in so far as it related to Air

India, was just not feasible. The reason I gave was simple: Air India was not a company in the ordinary sense, nor did it have any share capital to disinvest; it was a statutory corporation created by an Act of Parliament. I said this out of my general awareness and the Minister wondered how such an absurd proposal was submitted for approval at the highest level of Government. He asked me repeatedly if I was sure of my facts. When I was reassuring the Minister, we both alighted at the PM's house. Dr. Manmohan Singh, who was then the Finance Minister, was also getting out of his car. Mr. Scindia confronted him immediately and asked how this unworkable proposal was sponsored; Dr. Singh looked enquiringly at me. We had known each other since the 1970s, when he was Economic Advisor in the Ministry of Commerce. When I reminded him of the status of Air India as a statutory Corporation having no share capital to disinvest, he readily accepted and was visibly embarrassed. It was left to Scindia to bring up the issue in the Cabinet where Prime Minister Narasimha Rao desired that a separate note be put up by the Ministry of Civil Aviation in respect of Air India.

Under normal practice, whenever a proposal is placed before the Cabinet, it becomes the duty of the sponsoring Ministry to first have prior consultation with the other Ministries concerned and incorporate their views in the note submitted for consideration. Had the right procedure been followed, the Finance Minister would have been spared the embarrassment of being caught unaware of the status of Air India that rendered his proposal infeasible. At the inter-Ministry consultation stage the Ministry of Civil Aviation would have pointed out the factual position and Air India could have been dealt with differently, which is what happened when the Cabinet ordered it.

Those were the early days of economic liberalisation. India's balance of payments situation having become precarious, we had sought comfort in the lap of the International Monetary Fund. Fiscal stabilisation and economic liberalisation, which we ourselves should have initiated long before in our own national interest, were now being forced on us by the IMF. A lobby had also developed advocating liberalisation indiscriminately and at times merely to please external forces. I was already aware of this, having served as Additional Secretary (External Finance) in DEA and Special Secretary (Commerce). How the Air India disinvestment issue played out is a story worth telling in this context.

A policy decision had been taken by the government to go for disinvestment in selected PSUs up to a maximum of 20%. Since a separate note was called for in the case of Air India, I examined the matter with reference to relevant statutory provisions and put up a draft Note, setting out a series of steps that were required to be taken in order to bring Air India within the ambit of disinvestment. On the day I was finalising the note for submission to my Minister, there was a surprise development, I received an overseas call from our Executive Director at the World Bank who tried to persuade me to seek approval for disinvestment in Air India of up to 51% instead of 20%. I explained to him that as far as I could visualise, it would take a long time to first carry out the requisite amendments to the Air Corporations Act, to enable disinvestment and then to create equity capital before a part of it could be disinvested; I thought it was premature to debate whether the ceiling of disinvestment needed to be raised to 51% from the generally applicable 20%.

The Executive Director was known to me for years. I had no difficulty in getting him to accept my view. But the forces that made him speak to me did not rest there. The suggestion given to me was made to my Minister. He did not tell me who made the suggestion to him though I could easily guess who it was. Scindia asked me if there was any harm if the suggestion was incorporated in the note. I mentioned to him the reasons I had given to the Executive Director and added that while I had no problem if the Minister asked for the ceiling to be raised to 51%, I would find it difficult to give cogent reasons in support of the higher ceiling for Air India while it remained at 20% as the general policy of the Government. He looked at me with a twinkle in his eye and substituted in his own hand the 20% mentioned in the draft note by 51% without spelling out why. The amended note was sent for consideration by the Cabinet. About the twinkle in Scindia's eye, I must say that this gesture became a lovable indication to me whenever he was about to express a view that was at variance with mine. Needless to say, it promoted better understanding between us while allowing adequate space for honest difference of opinion.

Our note on the issue of disinvestment in Air India came up for consideration of the Cabinet a few weeks later. The Cabinet endorsed all the preparatory steps that we had spelt out in order that a stage could be reached to undertake disinvestment but the proposed enhancement of the disinvestment ceiling to 51% was not approved. The disapproval came to me as a big surprise. The Minister himself had proposed the higher ceiling, in the face of my advice against it. I had thought that he would have done so after making sure that it would find acceptance by the Cabinet. He was deeply embarrassed by the disapproval.

I never asked him what transpired in the Cabinet but I felt disturbed that certain elements within the government had interfered in the working of our Ministry and succeeded in forcing their agenda on my Minister, instead of taking the straight-forward route of proposing the measure themselves. Those who caused the embarrassment were obviously keen to demonstrate that our public enterprises were up for grab. There could not be a better choice than Air India with its international visibility. Having failed to enlist my support through the Executive Director in Washington DC, they managed to brainwash Scindia. But the Cabinet decision came as a clear signal that the Narasimha Rao Government favoured calibrated reform, not reform of the gung-ho type that followed the collapse of the Soviet Union.

Another incident of my early days in the Ministry needs to be mentioned. One afternoon a Joint Secretary brought a file and told me that I might endorse a proposal which the

Minister had asked him to put up for the reconstitution of the Boards of Directors of Air India and Indian Airlines, inducting non-official members chosen by the Minister. The two Boards were composed of only part-time official members, apart from the Chairmen, and there was need to expand the Boards. While I had no objection in principle to the induction of non-officials, I was of the view that the Boards should also have whole-time functional Directors as members, in areas such as Operation, Finance, Planning and Commercial. As a matter of fact, in the light of my experience in the management of successful public enterprises like BHEL and HMT, I had thought of creating whole-time posts of functional Directors in the two air corporations to strengthen top management and policy making. I had not been able to initiate this action as other issues needing urgent attention had cropped up.

When the Joint Secretary brought up the matter of Board-level appointment, I thought of putting up my comprehensive proposal and asked the Joint Secretary to leave the file with me. That very evening I submitted the case to the Minister with my proposal in a reasoned note. Later on, in the evening when I was about to have dinner at home, the Minister rang up to say that he wanted to have the appointment of non-official Directors announced soon and wondered why I had brought up other matters. I clarified that the announcement could still be made without waiting for the creation of the posts of functional Directors, as I had made no comment on the suitability or otherwise of the non-officials proposed. While agreeing with me the Minister desired that we discuss the matter in the office next morning.

The following day we had a prolonged discussion in the office. Mr. Scindia tried to persuade me to withdraw my note and merely endorse the proposal to reconstitute the Boards by inducting non-officials. His view was that, orders could be issued inducting the non-officials and the matter of appointing Functional Directors could be processed separately. I explained to him that what he wanted could still be done if he passed a brief order on the file to that effect and there was no need to withdraw the note which I had recorded. I even offered to record the note myself, referring to my discussion with him. But he was reluctant and raised the larger issue of the impact that the file noting would have in the Ministry.

He felt that if my recorded note remained on file, it would appear that the Minister and the Secretary had a difference of opinion and were not on the same wavelength. He was of the view that no such signal should be given. He went on to suggest that ordinarily I should discuss an issue with him before recording my view, to avoid any impression of difference of opinion. Recalling his earlier experience in the Ministry of Railways, he said that the Chairman and Members of the Railway Board invariably held prior discussion with him before sending up any proposal for approval. The same practice, he added, was followed even by my predecessor in the Ministry of Civil Aviation. Although our conversation was marked by extreme cordiality, the underlying thought was alien to me.

It went against the basic principle which required all relevant material and viewpoints brought on record to enable the Government take a conscious decision in a matter. I said so, adding with due respect, that had it been otherwise, only a few stenographers would be adequate to run a Ministry and a large complement of officers would be redundant. What I said could have annoyed any Minister, not to speak of Mr. Scindia, who was a Maharaja! But it goes to his credit that he gave no indication of annoyance; on the other hand he complemented me. We went ahead with the appointment of non-official Directors, delinking the issue regarding Functional Directors. Thereafter we got so busy in tackling more urgent issues, diffusing agitations and facing rough weather in the Parliament that my favourite plan of management strengthening remained dormant.

The pernicious effect of the Railway Board practice of 'prior consultation' became known in public twenty years later in course of investigation into what came to be known as Railway Board Appointments Scam that forced Minister Pawan Kumar

Bansal to resign in 2013. In course of this investigation, the Chairman of the Board confessed that he could not formulate his recommendation for appointment of a General Manager because every time he broached the subject with the Minister, Bansal deferred discussion and no proposal for the appointment could be made for want of prior consultation with him.

I wonder why a Chairman or a Member of the Railway Board should give up his responsibility to make recommendation on file and wait for prior consultation to know the mind of the Minister unless the objective is to tailor the proposal to suit the Minister's wish rather than requirement of the administration. Yet, 'prior consultation' with the Minister had apparently been invested with the sanctity of rule by sheer servile practice in the Railway Board (perhaps in other Ministries also), to the detriment of good governance. Such abdication of responsibility invariably leads to lethargy and corruption if it becomes the established practice in Government.

Soon after joining the Ministry of Civil Aviation, I had noticed a practice, unusual in the government, of notes being submitted to the Minister with the prefix Honourable. I found this rather odd in a republic like ours where the earlier practice of Ministers officially being addressed as Honourable Minister was consciously given up when India became a republic in 1950. Important persons continued to be addressed at public functions with the prefix of Honourable as a mark of respect but its use in Government was abolished. In my long civil service career I had not seen its use in government papers until I came to Civil Aviation. I did not wish to continue the servile practice and started submitting papers to the Minister with the endorsement M(CA), M standing for Minister and CA for Civil Aviation. A senior colleague cautioned me that the Minister may not approve of the change and I should revert back to the previous practice but I did not do so. It goes to the credit of Mr. Scindia that, even in the unlikely event of his dislike over the change, he never gave expression to his displeasure. It is only a servile mindset that gives unwarranted importance and generates inflated ego.

My most challenging problem, however, was the mushrooming of air-taxi companies, which had assumed disturbing proportions. These companies operated mainly on the lucrative routes between metros, particularly the most profitable Bombay-Delhi sector. Several of these companies had come up over the past year. They provided welcome alternatives to passengers who were tired of the deteriorating service of Indian Airlines. But there was a serious legal issue involved. Only the state-owned Corporations—Air India and Indian Airlines—were allowed, by law, to operate regular air services with predetermined schedules. Even so, the private companies did with impunity what was prohibited under the law. To refresh memory, it is worth recalling the names of some of these companies: East West Airline, Modiluft, Damania, NESCO, Sahara, to name a few. They are non-existent now but were widely known then. What surprised me most was that the patent illegality of the operation was not only in full knowledge of the government but was even encouraged by it, on the dubious ground that it benefited the public.

When I saw the file on the subject I was both surprised and saddened. The proposal to encourage air-taxi companies to operate as regular airlines had originally come from a senior officer in the Prime Minister's Office (PMO) during the tenure of VP Singh as Prime Minister. It was then put up on file to my predecessor, with a brief note referring to the relevant provision of the Air Corporations Act which needed amendment to enable the government go ahead with the idea proposed in the PMO's letter. The file ended with a minute by the previous Secretary that he had discussed the matter with the Minister. The law remained as before but air-taxi companies operated in contravention of it. When I questioned how Parliament had condoned this, I was shown the Minister's reply to a question raised in the Parliament, to the effect that air taxi companies were authorised to operate only non-scheduled operations. On paper this was undoubtedly so, but they operated scheduled services as well while government agencies looked the other way.

While I was deliberating the course of action to adopt, I received a phone call from the then Director General of the Confederation of Indian Industries (CII) inviting me to an interaction with the aviation industry. I had known him since my days in the Ministry of Industry, long before the formation of CII, which came to represent industry groups that advocated economic liberalisation. I replied to him that I would rather wait until the law permitted de-monopolisation of the airlines industry before I could purposefully interact with industry organisations as I did not wish to encourage scheduled operations by private companies in contravention of the law. He surprised me by saying that the industry was well aware of the legal position and added that since my predecessor had had several rounds of interaction with them on the expansion of air services in the country by private parties, I need not be inhibited by the law. I politely declined the invitation and preferred to wait until I got a clear policy directive on the course to be adopted, having regard to the law as it stood.

The papers on the subject in the Ministry were fragmented. One file started with the letter from the VP Singh PMO and ended with a brief note by my predecessor, which has been referred to already. There were other files as well, all running concurrently. One of these contained a formal Statement made in Parliament in April 1990 by the Minister of Civil Aviation in VP Singh Government, extensively liberalising the Air Taxi Scheme of 1986. This Statement, which closely followed the PMO letter referred to above and left the door ajar for poaching by the air-taxi companies, was a clear invitation to the mess created in the air transport industry. No one in the Ministry at that time could have missed the point that it was a clever trick consciously played by the then Minister (not Scindia) to circumvent the law without taking the legitimate course of first asking Parliament to remove the state monopoly.

Worse, the Minister avoided seeking Cabinet approval for

a whole year after the Statement was made in the Parliament. When the proposed amendment to Section 18 of the Act for removal of state monopoly eventually went to the Cabinet in March 1991, it was not approved. Perhaps the Cabinet was not glad that the Minister had taken unilateral action without consideration of the pros and cons. The papers thereafter kept moving back and forth between different Ministries. Scindia, as Minister of Civil Aviation, had several meetings with air-taxi operators along with senior officials of the Ministry and other agencies concerned. The minutes of those meetings explicitly emphasised the need to continue the liberalised policy, despite its legal infirmity, which the officers were asked to implement faithfully.

All these left me in no doubt that liberalisation, howsoever desirable, was being brought in surreptitiously by the back door. And the worse thing was that, the law was being violated with impunity because Government did not muster courage to ask for its amendment by the Parliament. I found it difficult to reconcile myself to this and explained this to Scindia. I made it abundantly clear that I would need to direct all my officers, including enforcement officials of DGCA, to prevent further abuse of the law unless urgent steps were taken to bring it in line with Government's policy of liberalised air-taxi operation.

I also emphasised that amending only one Section of the Air Corporations Act to permit scheduled operation by air-taxi companies, leaving the rest of the Act intact, would not do. It would amount to ringing the death knell of Indian Airlines, which would still be bound hand and foot by the subsisting provisions of the Act while air-taxi operators enjoyed all commercial freedom. It gave me a great relief when I found that Scindia too felt uneasy with the prevailing contradictions and uncertainties. He agreed with me that it would be better to repeal the Act as it had fulfilled the objective of nationalisation and state monopoly was proving counterproductive.

We lost no time in seeking Cabinet approval to repeal the

Air Corporations Act and restructure the two corporations—Indian Airlines and Air India—into limited companies to enable them have the commercial freedom to compete with private operators. We took just about three months to complete the entire process including drafting of the Bill and having it presented before Parliament. Action was initiated concurrently to have the two entities valued, articles of association drafted, names of the proposed companies—Indian Airlines Limited and Air India Limited registered—and so on. As statutory Corporations under the Act of 1953, the two carriers had no freedom either to fix their own tariff or to attract talent by offering attractive compensation packages. Government rules bound them to provide services on concessional tariff to specified areas such as the North-East. Furthermore, they had no access to the capital market and had to look for budgetary support from the government, which was hard to get. Meanwhile, for well over a year the air-taxi operators had been eating into their bread basket with impunity, under the watch of its owner—the government! We had hoped that the Bill repealing the Air Corporation Act of 1953 would be enacted soon and the period of agony would end; but that was not to be—more on that later.

Soon after it became known to all, that we were trying to get the Air Corporations Act repealed, there was a flood of requests from people whom I had never come across, seeking appointments with me. I learnt that they were senior executives of international consulting firms wishing to advise us on privatisation. They had taken it for granted that the Air Corporations would simply collapse and a killing could be made of their massive assets. My personal staff was instructed to say in reply that we would seek advice when needed. But there was no respite until I wrote down on one of the written requests for appointment that we were not interested in privatisation; what we were aiming at was de-monopolisation; we were confident that the two Airlines would operate successfully in a competitive environment.

While others may have had doubts over this robust

optimism, I never had any. I had seen from close quarters in the Ministry of Industry that, given genuine autonomy, a public sector company such as BHEL could successfully meet the challenge of international competition. I was also aware of South Korea's experience of achieving great success with government-owned companies in the early years of development of that country. There was no reason why, in my view, an opportunity could not be given to the government owned airlines.

It became clear that far from hastening the demise of the air corporations I was interested in rehabilitating them, albeit after de-monopolising the industry. But intrepid liberalisers were displeased as they wished to see the massive assets of the Corporations pass into private hands. Contrary to the superficial impression that the government had built the two Corporations by giving them huge funds, all that had been given was just about Rs. 5 crore each for their establishment, and some interest-carrying loans and guarantees towards servicing of commercial borrowings contracted by them for fleet acquisition over the years. With these meagre funds, the Corporations had managed to build massive assets which the privatisation lobby was keen to grab. But some of us who believed in the declared government policy of calibrated liberalisation stood as impediments, for which we were targeted.

My attention was drawn one day to the lead feature published in a major national daily, written by a journalist who is now a Managing Editor or Editor-in-Chief. The feature described how key Secretaries to the Government of India were treading the path of economic reform. While the narrative covered Secretaries of practically all economic Ministries and put them in two categories, pro-reform and no-reform, it carried colour photographs of only three secretaries: S Kanungo (Civil Aviation), MS Ahluwalia (Finance), and AV Ganesan (my predecessor, who had moved to Commerce). The latter two were depicted as leading reformers. I was not placed in the 'no-reform' category but it was stated that I belonged to 'that fast vanishing tribe of IAS officers hesitant about reform'. There was a further remark, perhaps to prompt me to join the ranks of the 'reformers', that being a 'true-blue bureaucrat' I would carry out to the logical extent any clear directions which the Government gave. I knew that journalist personally and rang him up to enquire how he had formed his opinion without any discussion with me in the matter. Skirting the issue, he replied with a counter question that answered my query. He questioned me if I was not aware of the impression my colleagues had of me. I could easily guess who could have been his source.

While this type of targeting was being done through a section of the media and elsewhere, the air transport industry was groaning under acute problems of over-capacity on the one hand and traffic stagnation on the other; replay of the pre nationalisation scenario of early 1950s. The industry had entered a recessionary phase globally by the time air-taxi companies in India were encouraged by the Statement of April 1990 to bring additional aircraft into the country, taking advantage of low lease rentals for aircraft rendered surplus in the international market. They made profits by concentrating operation on lucrative trunk routes, with very little investment. When traffic stagnation overtook the Indian air transport sector, they too came under pressure. In a stagnant market Indian Airlines lost traffic to them while carrying the burden of massive investment in equipment and infrastructure as well as the social responsibility of catering to the entire country, including remote areas, at concessional tariff.

The acuteness of the problem may be judged from the fact that during the period 1987-91, while passenger traffic in the country declined, aircraft capacity registered a growth of more than 50%. Initially the loss was suffered only by Indian Airlines but eventually the private operators also suffered since air traffic did not pick-up for several years. Thus the Statement of April 1990, put into operation as a progressive measure of liberalisation, became counter-productive. Its pernicious effect was neither examined before its announcement nor any mid-course corrective applied during implementation. The Government refused to reconsider the policy although its illegality was pointed out repeatedly.

In this situation of excess capacity I found, to my utter surprise, a proposal in the Ministry for acquisition of new aircraft by Indian Airlines and Air India. Massive purchase was envisaged for modernisation and expansion of the fleet. Details of the aircraft required had been worked out and the cost of procurement was estimated at Rs. 40,000 crore or thereabout, at 1990 prices. There was yet another disquieting feature of this fleet acquisition plan. It may be recalled that of the thirty odd Airbus A320 aircraft purchased by Indian Airlines at the time when Rajiv Gandhi was the Prime Minister, one had crashed at Bangalore shortly after induction. VP Singh had grounded the entire Airbus A320 fleet for a whole year following the crash, casting doubt on its reliability to malign Rajiv Gandhi.

After suffering the crushing financial burden imposed by the grounding of this entire fleet, Indian Airlines was still struggling to re-induct into service the grounded Airbus A320s. Just one or two of these had started flying when I joined the Ministry, leaving the major part of the fleet still grounded. The proposal for massive fresh acquisition of aircraft worth Rs. 40,000 crore looked strange, to say the least, while a large number of brand new Airbus A320s awaited re-induction—and all this at a time of recession in the industry! When I discussed the matter with the Minister I found that he was in favour of advance planning for fleet modernisation but was not keen on commitment for aircraft purchase. After further discussion on the subject I got the impression that he was under pressure to purchase from some quarters which I could not identify initially. One of the sources of pressure surfaced when a senior executive of the Boeing Company tried to convince me of the need to expedite action. Though my mind was firmly set against aircraft procurement at that stage, I continued to discuss the matter with the Minister.

Taking advantage of his expressed desire for advance action towards fleet modernisation I had the proposal recast as an exercise in perspective planning, not procurement. He agreed and we took a note to the Cabinet seeking approval in principle of the perspective plan, making it clear that actual purchase would be governed by specific approval, to be sought after examination of technical and financial details as and when necessary. By the time the Cabinet approval came, I had become aware of the source, apart from Boeing, of the high pressure lobbying that was working behind the scene. It was a god-man well known in government and media circles for his tremendous clout those days. I was no match for his prowess.

Even so, I saw to it that details of the purchase proposals were remitted from one committee to another and not a single aircraft was purchased until I retired some years later. My assessment was that the combined fleet of Air India and Indian Airlines, optimally utilised, was adequate to cater to a realistic traffic projection for several years to come and there was no need for any fresh acquisition in the next five years. As it turned out, the fear of kickback built into price offers in such cases, was so strong that even long after my retirement, officials avoided placing any order for fifteen years. Anyway, my becoming the fall guy was inevitable, certainly for the god-man. He is not heard of now but in those days it was said that almost everyone who counted in Delhi paid court to him.

Those who were interested in forcing the fresh purchase of aircraft, notwithstanding the prevailing excess capacity, were naturally unhappy with me. I had also become unacceptable to the privatisation lobby which had powerful support in the government. The objectives of the two groups may not have had much in common. The first group expected the air corporations to serve their interests by purchase of planes; the privatisation lobby, on the other hand, wanted to see their virtual liquidation. I suited the interests of neither group. Having failed to convert me to the pursuit of their objectives, they wanted me ousted from Civil Aviation.

Evidence of this came from none other than the Cabinet Secretary. I got an unexpected call from him enquiring if I would like to join the Central Administrative Tribunal. The retirement age for the IAS was 58 and I had crossed 56; by going to the Tribunal I could serve till the age of 62. The incentive offered was obvious. Even though Tribunal work did not suit my temperament, I promptly conveyed my willingness to go as there was no reason for me to hang on to Civil Aviation if I was not required there. A few days later an Under Secretary of the Cabinet Secretariat advised me to send him a written request for the Tribunal appointment. I felt a little irritated and responded by answering that while I was most willing to go wherever Government wished to send me, there was no question of my sending an application. This was not intended as a snub to him or to the Cabinet Secretary, who was a friend. I could see that the latter was under pressure but there was no further development in the matter. Had the pressure been from the Prime Minister or my own Minister I could have been shifted any way. It was clear that those who wanted to remove me from Civil Aviation were elsewhere in the government. I continued to work undeterred after ascertaining from Mr. Scindia that he did not wish to have me removed.

Hes was Minister of Tourism as well and was keen to promote the flow of foreign tourists into the country. Tour operators were pressing him to open up the Indian skies to foreign airlines as Air India was seen as a constraint on growth. To revamp Air India, Scindia had brought YC Deveshwar as its Chairman, who later became a highly successful head of ITC Ltd. Deveshwar brought about some improvement but pressure continued to grow to open up. My review of the situation showed that while foreign airlines operating services to India were concentrating on Delhi and Bombay and some of them wanted more frequencies to these two places, they were hardly utilising their entitlements to other international airports in India. Not a single European or American airline was operating to Kolkata.

The flow of foreign tourists to India was substantially lower than the combined entitlement of the various airlines. Where Air India was not in a position to use its entitlement fully, it had leased out some of its rights to the corresponding foreign airline to operate on payment of a fee, in accordance with international practice. While I was all in favour of enlarging the opportunity for international airlines to promote tourism, I wanted reciprocal rights for Air India. I took pains to explain this to the Minister who shared my view. We started bilateral negotiations with various countries with the stated objective of opening up the Indian skies while securing commensurate rights for our national carrier. As a result of these negotiations, additional rights were given to as many as 16 foreign airlines. In this connection I am tempted to recall how British Airways inflicted a strain on our nerves.

The representative of British Airways in India was an Englishman who used to articulate the views of foreign airlines in general, apart from serving the interests of his own airline. He had access to Scindia, who often consulted him informally. Initially, I was not bothered as the consultations were on issues of tourism promotion. After sometime, I found that the Minister was being given motivated inputs on matters in the exclusive purview of the Ministry of Civil Aviation, such as tariff regulation and landing rights. Of course, Scindia had the salutary practice of getting those inputs cross-checked but I found it odd that the General Manager of a foreign airline, several rungs lower than the Chief Executive, should be interacting frequently with the Minister while the Chief Executives of prestigious government companies including Air India found it difficult to meet even middle level Government officials in America or Europe. I waited for a suitable opportunity to speak to Scindia on this issue.

The opportunity came sooner than expected, though in a peculiar way. One day the Minister asked me if it was not time for Air India to initiate the process of upward revision of tariff for flights going out of India. When I told him that no such idea had been mooted by Air India, I learnt that it had come to him from British Airways. He told me that I should have the matter considered in consultation with the GM, British Airways. I needed no consultation as it was clear to me why the GM was pushing for it. The practice generally followed In international aviation those days was for the national carrier to establish a tariff for outward flights, which no airline exceeded in its operation, although resourceful airlines often offered discounted tickets in various ingenuous ways to attract customers.

Some of the foreign airlines wanted Air India to take the initiative for upward revision of air fares out of India so that they could undercut Air India, which would be bound by public sector constraints. Even though, I arranged for a meeting, as desired by the Minister. The views expressed at the meeting were on expected lines. The GM, perhaps unwittingly, overstated his case by referring to trends towards globalisation and liberalisation. That gave me the opportunity to spring a surprise. I questioned the prevailing global practice of establishing common fares and asked him why we should not take the lead in completely de-regulating fares? This was not at all favoured by foreign airlines as they were happy with the prevailing system that gave them the opportunity of disguised cartelisation and undercutting the national carrier when it suited them.

The enthusiasm displayed by the GM for revision of tariff suddenly ebbed. The meeting ended with the conclusion that no action was necessary. After the meeting, when only senior officials of the Ministry and Air India were left in the room, we chatted for a while. In course of this, I made a rather indiscrete remark which could have landed me in serious trouble. Referring to the GM, British Airways, who had just left, I said that in dealing with Mr. Scindia, the GM perhaps fancied himself in the role that Sir Thomas Roe had played in the court of Emperor Jahangir. This remark was bound to reach the Minister, perhaps with some embellishment. Ordinarily, a Minister could have taken serious exception to such a flippant remark by his Secretary. But, it goes to Scindia's credit that he did not allow his attitude towards me to be soured.

On the other hand, when I sheepishly briefed him on the proceedings of the meeting held on the tariff issue, he surprised me by saying, with the characteristic twinkle in his eye, how he enjoyed my Sir Thomas Roe remark and the suggestion to de-regulate fares. Thus put at ease, I briefly discussed with him how powerful nations of Europe advocated economic liberalisation only where it suited them and not otherwise. After that day I noticed that the Minister started distancing himself from the GM. The desired objective was achieved without my taking up the issue frontally from my side.

Some time later, a suggestion came from our Ministry of External Affairs that we should hold bilateral negotiations with the British Government to sign an Air Services Agreement during the forthcoming visit to India by the Queen of England. On checking up the pending proposals I found that the British had pitched their demands so high, while stubbornly refusing additional rights sought by Air India, that it was not possible to complete the negotiations within the short period left for the Queen's visit unless we were resigned to a meek surrender. MK Dixit, the Foreign Secretary, whom I consulted, did not require much convincing. He immediately saw the suggested negotiations as an attempt by the British side to hustle through an unequal agreement, taking advantage of the VVIP visit.

The suggestion was dropped and we heaved a sigh of relief, only to be pressurised again soon, this time by our High Commissioner to the UK, LM Singhvi, pleading with Scindia. He found the pressure hard to resist but had the good sense to deflect it to me. I was at home when the Minister rang up and after a brief preamble handed over the phone to Singhvi who spoke to me for nearly half an hour pleading the British case. I assured him that we would schedule the discussion after the Queen's visit, not before it.

This we did as promised and concluded a balanced agreement securing for our national carrier additional landing rights at Heathrow (which they had resisted stubbornly for a long time) while giving them much of what they wanted. Even after that, Air India faced serious difficulty in getting landing slots at Heathrow airport to utilise the additional rights it got. Our High Commission in London could do precious little. The landing slots were released by the British side only when British Airways needed to be bailed out in India on a particular issue on which the High Commissioner of UK in Delhi sought my help and we provided them the requisite relief. The events narrated here were spread over several months and there were many annoying moments during that period but I admired the tenacity with which the British pursued their interest. I wish we could emulate them in this.

It is worthwhile referring to another event in the management of our external relations in the area of civil aviation. The International Civil Aviation Organisation (ICAO) is the apex body that serves a very useful role in the co-ordination and management of aviation safety in member countries. It has a Governing Council of which India had long been a member. In the election for the Governing Council in 1992, South Korea staked its claim for membership and a contest became inevitable. We requested our Foreign Ministry to advise our missions abroad to seek the support of all member-countries for our candidature.

We were surprised on being told that India need not offer her candidature as South Korea would have overwhelming support in the election. We informally learnt that according to MEA's assessment, with Americans and other western powers supporting South Korea, we were unlikely to muster adequate support and should not spoil India's case for the higher goal of a permanent seat in the UN Security Council by entering the contest for the Governing Council of ICAO. Not only was the logic far-fetched but their assessment was also seriously flawed, as results would prove later. We had our way in going ahead with our candidature.

The election was to be held at a meeting of ICAO's General Assembly at Montreal and I had to be present there.

Incidentally, contrary to an impression that Aviation Secretaries in India often went on foreign visits, that was the only foreign trip I made during my entire tenure as Secretary Civil Aviation. We vigorously lobbied with the delegations of other countries and the results were most rewarding. India won with a thumping majority. A large measure of credit for this must go to the untiring efforts of Ravindra Gupta, then India's Representative to ICAO, based in Montreal. Our efforts also got a major boost from an impressive fund of goodwill for India created by his predecessor, Vivek Pattanayak, who later joined the top management of ICAO as Director. Both of them had earlier served as Joint Secretary in the Ministry of Civil Aviation.

Meanwhile, we were making sustained efforts to get a whole time Chief Executive for Indian Airlines, which was being managed by a Joint Secretary in addition to his duties in the Ministry. While awaiting the recommendation of the Public Enterprises Selection Board (PESB) we had tried to persuade some senior officials to respond to the PESB's invitation of candidature for the post. But no one was willing to do so. We also explored the possibility of appointment on whole-time deputation. We short-listed two officers for this purpose, in which one backed out and the other one was not approved at the higher level. I had recommended about half a dozen of the senior most officials of Indian Airlines then working as Directors (below Board level) to be considered by the PESB.

After interviewing the eligible candidates the PESB selected L Vasudev, who was CMD of Madras Fertilizers or had just completed that assignment. He was appointed immediately and we felt relieved that a whole time Chief Executive officer had been found at last for the ailing airline after Joint Secretary Pradip Banerji had done a fine holding operation as Acting Chairman for about six months. Vasudev started his duties well and I was impressed by his analytical approach to problems but I did not realise that he had developed an adversarial relationship with employees, particularly pilots. To this I shall revert later.

While air-taxis continued to encroach on the exclusive preserve of the air corporations, causing a progressive decline in the passenger load and profits of Indian Airlines, there were excessive pressure on landing and parking facilities at airports, particularly at Delhi and Bombay where air-taxi companies concentrated their operation bringing in more and more leased aircraft from abroad. Air traffic management over Indian skies came under considerable strain because aircraft movement, particularly on trunk routes, registered significant increase, although the passenger load for the industry as a whole declined. This again brought out the inadequacy and inappropriateness of the faulty policy of promoting substantially more aircraft operations without providing matching terminal facilities and navigational aids.

There was an urgent need to modernise our airports and greatly augment the facilities there. The airports were mostly of the Second World War period and the facilities available at most, barring the international airports of Delhi, Mumbai, Kolkata, Chennai and Thiruvananthapuram, could barely qualify for modern aircraft operation. As a matter of fact the Pilots' Union of Indian Airlines was frequently resorting to industrial action on the pretext of being made to fly to airports with inadequate landing and navigational aids. The terminal buildings at even state headquarters were tiny little unimpressive structures without baggage conveyers or trolleys.

Airport facilities needed to be improved immediately; landing and navigational aids as well as passenger conveniences had to be provided. Scindia took personal interest in the implementation of these plans. At his instance, a plan was also drawn up for the construction of new terminal buildings with baggage handling equipment and other facilities at twelve relatively more important airports, which were to be model airports. Radar and communication equipment had to be procured, technical manpower trained and complementary facilities provided in order to institute an effective system of air space management for better regulation and guidance of domestic and international flights.

While trying to upgrade infrastructure at airports and provide modern facilities for route navigation and surveillance, I found a mismatch between requirements and availability of funds. Those days we had two separate Authorities for airport management and development—one for the five international airports and the other for all the domestic airports in the country. The International Airports Authority of India (IAAI) had surplus funds at its disposal because it was handling large numbers of jumbo carriers on which parking and other fees were being collected at international rates. On the other hand, the National Airports Authority (NAA), which was responsible for air traffic control in the entire country, faced severe constraint of funds. Ground Controllers and Communications Engineers of NAA often felt over-worked and were not averse to agitating for better conditions of service. In addition to these problems, NAA also had the responsibility of managing many small and medium airports which lacked even minimal facilities.

After considering various options I decided that the best way forward was to merge the two Authorities as a single unified organisation could better meet the enormous task of infrastructure development. Scindia approved of the idea. There were some murmurs based on apprehensions on personnel issues. A blueprint for integration was prepared to avoid any abrupt action that could have unnerved sections of employees of both the Authorities. To start with, we proposed a common Chairman for the two organisations, while still keeping them as separate entities. Integration at the level of the Board of Directors was to be the next step, leaving amalgamation of cadres of employees of the two organisations to be done later.

As both the organisations were statutory authorities, the objective of their eventual merger could be achieved only after Government obtained parliamentary approval. I was determined not to adopt the subterfuge through which the Air Taxi scheme had been enlarged by hoodwinking Parliament. We quickly drafted the Bill for amalgamation of the two Authorities and introduced it in the Parliament. I had to appear before the Parliamentary Standing Committee which went into a clause-wise examination of the Bill and approved it, after which it was enacted. The late Pramod Mahajan, then a leading MP of the BJP who chaired the Standing Committee, put many searching questions but after being satisfied with the replies he adopted a very positive approach. The Bill was cleared by the Committee and approved by Parliament without any modification. Meanwhile, the Chairman of IAAI was completing his tenure. Instead of appointing anyone else in that vacancy we placed the Chairman of NAA in additional charge of IAAI, as a preparatory step towards merger.

As a result, the amalgamation was smooth when Parliamentary approval came. Ardhanareeswaran, the common Chairman of the two erstwhile Authorities became Chairman of the Airport Authority of India, the amalgamated body brought into being by a new Act of Parliament. It must be added that though the proposal of amalgamation was approved by Scindia, the passage of the Bill through the entire Parliamentary process was steered deftly by his successor, Ghulam Nabi Azad, who possessed an extraordinary ability to manage MPs not only of his own party but also of the Opposition.

A story that appeared in an important national daily a few months earlier may be mentioned here. It relates to the initial appointment of Ardhanareeswaran as Chairman of NAA. He was a couple of years senior to me in IAS. I knew that Ardha (as he was referred to by friends) was being appointed. His appointment was notified a few days later when Scindia was on tour. I got a call from him enquiring about Ardha's antecedents. I gave the requisite details and added that he was a friend of mine and I looked forward to working with him. Next morning I saw the news report referred to above which said that Scindia had brought in as

Chairman NAA, an officer senior to the Secretary in order that "Kanungo's wings may be clipped". To this day I have not figured out if this story was planted by the 'privatisation lobby' or by self styled well-wishers of Scindia who wanted a wedge driven between the Minister and the Secretary. In this they did not succeed, for Scindia's attitude towards me remained exactly as before.

The unified Airports Authority of India (AAI), although well placed to undertake improvement and modernisation of existing airports, lacked resources to undertake the construction of green field airports, requiring massive investment. The airports at Bangalore, Hyderabad and Mumbai were reaching saturation levels and had little space for expansion. Private participation was necessary to meet the requirement of funds but no private party was coming forward. The law did not preclude private investment in this sphere, but private capital was shy because the investment requirement was high and the payback period long. Even so, we continued to explore possibilities of airport development with private participation. Hope of success came from a rather unexpected source. An enterprising group of people, supported by the Government of Kerala, took the initiative of setting up a green field airport at Kochi. I recollect the tireless efforts made for this purpose by a young IAS officer who, I think, was the local Collector and later made the Chief Executive of the project. They were able to mobilise the requisite resources and we were happy to provide technical guidance from AAI. The result of this effort, an early example of PPP (Public Private Partnership), is a fully functional airport for everyone to see.

Our efforts to strengthen the foundation for a healthy civil aviation industry continued. A well-ordered industry required an effective regulatory mechanism to enforce safety and prevent malpractice in operation. The basic legal frame-work was in place and the Directorate General of Civil Aviation (DGCA) had the responsibility of executing this vital task. But years of state monopoly had led to the marginalisation of the DGCA. While the technical competence of the personnel in the DGCA was not in question, the induction of new generation aircraft and the sharp increase in flight operations following unrestrained operation of air-taxis brought the regulator under severe strain.

At the head of the organisation was a Director General (DG), with a single Deputy Director General (DDG) to assist him. The DG at that time was Sivaraman, a highly competent IAS officer. He had initiated a proposal for a modest increase in the strength of DGCA, but procedures were so circuitous that it took ages to get the posts created and longer still to fill them up. I recollect that the posts created at higher levels were those of three DDGs instead of one and a single post of Joint Director General (JDG) where none had existed earlier. I must confess that I failed to make substantive appointments to these posts until I retired, thanks to procedural hurdles. The consolation was that archaic recruitment rules were revised, enabling high calibre professionals in the organisation to be promoted to different levels.

Over the years, the government had carried on with an understaffed and de-motivated regulatory set-up in the vital sector of air transportation, where safety is a paramount consideration. The inadequately staffed DGCA had a structure and promotion policy that hardly promoted career growth. Once we were able to create a few more posts, I was determined to put an end to the age old practice of appointing, to the highest position of DG, officers coming on deputation from the IAS or the Air Force. I was convinced that a technical organisation like DGCA needed a competent professional at their top. I therefore, resisted successfully another officer being offered on deputation to succeed Sivaraman.

Yet the two most senior professionals in DGCA, bottled up for long periods in lower posts, were still ineligible to be appointed on a regular basis to the posts of DG and JDG. I had to resort to promoting Khola, the senior one, to discharge the duties of DG on an officiating basis. He remained DG for many years and after him other professionals succeeded to that position. But lately the post seems to have gone back again to officers coming on deputation, which does not speak well of professional management in the organisation.

Let us go back to Air India and Indian Airlines again, where efforts were being intensified to improve the quality of service and withstand competition from private players. While most employees responded well to the challenge, certain sections, habitually prone to extract benefits by threat of industrial action, were creating problems. Inadequate initiative at middle management levels, possibly due to over-bureaucratisation within the organisation, accentuated the problems. Deveshwar and Vasudev tried to motivate the employees to attain higher levels of efficiency but the results were not very encouraging. Agitation by unionised employees continued to afflict both Corporations.

The agitation in Air India became quite serious when its Flight Engineers went on strike. Conciliation failed and services were crippled. The management's efforts to have the strike declared illegal did not succeed. Deveshwar suggested that I should mediate. I organised a meeting along with Deveshwar and the Flight Engineers' Union. The issues that had snowballed into a major confrontation leading to massive disruption of services were amicably settled and normalcy was restored.

Indian Airlines, however, was drawn into a crisis that might well have led to its demise. If I remembered correctly, the issue was of Meal Allowance for pilots, a hardy perennial issue that had given rise to agitations in the past too. As a part of their compensation package, the pilots were entitled to Meal Allowance while on duty. Initially the allowance was modest, but once the Income Tax department declared the Meal Allowance tax-free when Rajiv Gandhi was Prime Minister, repeated revisions took place on recurrent demand. It was already disproportionately high when further revision was demanded by the Pilots' Union. The management resisted it. Vasudev was in touch with us while negotiation with the Union was in progress. Later on, matters precipitated and negotiations broke down.

The Union threatened the Government to go on strike. A contingency plan was drawn up to maintain services, relying on Executive Pilots and calling upon air-taxi companies to intensify their operations. Scindia personally oversaw the preparations. The Executive Pilots, on whom the contingency plan hinged, were a peculiar lot. They performed exactly the same duty as airline pilots, i.e. flying aircraft. A legal fiction had been created, however, by giving them managerial status with the expectation that they would then identify themselves with the management and not resort to industrial action along with unionised pilots, who were workmen under labour laws. I was not at all hopeful that the Executive Pilots would remain loyal to the management in the event of a strike by line pilots. Mr. Scindia had some apprehension too. However he told me that since Vasudev was confident of handling the situation he must have made sure that flight operations would be maintained by the Executive Pilots during a strike.

The strike began and confusion followed. The worst sufferers were the passengers and the only ones who benefited were air-taxi operators. Far from making up even a fraction of the shortfall in flights, they exploited the situation by jacking up the prices of their tickets. A few of the Executive Pilots operated some flights on trunk routes but that was far short of requirement. It was perhaps the second day of the strike when Vasudev rang up late in the evening and informed me that the Executive Pilots had also joined the strike en block. My immediate reaction was to ask him if that did not mean suspension of all flights. He surprised me by saying that he had wet-leased a number of aircraft from Uzbek Airlines, which were expected to arrive next morning along with their full complement of crew and would be pressed into service to maintain flights under the contingency plan.

I felt quite upset and wondered how planes could be wet-leased at such short notice and whether the arrangement would work. I called the Air Chief (Air Chief Marshal Suri), with whom I had been in touch since the strike began, and requested him to keep in readiness some transport pilots from the Air Force to operate our flights if necessary. Thereafter, I spoke with Mr. Scindia and apprised him of what I was proposing. His reaction to the news of Executive Pilots having joined the strike was on expected lines. But I noticed that, unlike me, he was not surprised at the wet-leasing of Uzbek aircraft.

The Uzbek planes came along with their crew and were pressed into service. However, passengers continued to suffer as only a few services could be operated with the limited number of hired aircrafts. No connectivity could be provided to places other than metros because operations of the hired aircraft, like those of air taxis, were mostly on trunk routes and fell far short of requirement. As more and more passengers were stranded and dissatisfaction mounted, Scindia's patience was wearing thin. Though I had cautioned him in advance on placing reliance on Executive Pilots, he never expected the contingency plan to collapse so soon. Late one evening he asked me over the phone, in a highly agitated voice, how much longer we needed to bear the wrath of passengers. I had no clear answer. Nor could I remind him that I had repeatedly advised against confrontation with the Unions until the industry was legally de-monopolised and further that in the event of a strike we had to be prepared for the long haul.

The agony of the strike continued but worse was to come. A few days later, catastrophe struck. Well past midnight I was woken up by a phone call informing me that a grossly delayed flight from Hyderabad had crashed while landing at Delhi airport and the aircraft was in flames. I rushed to the airport, driving my little Maruti Car on that intensely foggy winter night. The closer I came to the airport the greater was the drop in ground visibility until it was reduced to just a few feet on the runway. Even at a distance of about three hundred feet, I could not see a trace of the fire, much less the plane, and repeatedly enquired if the aircraft was actually burning. The massive conflagration of the burning aircraft gradually unfolded as I proceeded closer.

There appeared to be little hope of any passenger surviving the crash. But I was in for a big surprise—a pleasant one. I saw a group watching the fire at a safe distance and was told that they were among the passengers of the ill-fated flight awaiting transfer to the terminal building while others had already been transferred. On reaching the group I was in for more surprise. It included several of my friends and senior colleagues in the government who were returning from Hyderabad in that disaster bound flight. When I asked one of them if he had any idea of the extent of casualty, the reply was reassuring. I was informed that no one had perished or sustained serious injury. The aircraft went off the runway while landing and split into two after it came to a halt. All the passengers came out of the plane before the fire erupted. The escape was miraculous.

On my return to the terminal building I found Mr. Scindia there, surrounded by a number of irate persons—passengers of the ill fated flight who had miraculously escaped and those who had come to receive them. Angry words were being hurled at the Minister. He was looking not only sad but also hurt and dejected. Soon after we met, he took me aside and said that he was proceeding straight to the Prime Minister to tender his resignation. I pleaded with him not to act on the spur of the moment, particularly since no casualty had been reported, but he would not listen. He rebutted me by saying that the information given to him was that one passenger had died. He got into his car and asked the driver to proceed to the PM's house. It was not even daybreak yet. I asked for a complete re-check on the status of casualty and felt relieved when it was re-confirmed that no one had perished.

After ascertaining that Mr. Scindia was still with Prime Minister Narasimha Rao, I apprised the PM of the correct status over the phone and requested him to ask the Minister to reconsider resignation. The PM handed the phone over to Scindia. He felt relieved that no one had died but refused to withdraw his resignation. Apparently the PM had accepted the resignation promptly.

To his query as to what we proposed to do next, I told the PM that I would suggest immediate grounding of all the hired Uzbek aircrafts as faith in their reliability had been shaken. I also added that while compensation payment to passengers of the ill fated flight would be expedited and the few passengers who had sustained injury would be looked after, we might wait and watch the course of the strike for some time. He gave his consent and I took it that the PM had assumed charge of the Ministry until it was assigned to someone else. Operations of Indian Airlines came to a complete halt. The management was shaken and the outlook was gloomy but the pilots remained unrelenting. I waited for them to tire out and soften their attitude. The strike continued.

A strange experience that shocked me to no end needs recounting here. While the strike was continuing, I was at a wedding reception at The Claridges hotel in Delhi one evening when Finance Minister walked down and asked me about the strike situation. I responded with an optimistic prediction that it would end soon and said that I was looking forward to the revival of Indian Airlines. But he cut me short and went away uttering words to the effect that as Indian Airlines had outlived its useful life, it hardly needed to be revived. I felt devastated on hearing these words from Dr. Manmohan Singh. I wondered if he was giving out a policy decision already been taken or was merely expressing a wish! Little did I know that the Prime Minister was shortly to entrust the Ministry of Civil Aviation to a Minister who would become the saviour of Indian Airlines.

Ghulam Nabi Azad who, as Minister of Parliamentary Affairs, was known to be the principal trouble-shooter to ensure the continuance of Narasimha Rao's minority government, was given charge of both Civil Aviation and Parliamentary Affairs. I recalled that when the strike intensified, with Executive Pilots joining it, Scindia had told me with a touch of sadness that the PM might ask a 'politically heavyweight Minister' to intervene and negotiate a settlement. At that time I had no idea who that Minister was but with Azad's appointment as Minister of Civil Aviation it became clear to me that he was the person Scindia had referred to. It did not take me long to discover that Azad genuinely wanted to defuse the agitation and restore normalcy. At my first meeting with him I was given a clear direction to re-start negotiations. I initiated this using a back channel. It was not difficult to agree on the broad parameters of settlement as the people with whom I spoke were convinced of our sincerity. In their turn they were able to get the concurrence of the striking pilots, after which I asked Vasudev to work out the details and formally settle with the Union. This he did expeditiously and Indian Airlines was back in business.

Those who wanted to see the end of Indian Airlines were obviously not pleased. The move to have me shifted from Civil Aviation was revived. A few days later I was informed by the Cabinet Secretary that the Finance Minister was willing to have me appointed on the Board of Industrial and Financial Reconstruction (BIFR) for which there was no need for any application from my side. I could clearly see the determined effort to shift me, not by the straight-forward process of transfer (which required wider consultation and approval at the highest level) but by the adoption of a subterfuge by which I might be tempted to leave so as to gain a few years of service in BIFR, where I could continue beyond the age of superannuation.

It was exasperating to find myself facing the wrath of powerful forces within the government only because I was pursuing the declared policy of the same government, namely rehabilitation of Indian Airlines. I met the Finance Minister and thanked him. By then I was tired of being targeted and wanted to leave. But again the proposal did not fructify. It remained simmering till I retired. Those who did not know the facts speculated that it was being kept ready as a parting gift on my retirement. Little did they know that it was intended not as a parting gift on retirement but as a parting kick to drive me out of Civil Aviation! I had no problem with my own Minister or the Prime Minister. I had no doubt in my mind that Indian Airlines, with all its weakness, was still a big national asset which needed to be saved from those in the government who, in the name of reform colluded, unwittingly perhaps, with unscrupulous elements anxious to make a killing of the assets built up over the years.

Even prior to the strike, Indian Airlines was going through a rough patch. The Bill that we had presented for the repeal of the Act of 1953 was not making any progress in Parliament. While the left parties were opposing it on ideological grounds, the BJP was also opposed to it, perhaps because of their allergy to Scindia. It may be recalled that these very parties had propped up the VP Singh government, whose Minister of Civil Aviation had placed in Parliament the Statement of April 1990, which enlarged the scope of the Air Taxi Scheme, severely impinging on the exclusive rights of the air corporations to operate scheduled services. While the fate of the Bill hung in balance, we could not take up the restructuring of the corporations. Employees of the beleaguered Indian Airlines, who were not paragons of disciplined conduct even at the best of times, became restive. Pilots started leaving, because they were attracted by the higher pay offered by air-taxi companies. The passenger load of the Corporation depleted and losses of Indian Airlines mounted.

The strike dealt a grievous blow to the airline. Air-taxi companies had not only usurped a large chunk of traffic but also enticed away technical manpower—pilots and engineers in particular—built up over years of effort and investment. Shortages in operating staff became severe. Salary hikes appeared unavoidable but the cash crunch posed a serious problem. On top of all this, there was a pervasive feeling of uncertainty arising out of the government's unwillingness to rein in the air-taxi operators and its inability to carry through the Repeal Bill in Parliament. Ghulam Nabi Azad brought hope in this otherwise gloomy scenario.

Mr. Scindia was a high profile Minister who believed in

hands-on management. He had been Minister of Railways earlier in the Rajiv Gandhi government. He told me more than once how satisfying it was for him to manage the Railways, which had a much larger spread and complexity of operation than Civil Aviation. I had to remind him that unlike the Air Corporations which were a creation of the post-independence era and were bedevilled by unremitting interference and indiscipline, the Indian Railways had a long history, well established procedures and a well structured organisation built up over the years. The habit of air corporation employees, particularly pilots, resorting to flight disruption even on minor issues caused Mr. Scindia much annoyance. He was keen on turning the Corporations around and changing the mindset of the employees. He also devoted a lot of his time and effort seeking quick results, but problems were compounded. Aggressive encroachment by air-taxi operators into the exclusive turf of Indian Airlines was rapidly weakening the airline.

Mr. Scindia was perceived as the architect of the policy that encouraged the air-taxi companies, to the detriment of Indian Airlines. His efforts to enforce discipline and secure improved performance were mistaken as repression. An adversarial relationship developed imperceptibly and that made matters worse. Uninformed people spread the canard that Scindia's single point objective was privatisation and he was willing to sacrifice Indian Airlines in the process. Nothing could be farther from the truth. In his early days as Minister of Civil Aviation he might have been misguided into believing that by promoting air-taxis he would bring in a competitive spirit in Indian Airlines and thereby improve the quality of its performance.

Having gone ahead, he found it difficult to step back lest his image as a 'reformer' suffered. Once he realised that the purpose could not be achieved without parliamentary sanction, he initiated action in that direction but it was too late. The opposition in the Parliament was so virulent to him that our Bill did not make any progress. But he did not wish to give up. He had a genuine interest in making Indian Airlines strong and vibrant and made strenuous, though at times ill advised, efforts in that direction. The results unfortunately were disappointing and culminated in his resignation.

Why did Mr. Scindia's efforts prove counter-productive? In my view, the answer lies in the cardinal mistake that he made in enthusiastically following up the Statement of April 1990 without making sure of its implications vis-à-vis the Air Corporations Act. However, it should be remembered that it was not he who had made that Statement, but a predecessor, belonging to a party opposed to his own. That Government had fallen and that Parliament was dissolved. A fresh Parliament and a different Government had been constituted and the new Minister of Civil Aviation was entitled to review the policy that impinged on the law of the land. He, as the new Minister, should have stayed further implementation of that policy until it got legitimacy in law. Meanwhile, the Air Corporations could have been restructured and strengthened to function effectively in a competitive environment. Private companies could then have been inducted to operate as regular airlines after fulfilling requisite conditions. Instead, he was persuaded to continue the subterfuge of encouraging air-taxi companies to function as if they were airlines entitled to operate scheduled services, in clear violation of the law.

By the time I came to Civil Aviation, about eighteen months after the Statement of April 1990 had been made, air-taxi companies were being encouraged vigorously to operate virtually as airlines. I repeatedly urged that clear orders be issued for strict enforcement of the Air Corporations Act but was told in no uncertain terms that it was too late to reverse the trend. I saw to it that the legislative proposal, kept hanging for a long time, was processed at long last. But our Bill made no progress in the Parliament as mentioned already. The 'reform' ushered in by stealth did not work. It only further damaged the health of the already ailing Indian Airlines and took a heavy toll on Scindia. Several years later a widely circulated news-magazine, in its anniversary issue recounting major events during the thirty years of its existence, mistakenly credited Madhavrao Scindia as the Minister who removed state monopoly in airlines operation. He undoubtedly tried his best to do so but he could not succeeded in the face of a hostile Parliament. The unfinished task was accomplished by his successor in office, Ghulam Nabi Azad.

Aviation, even though it constitutes a very small segment of the Indian economy, is glamorous and high-profile. It was therefore, an obvious target for the Liberalisation Lobby to show-case economic reform. There was nothing wrong in that; the sector was certainly in urgent need of reform. Problems arose because of the surreptitious manner in which reform was smuggled into this sector, even before Scindia came on the scene. He could have restored the rule of law and proceeded with reform in a lawful way, but he became a willing ally of the Liberalisation Lobby which was anxious to impress its mentors abroad. In any case his tenure as Minister of Civil Aviation came to a tragic end. An otherwise bright political carrier suffered a severe setback. His final exit from this world was equally tragic. Some years later he died in an air crash when he was rather young.

Ghulam Nabi Azad brought a different approach in Civil Aviation. He no doubt favoured liberalisation and opening up of the sector but refrained from actively promoting air-taxis. With his vast experience in parliamentary floor management he knew that the government was in no position to push through the Repeal Bill easily in the face of stiff opposition. He waited for tempers to cool down, had the Bill referred to the Parliamentary Standing Committee for detailed examination and meanwhile concentrated attention on bringing about qualitative improvement in the performance of Indian Airlines, particularly in the area of passenger care. The employees responded positively. It gave us great satisfaction to see the old mindset of taking the customer for granted changing. Not that the employees did not have grievances any more but the tendency to escalate into agitation was avoided. Azad also deserves credit for having got the new fleet of Airbus A320 re-configured to create the Executive Class that enabled Indian Airlines to regain high-end customers who had migrated to privately operated air-taxis. Morale was largely restored and it looked as if the airline was poised for healthy growth. But its financial condition had become critical.

Vasudev, who settled with the pilots after the strike ended, had continued to manage Indian Airlines in the midst of serious financial constraints. He used to meet me and discuss issues that cropped up. But I never got any inkling from him of deteriorating communication within the organisation. By the time I came to know about it, much damage had been done. Unhappy elements within the organisation were briefing not only non-official members of the Board of Directors but also Members of Parliament. Matters came to a head just ahead of a meeting of the Parliamentary Consultative Committee. Vasudev was reluctant to attend this meeting though it was the established practice for heads of public enterprises to be present. It is hard to recollect whether I spoke with him or had it conveyed to him but my message was clear: Vasudev should attend; he could bring to the meeting any senior colleague to assist him. Apparently he had made up his mind not to face the Committee. Perhaps he wished to avoid scathing criticism of his conduct, as I was told later. He resigned and left Delhi. Indian Airlines once again got an acting Chairman; a different Joint Secretary this time.

While leaving Delhi Vasudev made news by telling the press an utter lie. He referred to the crashed aircraft leased from Uzbek Airlines at the time of the Pilots' strike that led to Scindia's resignation and said that the leasing was done at the instance of Secretary (Civil Aviation). This made headlines in practically all major newspapers. On getting the news, my first impulse was to issue a contradiction but then I realised that it would be just one assertion against another. On cooler reflection, I asked Indian Airlines to issue a press note indicating the facts of the leasing based entirely on the records of the airline. The press note issued by Indian Airlines on the following day clearly brought out how the leasing was done entirely as an internal exercise of the airline which was in touch with the Uzbek Airline.

I had absolutely no prior knowledge of the leasing and our contingency plan to tackle the strike did not envisage any such leasing. I wondered why he made the preposterous statement of my involvement, particularly as there was no allegation of corruption or irregularity against him that he may have tried to deflect. The matter puzzles me even today as I write now after two decades. However, I do recall a cryptic remark made in this connection immediately following the news report that made the headlines. The venue was a dinner hosted by a close friend and attended by a number of senior officials, some Ministers and a senior journalist.

The morning papers had carried the news report in question that very day. Immediately on my arrival a friend anxiously enquired about the motive behind the news. Before I could respond, the journalist (now a well known Chief Editor of a large newspaper chain) interjected with a remark that suggested a role for Mr. Amar Singh, a Scindia-appointee on the Board of Directors of Indian Airlines. The Ministers at the party appeared to understand the implication but the matter was not discussed further and I was in no mood to follow up. For a self-respecting civil servant even a veiled allegation of the type made by Vasudev can be disturbing. I imagined all kinds of fabricated imputations orchestrated in the media. But nothing of the sort happened after Indian Airlines issued a rebuttal the next day, which again got wide publicity in the press.

Our efforts to improve the working of the aviation sector continued notwithstanding hiccups. While current expenses could be recovered, there was inadequate surplus In Indian Airlines to meet fixed costs, particularly the growing burden of debt servicing. Ordering of a large fleet of Airbus A320 had imposed a heavy debt burden and the grounding of that fleet soon after its acquisition had severely eroded the finances. It was no longer possible for the airline to bear the burden of lower fares ordered by Government for the North-East without any subsidy. Besides, the entire industry (including air-taxis) was saddled with excess capacity in a stagnant market, because of which there was little scope to raise fares in other sectors. The industry was facing the problems not only of uneconomic fares but also of high taxation and excessive fuel prices. The price of aviation fuel in India was more than double the international level. On top of this was the Government levy of Inland Air Travel Tax at 15% of the fare.

The problem was serious for the industry as a whole; for Indian Airlines it had become acute. Azad rightly considered it advisable that the Prime Minister needed to be briefed. He himself spoke to the PM, had an appointment fixed for the briefing and asked me to accompany him. The PM had two sittings with us, each of over an hour. I explained in detail, along with a slide presentation, the genesis of the problem, its subsequent development as it became acute and what our proposals were to tackle the situation. The PM captured the gravity of the problem, recognised the need for assistance and desired that a further meeting be set-up to consider the matter, along with the Finance Minister participating. That meeting, chaired by PM, was held soon. Knowing as I did that Dr. Manmohan Singh, the Finance Minister, had no sympathy for our efforts to rehabilitate Indian Airlines, we presented our proposals in the form of assistance to the airlines industry as a whole, admissible to private companies also. Specifically, we asked for removal of the Inland Air Travel Tax and a time-bound plan to bring down progressively the domestic price of aviation fuel to international levels.

For Indian Airlines we added two more proposals: (i) subsidy to cover loss in North-East operations at below-cost fares and (ii) cash support for a limited period to meet shortfall in the requirement of debt servicing. Both these proposals together would have cost less than Rs. 200 crore. This was by no means an excessive burden on the exchequer considering the size of the total budget and the dire need resulting from faulty government policy introduced surreptitiously. The PM made no secret of his unhappiness over the manner in which air-taxis were allowed to operate on trunk routes, to the detriment of Indian Airlines which was saddled with non-viable services to the North-East. He appreciated the need for assistance, referred to the fact that the Finance Minister himself represented the North-East in the Parliament, and stated that our proposals in respect of Indian Airlines would surely receive his sympathetic consideration. Thereafter, we referred our proposals to the Finance Ministry for concurrence, but the Finance Minister remained unmoved.

Azad did not give up. He took the matter back to the PM who remitted it to a Group of Ministers headed by the Finance Minister. There was much procrastination and no help. Indian Airlines was in no position to discontinue its uneconomic North-East operations nor could it raise fares. The Finance Minister also knew the consequences of default on debt servicing. Even so, he remained determined not to assist. The Airline was left with no option other than incurring further debt to service past debt and meet shortfall in its working results. Had he given the modest support we sought, there was every possibility of a financial turn round by Indian Airlines; Air India was profitable those days and needed no financial support from the Government.

Be that as it may. We continued to remain steadfast in our endeavour to improve the viability of operations. An important milestone we set for us was securing close cooperation between Indian Airlines and Air India. I had noticed that major international airlines, with diverse ownership patterns, combined together to form alliances to extend their market reach. The more successful of them also operated on the principle of what is known in aviation circle as the 'Hub-and-Spokes' pattern, by which an international carrier provided seamless travel facilities to a larger body of customers by tying up with airlines having domestic spread. The domestic airline served as a spoke catering to the hub to which the international carrier operated, to the mutual advantage of both. Although this was the preferred practice internationally, our two air corporations, Air India and Indian Airlines, demonstrated complete disinterest in coordination. They were not averse even to competing against each other in sectors where both wished to operate. It was really regrettable that the two entities, both of the same nationality, both owned wholly by the President of India and both fluent in the English language, were reluctant to speak with each other except through an interpreter—the Ministry of Civil Aviation!

I was convinced that the two had enormous potential for growth by close inter-linkage under the Hub-and-Spokes principle. They could also benefit greatly by sharing the available infrastructure such as ticketing arrangements, office space, marketing efforts and facilities for repairs, maintenance and training. Yet they showed little interest in this direction, preferring instead to function in air tight compartments. I noticed that, at a time when the brand new Airbus A320 fleet of Indian Airlines had surplus capacity, Air India invited international offers to take medium haul aircraft on lease to expand its operations to the Gulf area.

The readily available Airbus A320s of Indian Airlines were eminently suitable for the job and there was no justification for the hiring of aircraft from the international market. The mutual benefits of collaboration should have been obvious, and yet I had to spend many hours with the top management of the two Corporations before the parameters of the joint working could be settled. I must add, however, that once the broad decisions for joint operation were taken and a common group was set-up jointly to work out the details, the officials concerned did an excellent job. The joint operation to the gulf region started in record time, making significant contribution to the finances of both Corporations.

This made us think of the tremendous advantage that could be derived by fully integrating the working of the two entities, leading eventually to a complete merger, so that India could have at least one strong airline with a noticeable fleet size and a reasonably wide network of operation to function effectively in the highly competitive world of civil aviation. In those days the combined fleet strength of the two Corporations was just 60 or so, close to what Singapore Airline, with no domestic operation, commanded; larger companies like American Airline had over 400 aircraft in their fleet.

The way forward for the civil aviation industry in India lay in consolidation, not fragmentation. We already had the two air corporations under single ownership, with considerable experience and expertise in each. That advantage needed to be synergised to build the indigenous air transportation industry to international scale, in order to achieve full potential. The scheme we prepared and presented to the Cabinet for restructuring of the air corporations envisaged, not only their conversion into limited companies but also their eventual merger. We had visualised the problems that would arise in the process of merger, particularly issues relating to the employees. For the smooth running of the process we proposed to bring about the merger in stages. In the first stage, integration was to be achieved only at policy level by having a common Board of Directors and a Common Chief Executive for both the entities. In pursuance of this we had gone ahead and appointed a common Chairman and Managing Director (CMD) even before the Corporations became limited companies.

Utilisation of the infrastructure and equipment of both the corporations was sought to be optimised by the common CMD under the guidance of a common Board of Directors. Full integration was to follow only after personnel issues were settled in consultation with employees' organisations. The merger of Air India and Indian Airlines required, at the top management level, both commitment to the objective and the ability to see it through the various stages after securing goodwill of the employees. I had thought that Deveshwar, with his vast experience in the private sector along with the understanding of the aviation industry he had acquired as Chairman Air India, would be a good choice for appointment as common CMD of the merged entity. But he had fixed his sights on the top slot in ITC, his parent company. He wished to go back to ITC and I had no wish to come in the way.

The task of restructuring the air corporations and de-monopolising the sector was made more difficult not only by the delay in the enactment of our Repeal Bill and the agitation by employees but also a number of accidents and air crashes that occurred in quick succession. Hijacking and other acts of terrorism also put severe strain on us. The air crash in Delhi that led to Scindia's resignation has been referred to already. There was another air crash, this time of an Indian Airlines plane going to Chennai. In both cases the large number of passengers and crew on board had all luckily escaped. But there was yet another crash, again of an Indian Airlines flight, while the aircraft was taking off from Aurangabad. Destiny was severely harsh this time. The crash was much more tragic as a number of passengers and crew members perished. There were other mishaps too. As Secretary (Civil Aviation), I was perhaps singularly unlucky to endure the highest number of calamities.

Security conditions in the country had also deteriorated and our flights were becoming increasingly vulnerable. The level of professionalism in aviation security left much to be desired. Security at airports was almost entirely in the hands of local police and the personnel deployed on airport security were often found to be an unhappy lot, neither trained in anti-hijacking and anti-sabotage work nor adequately provided with electronic aids to detect possible threat and mischief. Their interchangeability with those deployed on normal policing functions and frequent transfers by the state police made things worse. The performance of the security personnel posted at airports, barring exceptions, was generally below par. We also did not have any rigorous system in place to provide Flight crews with anti-hijacking support. In these circumstances it was easy even for a prankster or a novice to hijack a flight easily or cause disruption.

Several incidents of security hazard actually took place. If

I remembered correctly, an Indian Airlines flight from Delhi to Lucknow was taken over in mid-air by a person brandishing what looked like a gun. He made some weird demands and insisted that he would negotiate only with Atal Bihari Vajpayee, who was then an opposition MP. This was puzzling. I hesitated to contact Mr. Vajpayee and gained time. Meanwhile the fellow either gave up or was overpowered and his weapon turned out to be a fake. The flight landed safely. Prior to that, a potential disaster was averted at Delhi airport. An Air India flight to New York was being made ready when one of the ground staff noticed a wire jutting out from a food trolley. The boarding of passengers was deferred and a complete search of the aircraft carried out. The wire and its attachment turned out to be a component of an Indigenous Explosive Device (IED) which luckily had no explosive. A more serious incident of sabotage was attempted some months later by way of a partially successful hijack.

An Indian Airlines flight leaving Amritsar was hijacked shortly after takeoff by a terrorist demanding release of some prisoners. Dealing with that situation was a nerve-wrecking experience lasting till midnight. The aircraft had been forced to land at Chandigarh for refuelling in order that it could be flown out of the country. The Punjab Police started negotiation with the terrorist and carried it on skilfully while the aircraft was on the ground. Ultimately the man either gave up or was overpowered and shot dead while escaping. The passengers and crew members alighted unharmed. Apart from these, there were frequent hoax calls from pranksters causing bomb scares at airports, particularly the busy ones. Severe flight dislocations were caused by the prolonged search and sanitisation exercises that used to follow. Managing the security scenario with personnel not adequately trained or equipped for the job was becoming increasingly wearisome.

On close examination of the security issues we came to the conclusion that it was high time a dedicated force was entrusted with the task of aviation security. I had several rounds of discussion with Cabinet Secretary and Home

Secretary. When I found that things did not move fast enough, I got a scheme prepared to set-up a separate Aviation Security Force under my Ministry and presented it for approval. Things started moving thereafter and the Ministry of Home Affairs was entrusted with the job of identifying a suitable Central Police Force to handle aviation security. Sometime later, the Central Industrial Security Force (CISF) was assigned the job which, hopefully, it is doing professionally.

Like aviation security, air safety is a major issue in civil aviation. Incidents and accidents sometime do occur. Tragic consequences of air crashes are also well known. But countries serious about prevention of mishap have set-up strong institutions to ensure air safety. In India this responsibility traditionally rests with the DGCA. This organisation, one of the agencies inherited from the colonial era, has laid down internationally accepted norms of safety, but it is unclear whether DGCA is in a position to enforce them. The anaemic condition of DGCA, alluded to already, is one of the principal causes of its feeble conduct. I was able to take some measures by way of providing incremental staff to that organisation and placed a competent professional at the top as DG, but I had no doubt that much more strengthening was required.

Private airlines brought enormous expansion in the number of aircrafts, considerable variety in technology and new work practices. DGCA should have kept pace both in terms of staff strength and professional competence. Lately, Air India (which now includes Indian Airlines) also has undertaken massive fleet expansion. The irregularities noticed in recent years in the enforcement of regulatory measures in the areas of airworthiness of equipment, certification of flight crew, conduct of examinations etc. can largely be attributed to inadequacy in the building up of DGCA as a strong, vibrant and professionally competent regulator capable of disciplining a fast growing, high profile, technology-intensive aviation industry. DGCA being squarely under the government is also an impediment to the discharge of its role as an independent regulator. This was recognised even while we were engaged in the work of removing state monopoly over air transportation. A note I had drafted those days on 'Policy for Civil Aviation in a Competitive Environment' envisaged a statutorily autonomous regulator instead of a departmental DGCA. Action had been deferred as our hands were already full with two legislative measures: one for removal of monopoly and the other for unification of Airports Authorities.

Our most urgent task was to restructure and strengthen the air corporations. The Bill to repeal the Air Corporations Act and restructure the corporations was before the Standing Committee of the Parliament, as also the other bill for unification of the two airports authorities. The latter Bill had a relatively smooth passage but even that took time. The Bill to repeal the Air Corporations Act was still facing opposition. It goes to the credit of Ghulam Nabi Azad that opposition to the Bill was skilfully worn down as it remained under the consideration of the Standing Committee, chaired again by the late Pramod Mahajan of the BJP.

The strategy adopted by Azad was admirable, though I was unable to comprehend it then. He patiently had the Bill steered through the Committee where Mahajan, who understood the implications well, played a positive role. After the Standing Committee endorsed the Bill for the approval of Parliament, Azad took the matter again to the Cabinet, this time to have an Ordinance promulgated on the ground that the Bill had remained pending for a very long time and further delay in bringing the provisions of the Bill to fruition would be injurious. There was no difficulty in getting Cabinet's approval. The Ordinance was promulgated, if I remember right, in January 1994. It was replaced as a matter of course, by an Act at the next session of the Parliament. The strident opposition encountered in the past had dissolved because of Azad's fine parliamentary strategy.

Thus, it was Ghulam Nabi Azad who brought to an end the forty year old state monopoly in the Indian air transport industry and ushered in a competitive regime by repealing the Air Corporations Act of 1953. We lost no time in removing the avoidable burden imposed on Indian Airlines under the monopoly regime. One such measure was equitable sharing of obligation to provide air services across the country. As stated earlier, air-taxi companies had concentrated their operation on highly profitable trunk routes connecting metropolitan cities, with hardly any presence in the rest of the country and none at all in the strategically vital North-east. Indian Airlines, on the other hand, was carrying the burden of operating a number of flights connecting the North-east with the rest of the country and that too at concessional tariff. In addition, it provided connectivity to various state capitals and other places by air routes, some of which were hardly remunerative. The air-taxi companies could not be made to share the responsibility of providing services in the north-east as long as the Air Corporations Act remained in force.

I am tempted to recall in this context a sharp interaction I had with Prime Minister Narasimha Rao at a meeting called to brief him prior to the visit of a foreign dignitary. Towards the close of that meeting the Prime Minister told me to arrange more flights of Indian Airlines to the North-East as MPs from the region were making persistent demands. He obviously expected me to take an early action. I should have readily offered to do my best, had I been politically correct. But by that time I had already met with stubborn refusal from the Finance Minister to provide legitimate support to the financially starved airline, even after the intervention of the PM himself.

My frustration got the better of me and I argued with the Prime Minister, telling him rather bluntly that Indian Airlines was in no position to increase the frequency of its operations because the more it flew to the North-East the higher would be its losses. The PM, naturally, was not pleased. A colleague who was an eye witness asked me later why on earth I had joined issue with the PM, just a couple of weeks before my retirement, and got into what he aptly termed 'flight turbulence' when I could have easily left a note to my successor on what the PM had desired. I had no answer as I myself felt sorry for my conduct, particularly because the PM had supported us in our endeavour to get funds for the airline.

After the repeal of the Air Corporations Act it became a statutory obligation for all scheduled operators, including air-taxi companies, to share equitably the responsibility of providing air service to different parts of the country, including North-East Region. A set of simple, transparent and easily enforceable rules was drawn up for this purpose. I had asked for such a scheme even prior to the passing of the Repeal Law. But it was not ready by the time the Act was repealed. I was not willing to brook further delay in this matter. Khola, the acting DG, CA and I both sat together in my office one morning and drew up the scheme. The country was divided into three broad groups for this purpose.

Category I, comprising the highly profitable trunk routes, Category II, covering the North-east, Jammu & Kashmir, Andaman and Lakshadweep islands where air services were a necessity but unprofitable in those days, and Category III, covering rest of the country with routes where profitability was moderate or low. Those operating on trunk routes (Category I) were required to provide service compulsorily in Category II and Category III in a prescribed ratio. I understand that this hurriedly worked-out formula remained in force for the next fifteen years and perhaps even now.

Another major step taken was the appointment of K Padmanabhaiah as common Chairman of Air India and Indian Airlines, with a common Board of Directors. Meanwhile, PC Sen, an officer with extensive prior experience in civil aviation, had been appointed as a whole time Managing Director of Indian Airlines, terminating the *ad hoc* arrangement under which Joint Secretary Brijesh Kumar ably functioned as Acting Chairman, following Vasudev's exit. Thus, both Air India and Indian Airlines were provided with whole-time top executives: Mathur as Managing Director of Air India, Sen as Managing Director of Indian Airlines and Padmanabhaiah as the common

Chairman of both. Many more measures had been lined up but my time was over.

I retired in March 1994. There was the usual round of farewell parties where nice things were said, as expected on such occasions. I am however tempted to recall one remark made by Ghulam Nabi Azad. He mentioned that at meetings held in the Ministry periodically to review working of various organisations, he often found me severely taking to task persons, howsoever senior, if their performance fell short of expectation but at exclusive discussions with him, in their absence, I stoutly defended and often praised them for their positive contributions. I valued this remark because what the Minister said was truly based on his observation over a long period. All through my career I seldom failed to acknowledge the contribution of my colleagues and invariably tried to spur them into attaining greater heights by telling them, even sharply, if found wanting. This may not have been an endearing quality but I was made that way and never tried to be what I was not.

The tenure of Padmanabhaiah, was short. He was posted elsewhere a few months later and was succeeded as common Chairman of Air India and Indian Airlines by Russi Mody who had served Tatas with distinction for long years before he came to Civil Aviation with a formidable reputation of competence. I was therefore, hopeful that he would provide the much needed leadership and ably steer the two airlines to merger and steady growth. But that hope was soon belied. As I learnt from news reports, Mody was preoccupied in trying to establish his personal supremacy. Instead of deploying his considerable experience and ability to resolve conflict within the organisation, strengthen management capability, improve internal working, build consensus and provide better quality of service to passengers by seeking cooperation of all concerned, he got dissipated in challenging authority. One cannot be sure if this was true but there was no visible improvement in the working of the airlines during his tenure. An opportunity was again lost.

Several years have passed; meanwhile there have been many changes of Ministers (across political parties), Secretaries and Chief Executives. But the condition of the two national carriers, also the single entity into which they were merged at long last, is no better; in fact it is worse. Air India, in its new avatar, has accumulated massive losses. Its market share in the domestic sector has fallen to 15% from 75% in 1993. In international operations also it has had to shed profitable routes to private operators. It may be recalled that both Air India and Indian Airlines recorded profits until about 1990. While Air India continued to be profitable for some more years, Indian Airlines was weighed down under the burden of debt it had incurred for the acquisition of a large fleet of Airbus A320 and the subsequent grounding of the fleet. That inflicted on the airline a financial burden of Rs. 300 crore. Even so, the two carriers together did not have accumulated loss until 1993. That was the time when we in the Ministry of Civil Aviation asked for a one-time support of Rs. 200 crore, which Finance Minister Manmohan Singh refused, leaving the airline to bleed.

Indian Airlines went on suffering loss of market share, continued piling up losses and incurred more and more debt. Governments, run by parties across the board, went on watching. Then a crushing blow was dealt by the government of the same Dr. Manmohan Singh, who had by then become Prime Minister, and Praful Patel became the Minister of Civil Aviation in his Cabinet. Together they found it prudent to burden the two airlines (merged into Air India) with a massive purchase of 111 new aircraft at a cost of Rs. 50,000 crore. Mind boggling indeed! Air India came to be saddled with staggering accumulated losses of Rs. 20,000 crore, a loan burden of Rs. 60,000 crore and forced to curtail flights and face agitation owing to its inability to disburse pay and buy fuel.

In popular perception, Air India's woes are on account of indiscipline among its employees. Indeed the conduct of sections of its employees, pilots in particular, has often been deplorable. But the conduct of the owners, namely the Government of India, has not been praiseworthy either. The sad story of betrayal of Indian Airlines by the Government under the pretext of the Statement made in the Parliament in April 1990 has already been narrated. Mention has also been made of the acquisition by the airline of a large fleet of Airbus A320. What needs to be pointed out is that the burden of acquiring a high-technology 'fly-by-wire' fleet was thrust on the airline by the government without even ensuring the recruitment of competent avionics engineers capable of maintaining the new fleet! Even one year after, delivery of these aircrafts, Indian Airlines had only nine avionics engineers against the requirement of more than 100. As a result, induction of the planes into flight schedules was seriously hampered, with consequential loss.

In the wake of economic reforms in 1991, Finance Minister Manmohan Singh was pushing hard for divestment and privatisation of public enterprises and Air India was on the top of his list. It was argued that this was necessary if under-performing assets of the government were to be harnessed for greater good of the nation. If so, why was no action taken during nine long years of Manmohan Singh's stewardship as PM to have even a token disinvestment done in Air India? Obviously no one would come forward to subscribe to the share capital of a sinking ship. Yet the Government burdened it further with the biggest ever purchase of planes, when the airline was in no position to bear this massive burden. It is common knowledge that aircraft manufacturers and their agents mount marketing pressure to push their sales.

The government was duty bound to critically examine whether or not the airline was capable of bearing the burden of acquisition, even if credit was forthcoming to finance the purchase. Planes were delivered but there were not enough pilots to fly them. Expatriate pilots were hired on significantly higher wages which accentuated disparity and created discontent culminating in strike. Pilots were sent for training abroad to fly the newly-ordered Boeing 787 Dreamliners without sorting out contentious issues of their relative seniority. This inevitably led to another agitation and a prolonged strike. Could the problems not have been anticipated prior to the placement of orders for the new aircraft, or sorted out before the long simmering discontent over the issues finally exploded? Although the merger of the two airlines was envisaged close to 20 years earlier and the massive order for purchase of aircraft was cleared by the Government almost five years ago, a Committee chaired by Retired Justice Dharmadhikari was appointed too late to consider various aspects of personnel issues involved and make suitable recommendations. Could such a committee not have been set-up earlier? What was the urgency in clearing the aircraft purchase, not matched by a similar concern to sort out personnel issues in the merger of the two airlines?

Was the Government's decision tainted by extraneous considerations? After all, there has been a dismal record of serious allegations of kickback in aircraft purchases. The Central Bureau of Investigation went to the extent of registering a criminal case against specific individuals involved in the purchase of Airbus A320s by Indian Airlines. A news report published in 2011 alleged that the Enforcement Directorate had found that one Hasan Ali, accused of extensive money laundering, had received a commission of US $ 11.5 million to facilitate the sale of just two planes to Air India while the latest order was for as many as 111 planes, valued at Rs. 50,000 crore. It continues to be a mystery why Government chose to cast aside prudence in making the decision to investment in the massive purchase. Government is already accused of several mega-scams. Could this be one more, or would it continue to remain under wraps as another case of 'coalition compulsion'?

Dr. Manmohan Singh had stubbornly refused to give, as Finance Minister, Rs. 200 crore when it was needed to rehabilitate Indian Airlines in 1990s. He wanted the airline to die, as I have narrated earlier. But, as Prime Minister, the same Dr. Singh is committed now to give Air India (the merged entity) Rs. 7,000 crore from the Budget and a massive bail out package of Rs. 30,000 crore. And having done that, the

Government subsequently gave away to a foreign airline a massive bonanza of highly valuable traffic rights to the Gulf region that threatens the very existence of Air India!!! Is it a fresh attempt to destroy the national carrier after pumping in large amounts of public funds?

Chapter 20

Orissa Public Service Commission

The Chairman of the Orissa Public Service Commission (OPSC) had been sick for a long time before he died in harness. A temporary arrangement had been made to carry on with the Commission's work, which naturally suffered a setback. It was in these circumstances that I was invited in 1996 to become the Chairman. Having been in Delhi for long, I had no clear idea of the actual state of affairs in the OPSC, which had its headquarters at Cuttack. Friends and well-wishers cautioned me that the situation there was far from satisfactory, with charges of favouritism being openly made and inordinate delays in making recommendations for recruitment to public services. The prevailing impression about the functioning of Public Service Commissions in other states was also not inspiring. I was therefore, hesitant to accept the offer. Besides, after retiring from IAS I was chairing two Committees based in Delhi and did not wish to abandon the work midway. However, when told that I should not spurn an opportunity to re-establish the credibility of an important Constitutional body that was languishing in my home state, I decided to take up the challenge. The work of one of the two committees I was chairing was nearing completion. I was able to present its report within a few weeks but an alternative arrangement had to be made for the other Committee by the Government of India to enable me join the OPSC.

A day before I assumed the office of Chairman OPSC, in March 1996, there was an incident which surprised me completely. I was waiting to take delivery of my Maruti 800 at the workshop of a dealer in Bhubaneswar who had arranged its transportation from Delhi. A young man came up to me and enquired if a widely circulating rumour that I had cancelled the examination held last for recruitment to the civil services of the state was true. I informed him that the rumour was entirely baseless because I had not assumed the office of Chairman yet and knew absolutely nothing about the matter he was referring to. The very next day, when I made enquiries after assuming office, I was in for a bigger surprise. I learnt that the answer-papers of the examination conducted a year earlier were all kept in safe custody as no orders had been given by the Commission to commence evaluation.

I sent for the Commission's Secretary and other concerned officers and asked them if there was any cause for cancelling that examination. On being assured that there was no such need, I told them to work out a schedule for declaring the result at the earliest. They promptly came back with a detailed schedule but I was shocked to find that if we followed the usual practice we would not be able to declare the result for at least one more year. As the OPSC staff tried to explain to me how much time was required for each stage of the evaluation, I stopped them and said that the time would have to be reduced drastically. I wanted the final result, after completion of the prescribed viva voce, to be declared before the forthcoming Dussehra holidays, which were six months away. As they looked puzzled, I added that this target was inflexible. I told them that I wanted them to brain-storm among themselves and then come back to me to let me know what policy decisions they needed to make the target attainable. As they were about to leave my room, I added that in case they came back to report that the target was unattainable, I would resign and go away.

Whether or not they believed in the sincerity of my resignation resolve, I had no idea, but they appeared shaken. Within twenty four hours they reported back that the target could be attained with a change in the practice of evaluation of answer papers. They explained that much time was wasted in getting back the answer books from examiners after they had been evaluated as they seldom adhered to the prescribed timeline. I was informed that if we switched over from the practice of sending answer papers to examiners for evaluation at their sweet will and adopted a system of Central Valuation, already in vogue in many Universities, we would be able to declare the final result before Dussehra. I saw no reason why we could not do it and asked them to go ahead. The entire Commission—Members and the Staff—rose to the occasion and we succeeded in declaring the long pending final result for recruitment to the Orissa Civil Services (OCS) before Dussehra 1996.

The results that were declared in 1996 were for vacancies reported for the year 1992. I also learnt that such delays were a regular feature, as a result of which many field posts in the government were always lying vacant, with consequential deleterious impact on administration. When I enquired why the backlog could not be cleared in one lot, a Rule Book was shown to me which did not permit it. Since rule making was the government's privilege, I spoke to the Chief Secretary who readily responded to my suggestion to amend the rules and intimate the Commission the entire accumulated vacancies so that action could be started to fill up all by the next examination, for which we had already started preparations.

Meanwhile, I had discovered another wasteful practice that was being followed. The OCS examination included, apart from papers in elective subjects, compulsory papers in Oriya and English in which candidates were required to secure minimum qualifying marks of 30%, which did not count towards ranking. The candidates took the examination in all the papers including elective and compulsory ones but at the evaluation stage their answer papers in Oriya and English were evaluated first; all other papers being kept aside. The answer sheets in the papers which mattered for ranking purpose were not evaluated in case a candidate had failed to secure qualifying marks in Oriya and English. Thus, the answer sheets of thousands of candidates in subjects other than Oriya and English were never taken up for evaluation. Their entire labour undertaken in preparing for the elective and compulsory papers was rendered futile and they were not even aware of it.

I saw no justification in continuing this wasteful practice. It occurred to me that while keeping intact the content as well as the basic objective of the examination, one could introduce a transparent system of preliminary screening by merely splitting the papers into two groups, the first consisting of papers in Oriya and English where only qualifying marks were required and the second comprising papers on all the main subjects that counted towards ranking. In the modified system the first part was named the OCS (Preliminary) Examination and the second part the OCS (Main) Examination. Results of the Preliminary examination would be formally declared and only those who qualified in that would be allowed to sit for the Main examination. My colleagues in the Commission gave instant support to the idea and the state government promptly amended the rules, incorporating the changes suggested by us. The stage was thus set for not only filling up multi-year vacancies but also introduction of a two-part examination for the written papers. Since central valuation of answer sheets had already been established by us we were confident of prompt declaration of results even though the number of candidates was far greater.

The result of the Preliminary Examination was declared within a month or so, but it caused widespread surprise and consternation. Even I was quite surprised to find that barely

25% of the candidates had qualified in Oriya and English. The questions set were of matriculation standard while the candidates were all graduates and most of them postgraduates; the qualifying marks were just 30%. My surprise was on two accounts: first, at the low level of comprehension and expression on the part of the candidates revealed by the result not only in English language but also in Oriya. Secondly, I was intrigued at the intensity of anger it caused among the unsuccessful candidates and their resort to agitation which was not in evidence when we had declared the long delayed results of the earlier examination.

I required a comparative data for previous years to see how candidates had fared in the two language papers. The mystery unfolded after I analysed the data over a period of ten years or so. While the percentage of candidates who had qualified in Oriya and English in earlier years had ranged between 13% and 18%, the success rate in the current result was 25%, the highest ever. And yet there was discontent and agitation! After extensive discussion with colleagues we came to the conclusion that since the results of the examinations in Oriya and English were not published by the Commission in the past, the candidates were unaware of their poor performance. The Commission used to publish only the final ranking of candidates for recruitment purpose. That was the only result they knew of. The thousands who did not figure there took it that the successful ones had done better in the elective and compulsory papers which counted towards ranking. The unsuccessful candidates never knew how they had fared in the qualifying papers.

The credibility of the Commission had taken much beating over the years. The massive failure rate, revealed for the first time by the result of the Preliminary Examination, came as a shock which the unsuccessful candidates, 75% of the total, could not absorb. Some of them resorted to agitation by shouting slogans, taking out rallies, squatting at the Commission gate etc. I did not appreciate what the agitators were doing but I had sympathy for the unsuccessful candidates who (including those in past years) were not made aware of their inadequate proficiency in Oriya and English languages. I did two things: random checking of the evaluated answer sheets by a special cell closely overseen by a Member of the Commission to find discrepancy in valuation, if any; and secondly, I made it known that I was willing to meet all those, including the agitators, who wished to place their grievance before me.

A number of candidates and in some cases their guardians met me. While most of them wanted revaluation of the answer sheets, I would like to recall two cases in some detail. One of the candidates told me that he was a Lecturer in English in a college from which one of his students and he himself had appeared in the Preliminary Examination. He was aggrieved that he had failed to qualify in English but his student had qualified; this he felt was unacceptable. He spoke to me in English though I had started the conversation in Oriya. That helped me in forming my own impression. The English he insisted on speaking was so atrocious that I wondered how he had even graduated. He certainly did not deserve to qualify and his student who qualified must have done so in spite of the Lecturer.

The other case was more startling. A person who had worked with me many years earlier met me and represented that his nephew who was pursuing a Ph.D. programme in a well known university had failed to clear the Preliminary Examination. I promised to ascertain the position personally. When I read the essay he had written in English, I found that although he knew the subject well, his sense of grammar and power of expression were utterly poor; there was no way he could have been given qualifying marks by the examiner. I explained this to the candidate when he met me later.

While both the processes were in progress which I had started and the agitation was also going on, the media joined in; a section of it not only questioned the result we had declared but even went to the extent of alleging a scam. Meanwhile, some one petitioned the High Court and a Public Interest

Litigation (PIL) commenced. At a briefing on this issue I was advised that in a matter like this the Commission should claim privilege before the Court. That approach however did not appeal to me as it would appear that we were trying to take shelter behind a veil of secrecy and were not open to judicial scrutiny. I considered the PIL a blessing in disguise and instructed our Standing Counsel to lay bare before the Court the entire series of steps taken by us in the matter of the Preliminary Examination. I further instructed that, far from claiming privilege, we ourselves should produce before the court on the very first day of hearing all the answer sheets, barring those picked up already to re-check if there were discrepancies in the evaluation process. I thought, that would convince the people that we had nothing to hide. It had the desired impact. The bench headed by the Chief Justice entertained the PIL but refused to pass any peremptory order and declined to stay further proceedings for conduct of the OCS Examination of which the Main Examination was still to be held.

We went ahead with preparations for holding the Main Examination while the agitation continued and, encouraged by tendentious reports in a section of press, the demand for revaluation of the answer sheets gathered further momentum. I had also been informed that the revaluation demand had veiled support by a small section within the Commission that was involved in malpractices in the past and thought that they might stand to gain if mass revaluation was to be ordered. They were unable to manipulate the results because the earlier process of valuation was replaced by a multi-layered central valuation system under strict vigilance. Perhaps they believed that advantage could be taken of the agitation to discredit the new system and go back to old ways. To counter this I made it known that if the sample check we had started already or scrutiny by the High Court revealed any shortcoming in evaluation, the Commission would promptly cancel the Examination that had been held and hold a fresh examination, but there was to be no revaluation.

With the High Court seized of the PIL, the agitation was losing steam. As if to provide a fresh impetus, a baseless and tendentious 'news' was published in an important daily that the State Cabinet was going to issue a directive to the Public Service Commission to undertake revaluation. Anyone with a modicum of common-sense would know that the Commission is a constitutional body and Government has no right to direct it one way or another. As I wondered how that preposterous report could be published in a well circulated newspaper, misuse of the media for personal gain came to light. Publication of that baseless report was traced to a person who, after a long career in journalism, had joined that particular paper in a senior administrative position. His son (or daughter) who had sat for the examination had failed to qualify and believed that a revaluation could smuggle him in.

The sample check that we had undertaken revealed no discrepancy. Since the High Court had not issued any stay order, we confidently went ahead. The agitators, whose number had dwindled by now, failed to secure any political support to pressurise me. Leading lights across party lines had contacted me and got themselves briefed of the facts. They knew that I was not amenable to pressure and therefore made no attempt to influence me. The Main Examination was held peacefully as scheduled and the final results of the OCS Examination created no controversy. I could not remember how exactly the PIL was disposed of by the bench comprising the Chief Justice and a senior Judge, both of whom were later elevated to the Supreme Court, but the Court at no stage made any intrusive demand that could even remotely encroach upon the jurisdiction of the Public Service Commission. Likewise, the state government never interfered or tried to exert the slightest influence, thanks to Chief Minister JB Patnaik's dignified stand in the matter. Both the government and the High Court remained well within their Constitutional limits and acted with dignity and restraint. I wish the press, particularly the vernacular press, had observed similar restraint and reported developments with fairness and objectivity.

While passing through the stressful period of the agitation in connection with the OCS Examination, we were also engaged in discharging other functions of the Commission that included recruitment to professional services such as those of doctors, engineers, judicial officers and a variety of other posts. We also adjudged the suitability of officers for promotion to higher positions beyond the entry level. Unlike recruitment to the state civil services where the OCS Rules laid down detailed parameters and procedures, in most other cases the recruitment rules incorporated only barely essential requirements and in many cases the Commission was left entirely free to decide upon the manner of recruitment.

I noticed that much refinement had come about over the years, following judicial pronouncements and other measures, in the recruitment rules for the state civil services. But similar changes had not been adopted in other cases, particularly where the Commission had unfettered discretion. This was quite glaring in the matter of personality assessment by viva voce. In the old days, a great deal of emphasis was laid on the marks a candidate scored at the viva vice. As times changed and deprived sections of the society started asserting their right to a fair share in higher bureaucracy the emphasis given to viva voce started diminishing. By a series of decisions the maximum marks set apart for viva voce in competitive examinations were brought down. Finally, the Supreme Court ruled that the maximum marks set apart for viva voce could not exceed a certain percentage (perhaps 25%) of the total.

Recruitment Rules in Orissa, like those elsewhere, were framed accordingly. But I was surprised to find that where statutorily laid down rules did not exist—and there were many such cases—the OPSC was merrily exceeding the limit in exercise of its discretion, so much so that in several cases the marks set out for viva voce were as much as 50% of the total. I considered this odd; though it was not illegal, it militated against the principle underlying the law laid down by the Supreme Court. I also noticed that in several cases viva voce marks awarded by the Commission radically altered the ranking of candidates and individual members of an interview board differed widely in awarding marks to the same candidate. I could not reconcile myself to this practice. In my effort to minimise if not eliminate free play of subjective elements, bordering on arbitrariness, in the selection process I suggested two measures: drastic reduction of marks set apart for viva voce and award of marks at viva voce on agreed basis by all the members of an interview board instead of each one giving marks separately. My colleagues accepted both the suggestions given by me and promptly implemented that.

One other practice that we changed soon after my joining the Commission was the method of evaluating the career attainments of candidates. This was necessary for recruitments, particularly of professionals in different disciplines, where written examinations were not prescribed but the marks secured by candidates at public examinations were taken into consideration for ranking. Under the prevailing practice values were being assigned on an *ad hoc* basis to candidates depending upon what they had scored at different stages of their academic career. To have it substituted by a more rational system we constituted an inter-disciplinary committee of experts, headed by Gopal Mitra, a Professor of IIT with intimate knowledge of the working of the state government, to recommend a suitable framework. The Committee gave its recommendations unanimously which we gladly implemented.

Apart from selecting candidates for direct recruitment, the Commission also judged the suitability of serving officers for promotion to higher positions. The Commission had come to a grinding halt prior to my joining because of my predecessor's illness and his death in harness. The government had referred to the Commission a number of proposals for the promotion of officers of different departments. Since the Commission had made no recommendation on their promotion, the government carried on merrily with promotion of officers on *ad hoc* basis. By making strenuous efforts we were able to clear the backlog in a short time. Thereafter, our disposal of references was so prompt that it made government departments work overtime to hold Departmental Promotion Committees to clear cases that had accumulated at their end.

We had also taken a number of measures to plug loopholes in our internal working, apart from the single most important reform of the examination system already dealt with, to quicken the pace of disposal and improve the Commission's credibility. I came to know that after the finalisation of results by the Commission unscrupulous elements within the OPSC were in the habit of indulging in the unethical practice of offering their services to facilitate the selection of individual candidates who already stood selected by the Commission. This was possible by taking advantage of avoidable delay in the transmission of the Commission's recommendations to the government. To eliminate this possibility we ensured that the results of selection were declared immediately following completion of viva voce and posted simultaneously on the notice board of the Commission for general information. This small step had a decisive impact. It completely blocked the possibility of the type of malpractice that was prevalent earlier. The reform of the examination process, with multilayered vigilance built into the system, had already made it fool-proof. The credibility of the Commission improved rapidly once candidates and people in general came to know about these measures.

Another important job to be attended to was preparation of Annual Reports of the Commission for presentation to the State Legislature; reports had not been presented for three or four years. We not only cleared the entire backlog but promptly presented the report for the latest year, soon after the year was over. Annual Reports are meant to be presented to the Legislature so that Members might debate cases where Government acted in contravention of the Commission's advice. In the reports which we submitted there hardly was any matter for debate. The reason simply was the fact that our recommendations gave no opportunity to the Government to differ.

Among matters which called for urgent attention when I joined, were also issues of basic infrastructure and housekeeping. Not only did I find the Commission's budget allocation slashed down to a token amount which fell far short of even the staff salary, not to speak of conducting recruitment examinations. The State Government could not be faulted because the Commission itself had been surrendering money provided earlier, having slowed down almost to a halt. The Government's response to my request for funds was prompt and positive. As a matter of fact, I never felt thereafter any constraint of funds even though we took a number of measures to enhance substantially the fees admissible to paper setters, invigilators, examiners, and other key personnel in the examination process to attract suitable people to perform these important functions. This confirmed my belief, grown over the years, yet again that finance is seldom a constraint if the objective is well established and not over ambitious.

Another matter that required urgent attention was acute dearth of space. The office did not have space even for reception or visitors. Experts invited to assist in interviewing candidates had no waiting room. There was no conference room for interaction. When I requested for suitable arrangements to be made for these purposes I was informed that it would be possible to do so when a new building was constructed for which a proposal had already been sent to the Government. I was surprised as the existing building was constructed not too long ago and there could not have been too much of an expansion in the size of the Commission's office in the intervening period. The reality revealed itself when I took a round of various rooms. I found that a hall large enough to relieve congestion among the entire staff sitting cramped in a few small rooms using primitive furniture was occupied by police personnel on sentry duty at the Commission's office.

What was more amazing was that of the four-storied office building, rooms of an entire floor were all kept under lock because answer sheets of examinations conducted in the past had been stacked in those rooms. I was informed that cases were pending in courts where some candidates had challenged their results in the past and that was the reason why old answer sheets had all been preserved though neither any court had ordered this nor was there any justification for keeping all answer sheets stacked up for years. To my query about any standing order of the Commission laying down the period for preservation of such papers the reply I got was that no such order existed. Standing Order was issued immediately to the effect that such papers should be preserved only for three years and destroyed thereafter unless there was a specific order to the contrary by a competent authority in any individual case. Implementation of this order not only provided ample space in the existing building but also yielded a cash dividend of over Rs. 1 lakh in sale of shredded answer sheets that were discarded. It was amusing to watch truck loads of waste paper being shipped out of the office for weeks.

The armed police personnel occupying the large hall were relocated in outhouses lying vacant behind the main office building and we had a well appointed Reception hall where visitors could be attended to. A room could be provided for experts to wait in comfort and dignity. A conference room could also be set-up for interaction in larger groups. All these were possible without adding a single room to the existing building, not to speak of adding a new building. I was also able to replace all the old oversized furniture used by the staff with modern functional office furniture and had the rooms repainted and furnished suitably to light up the working environment. The staff members who earlier languished or were engaged in unethical practices responded admirably in carrying forward the onerous task of recruitment to higher civil services of the state in a fair and transparent manner to which we all were dedicated.

In course of interaction with candidates, particularly at viva voce, I found that while the standard of performance of those who qualified for interview was quite good in cases of recruitment to civil services and of doctors, it was not so in most other cases and was particularly disappointing in the case of judicial officers required to man subordinate judiciary of the state. There were two streams of recruitment for these: one by written test of Law graduates with a couple of years of practice followed by viva voce and another from among lawyers with minimum practice of perhaps seven years who appeared only for viva voce. In all these recruitments a serving Judge of the High Court joined us on the interview board.

The result of the written test we conducted surprised me to no end. Out of over a thousand candidates who appeared in the examination only 11 could secure qualifying marks to be called for viva voce. To ascertain if the standard of valuation by the examiners was too stiff, I sent for the Chief Examiner who assured me that it was not so; on the other hand he said that the valuation was lenient. He attributed the poor results to the unusually strict invigilation we had instituted to prevent copying at the examination as I was very particular to eliminate such malpractices. The number of vacancies notified by the Government was over 30 and it was suggested to me that the cut off level could be brought down to call more candidates for interview but that was unacceptable. However, we adopted a liberal attitude at the viva voce and cleared all the candidates who appeared. But there was no alternative to carrying forward the vacancies for which qualified candidates were not available.

Disappointed as we were with the result, I pinned my hope on the next recruitment scheduled by us to test suitability of candidates with much longer experience at the bar on the basis of their performance at interviews only. The candidates who appeared were more than adequate. All of them were of course Law graduates with at least seven years of practice, but many of them had LL.M. degree in addition and at least one was a Ph.D. Impressed by their bio data we naturally expected them to do well at viva voce. But their performance disappointed us in most cases. I was amazed that a large number of them had no grasp of even elementary principles of civil or criminal law or important elements of even procedural law, not to speak of higher issues of jurisprudence or constitutional law. Very few of them including those who held LL.M. degree impressed us; the one who was a Ph.D. was perhaps the worst specimen.

We managed to recommend the requisite number for appointment. But I felt deeply disturbed imagining the quality of people that eventually would determine the standard of justice delivery. Appointed initially as Civil Judges and Magistrates, some of them would in course of time be promoted not only as District and Sessions Judge but also elevated to High Court and even Supreme Court perhaps. To share my concern in this matter I invited Vice-Chancellors of the three universities that were awarding law degrees in the State. After an extended discussion we all agreed that the principal cause of deterioration in standard was mushrooming of law colleges and inadequate supervision. When I raised the question of disaffiliation of Colleges that did not fulfil the prescribed standard, I was disappointed to notice that the Vice-Chancellors were indifferent. I thought the matter could be pursued elsewhere. So I met the Chief Justice and found him equally concerned. He told me that some initiatives had been taken at national level to improve the standard of teaching of Law by setting up new institutions with competent faculty and modern curriculum. The Law School at Bangalore was the outcome followed by several more institutions, including some in Orissa. I suggested that steps could also be initiated to have in-service training of recruits to equip them better for discharge of their duties for which a training school was required in the state. He agreed with me and said that such an institution was contemplated but suitable premises were not in sight. We discussed some alternatives based on my local knowledge and a training institute came up later at one of those locations.

Another cause for concern related to recruitment of faculty for medical colleges. It was not that, I was disappointed with performance of the candidates but what worried me was that in some disciplines there were hardly any candidates to be interviewed. The advertisement issued inviting applications to fill vacancies of over 30 posts of Lecturer in Anatomy and Physiology evoked response from only three candidates. The expert we had invited to assist us in that recruitment was a former Principal of Medical College whose own specialisation was in a non-clinical stream. To my query on the utterly inadequate response to our advertisement he replied that medical graduates were no longer willing to specialise in non-clinical subjects with practically no possibility of private practice. He added that medical colleges in the state were managing with only a few senior teachers in those disciplines who were close to retirement as younger ones were just not available to fill up vacancies. He regretfully said that no remedial action by the Government was yet in evidence despite repeated proposals to improve the attractiveness of these positions. He bemoaned the possibility of no teacher being available in these subjects after those in service retired, if the prevailing trend continued unabated.

The Commission had little jurisdiction in the matter but I could not rest content by only writing about it in our Report. I sought an appointment with the Governor to invite his attention to this unacceptable situation. He not only appreciated the need for early remedial measures but also advised me to invite the personal attention of the Chief Minister to this important issue which was obviously not getting the close attention it deserved in the Government. He also offered to speak with the Chief Minister. With his keen perception the Chief Minister immediately recognised the gravity of the situation and assured an early action. Soon thereafter, the State Health Secretary came to me and we had a long discussion on the lines of action warranted. The Secretary was energetic and sincere. I was assured that the problem would be squarely addressed and solution would be found since Chief Minister had evinced keen interest in the matter. I do not recollect the outcome, but there was perhaps nothing more that I could have done.

Towards the end of my tenure, a journalist asked me how I managed to resist pressure from politicians in matters of recruitment and promotion. He was surprised at my reply that far from being a problem, it was a non issue for me as no politician ever tried to influence me in such matters. And this was the truth though the journalist seemed unconvinced. He questioned me specifically, if the Chief Minister made no recommendation. My reply to him was that not only he recommended no one or even obliquely tried to influence me in any matter during my tenure as Chairman but earlier also when I worked under him in the Government. The journalist perhaps did not believe this. However, it was nice of him to tell me after I had demitted office that in a conversation he had with a senior journalist much older in age, where he made some snide remark on my assertion in the matter of political pressure, he was upbraided by the senior who apparently had watched me from my young days in the Government. He told the younger colleague that I was indeed immune to pressure and that was the reason why politicians seldom approached me for undue favours.

That of course was the fact and for me it was a great blessing in disguise. It saved me the trouble of being approached. I had seen several cases of officers, keen to be popular, spending much time and effort to oblige others, mostly those in public life. They earned some goodwill. But demands for favours invariably kept mounting on such officers who found it increasingly difficult to cope. They got drawn more and more into doing irregularities for which some of them faced serious consequences. On balance of considerations I have found it advantageous in the long run to have the image of being unapproachable for undue favour. If in addition one is able to build a reputation of fair conduct and unimpeachable integrity, there is every possibility of getting appreciation.

My tenure at the OPSC was of just two years. Parts of those two years were undoubtedly most stressful, but as I looked back at the volume and content of the work done by the Commission during that period, I felt satisfied. Not only were we able to clear the entire backlog of recruitment to Orissa Civil Services covering vacancies of five years but also recruited a record number of professionals like Doctors, Engineers, judicial Officers and other professionals. Besides, the recommendations we made for promotion of officers of different departments and grades to higher positions were the highest ever. The biggest source of my satisfaction however did not lie in the numbers. The priority for me was to restore credibility of the OPSC which had taken a severe beating. We took a series of measures by which the objective was achieved to a large extent.

We were committed to transparency, promptness, diligence and unimpeachable fairness. Selfless desire to attain the higher goal of rebuilding the institution was the primary force. There was need for sheer hard work too. Some of my friends used to wonder why I engaged myself in hours and hours of work, in the office and at home, much of which they thought would go waste and the Commission would revert back to old ways when I ceased to be the Chairman. That may well have happened. But I persisted in my effort and was fortunate to get full co-operation of my colleagues on the Commission. The staff, not particularly known for dynamism, also rose to the occasion and did exceedingly well. Two excellent officers who bore the brunt of my relentless pressure were the Commission's Special Secretary Jyoti Prakash Das and Secretary Kashinath Sahoo who worked ungrudgingly with unflinching loyalty.

I may have had some satisfaction from the hard work during my tenure as Chairman to streamline the working of the Commission but as I look back, I feel deeply distressed at the functioning of Public Service Commissions in the states in general. The Orissa experience of course is known to me personally. A few years after my demitting the office of Chairman in Orissa, an incumbent Chairman of the Commission had to be placed under suspension on charges of misconduct. There were allegations of corruption in recruitment and to add to that, criminal charges of misbehaviour were also brought against him by a colleague of his. Serious allegations of corruption were made against Chairman of the Public Service

Commission of Bihar and of Punjab. Scam in recruitment by the Public Service Commission of Karnataka has been alleged as a result of which there is widespread resentment there. If this trend continues, there would be no credibility left in the recruitment to higher services by the Union Public Service Commission even. Officers recruited under the flawed system can hardly be expected to refrain from engaging in corruption, not to speak of curbing corrupt practices with a heavy hand.

That brings me to the urgent need to combat on all fronts the single most debilitating force of corruption which now threatens to destroy governance and ruin the society. I propose to address this issue in the concluding chapter which follows.

Chapter 21

Corruption

Contemporary India faces the challenge of humongous corruption which severely weakens the social fabric and prevents realisation of our economic potential. It is not too late for us to pull back from the impending crisis but the collective resolve required to do so does not seem to have crystallised yet. Judging by the extent of rot permeating electoral politics in our country little reform can be expected in the conduct of political leaders, most of them being guided by insatiable desire for self preservation. Only the larger society and the youth in particular, can make a difference in their search for a better destiny. The bureaucracy, with assured security of service guaranteed to it by the Constitution, has a special responsibility to discharge. Abdication of this responsibility, especially by higher civil services, would cause irreparable harm to the nation and damage to the bureaucracy itself.

My batch of IAS had its golden jubilee reunion in 2010 at the Lal Bahadur Shastri National Academy of Administration, Mussoorie, where we all had started as probationers in 1960.

Meeting friends after a gap of many years was of course enjoyable but a striking feature of the programme was a structured discussion on the subject of Corruption. I happened to initiate the discussion by recalling that when we entered the Academy as trainees, corruption was not an issue; it seldom, if at all, came up in serious discussions among probationers. But I also added that corruption had raised its head during the time we served as members of the higher civil service and over the years assumed such alarming proportions as to warrant a full session for deliberation at the Golden Jubilee meet. Having spent almost our entire working life in the higher civil service I wondered if we could escape responsibility for the alarming growth of corruption in government.

I did not fail to notice signs of uneasiness bordering on disapproval at my opening remarks. But by the time everyone had spoken, it was clear that no one disagreed seriously. I genuinely believe that senior officers in my generation did not do enough to stem the tide of corruption that crept into higher levels of administration, almost imperceptibly at first but engulfed it over time. At the lower levels, particularly in departments like Revenue, Police, Forest and the judiciary, corruption had existed since times immemorial. People had got used to making nominal payments to petty officials to get their work speeded up. Demands for payment were generally not necessary because people gave without demur. But a more serious view was taken when a bribe was insisted upon under threat of denial of the admissible service. Close supervision at higher levels and firm action against bribery had kept the evil practice within tolerable limits. The higher civil services were largely free from the curse of illegal gratification.

The first case, in my knowledge, of corruption in independent India by an ICS officer was of SA Venkataraman who served as Secretary to the Government of India. The allegation of illegal gratification was proved against him and he was dismissed from service. The dismissal was followed by conviction under the colonial precursor to the Prevention of Corruption Act and he went to jail as he failed to convince the Supreme Court that his prosecution was unconstitutional. The entire process, which took place in early 1950s, was completed most expeditiously and served as a major deterrent. In a subsequent matter that came to be known as the Mundhra Scandal, no allegation of illegal gratification was made but irregularities were established that led to resignation of TT Krishnamachari, the then Finance Minister. There were also the cases of Partap Singh Kairon in Punjab and Biju Patnaik in Orissa, who were eased out of the office of Chief Minister because of serious doubts on their conduct, though no criminal charges were established against them.

As tall leaders of the freedom movement passed away and the moral fibre of the leadership frayed, the tendency on the part of the political class to leverage their power and influence over the government for personal gain grew. They needed the support of willing allies in the bureaucracy to cut corners and bypass rules. Elements in the provincial civil services became easy targets first because of greater vulnerability. Political functionaries at the grass-root level started coalescing with officials of questionable integrity and those who did not willingly fall in line were made to do so by threats of transfer. Ministers, barring some principled ones whose number dwindled with the passage of time, took the power of transfer and posting into their own hands and enjoyed exercising that power. There was progressive erosion of the authority of senior officers over subordinates.

The seniors who wished to sail with the tide took the line of least resistance and lost their personality. They failed to exercise control and supervision over juniors and allowed the system to deteriorate. Some senior officers, ignoring the risks involved, saw advantage in collaborating with unscrupulous politicians to improve personal fortunes and did so at the cost of the public good. The numbers of those officers who preferred the straight path of duty and chose to enforce discipline and maintain dignity, while denying themselves support and patronage, gradually went down. Malignant forces were steadily at work weakening the administration from within, infecting it with the virus of corruption in different forms. The process got greatly accelerated by another factor.

International lobbyists and power-brokers became active in India with the object of making big money by peddling high value imports for defence and other projects. Their multi-level operations, with offers of large kickbacks, could reach even the highest levels in the government both at the Centre and in the states. Some of them succeeded in swinging purchase decisions in their favour by subverting the system and compromising the government. The disgraceful saga of the Bofors gun procurement scandal that rocked the nation and its cover up spread over a period of three decades, culminating in the escape of the principal agent with part of the loot in 2010 is well known. This was just one case that came to be discussed widely because the agent was known to have had access to the Former Prime Minister and his family. There were many other cases that did not come to limelight as they involved lesser personalities.

The cumulative effect of all those forces damaged the credibility of the government and undermined the morale of dutiful officials with character and integrity. Whatever was left of the image of the government, was destroyed by numerous scams that surfaced in recent times, whether in the area of allocating natural resources like land, airwave spectrum, mining rights or contracts for the Commonwealth Games, or burdening Air India with massive aircraft purchases, or giving away undue benefits to private entities under Public Private Partnership (PPP) mode. Much of the malpractice, if not all, could have been avoided had senior officials in key positions not collaborated with those who acted against the public interest. It was not as if officers of character and integrity were totally missing, but they were rendered ineffective by the powerful nexus of unscrupulous Ministers with civil servants who lacked courage or integrity; or possibly both.

My exposure to corruption at the highest level in the state

came rather early when I joined the Finance Department as a Under Secretary in January 1964. Biju Patnaik had resigned at that time as Chief Minister and become Chairman, State Planning Board; he was succeeded as Chief Minister by his former deputy and close associate, Biren Mitra. While Patnaik was the Chief Minister, holding the Finance Department as well, he and Mitra together instituted a clever arrangement to route major government purchases through a private agency which made large profits. This became possible by a disingenuous circular issued by the Finance Department with Patnaik's approval as Finance Minister. The profits made by the private agency, adversely commented upon by the Audit, led to public criticism and it was alleged that Patnaik and Mitra were the real beneficiaries.

The matter was brought to the notice of Prime Minister Pandit Nehru who, even though fond of Patnaik, got it examined, if I remembered correctly, by his Cabinet colleague MC Chagla, former Chief Justice of Bombay High Court. Shortly thereafter, Patnaik resigned the office of Chief Minister under the well known Kamaraj Plan. Even Biren Mitra, his successor, could not remain Chief Minister for long and had to make room for Sadashiva Tripathy who succeeded him. Thus Orissa had three Chief Ministers—all of the same party—during the life of a single Legislative Assembly. No serious charge of corruption was levelled against Tripathy but Congress became discredited because of earlier corruption charges against the Party and lost badly in the election that followed.

As a young officer in the Finance Department I had opportunity to see the file from which the impugned Finance Department circular had issued, though after its withdrawal. It was indeed a cleverly contrived circular designed to benefit the private agency in question under the garb of protecting sales tax revenues of the state. No suggestion for such a move had come from any official source; nor was there a record of the expected revenue gain or possible adverse consequence. It was obvious that an obliging Finance Secretary had willingly issued the circular at the behest of his Minister who was also the Chief Minister. Much later, perhaps only after the controversy erupted, the Chief Secretary called for the file and recorded a cryptic remark seeking approval of the Chief Minister. The Chief Secretary's remark which I remember to this day was: "Finance does not foresee the pernicious effect of its circular which needs to be withdrawn". The file apparently had remained in the Chief Minister's office and came down only after he resigned and the circular stood withdrawn.

My first direct brush with corruption at high levels occurred during that same stint in the Finance Department, where I had become a Deputy Secretary. It concerned the purchase of crawler-tractors by the Irrigation Department, of which I have given some details in an earlier chapter. The State Irrigation Secretary and some junior officers were prosecuted in this case. They suffered protracted criminal prosecution and ignominy over a long period while the political bosses, including a Cabinet Minister in Delhi who gave the biggest push to the purchase, remained unscathed.

This perhaps served as a deterrent and one did not hear, for quite some time, about the involvement of senior officers in acts of corruption in the state. Of course there were a few who were known for their proclivity to cut corners but their number was so small that they could not contaminate the larger body of the higher bureaucracy. This was also helped to an extent by a slogan of 'Clean Governance', on the strength of which a coalition of two political parties came to power after the Congress was split in the state and got routed in the general election of 1967 because of corruption charges.

The leader of one of the two coalition parties which had split from the Congress and became Deputy Chief Minister in the new government was a man of impeccable honesty. He toured the state extensively and took great pains to spread the message of clean administration. I remember how some young officers like me made snide remarks on the fetish he made of honesty. We did not realise at that stage how important it was to emphasise the need for honesty in the delivery of good governance.

When I went back to the Secretariat in Bhubaneswar I found that the Deputy Chief Minister's passionate campaign against corruption had lost steam, though his personal conduct remained beyond reproach. Those days Orissa had hardly any industry worth the name, except a paper mill, an aluminium plant and a steel factory. Industrialists did not evince much interest in Orissa. Target groups for skimming by corrupt elements were principally two: Rice Millers and Kendu Leaf traders. The collection from rice millers had already reached a plateau. Trade in Kendu leaf however, had became increasingly attractive. With spread of Bidi smoking, demand for Kendu leaves grown extensively in the forests of Orissa had registered vast increase as these leaves were required for rolling tobacco into Bidi. The annual fixation of royalty on the leaves collected and the allocation of areas for collection of leaves provided excellent opportunities to unscrupulous elements in the government at high levels, to make private gain at public cost. It eventually became a major issue of political corruption in the early 1970s. A Commission of Enquiry set-up in this matter made caustic remarks on the conduct of the government at high political as well as bureaucratic levels.

Political instability and progressively high expenditure involved in facing elections brought into corrupt ways even those political activists who were not motivated by the desire for personal enrichment. Corruption grew in different states as if on a competitive basis. Some of the more glaring cases involving Chief Ministers included, apart from Biju Patnaik of Orissa and Partap Singh Kairon of Punjab, in other states too, like Antulay's cement scam in Maharashtra, Lalu Prasad's Fodder scam in Bihar, Palm-oil import scam in Kerala involving Chief Minister Karunakaran, Madhu Koda cases in Jharkhand, cases against Karunanidhi and Jayalalithaa in Tamil Nadu, Mining scams in Goa, Karnataka, Orissa and Andhra Pradesh and disproportionate assets cases against Mayavati and

Mulayam Singh in Uttar Pradesh.

Higher civil services in states no longer could claim any degree of effectiveness in curbing corruption. Many of the upright officers were tossed around if they did not lend themselves to misuse and others who remained on the sidelines preferred to drift, having lost initiative and interest in administration. Those with less regard for scruples happily collaborated with unscrupulous political masters to milk the State. However, as the bulk of the bureaucracy was composed of officers with competence and character, administration still remained on an even keel despite the depredation perpetrated by corrupt elements. But over the years the strength and character of these officers and sadly their numbers as well, declined as the extent and intensity of corruption grew. Officers with competence and character who could resist wrong and promote clean and good governance found their space shrinking. Many of them preferred to move to the Centre where working environment had not been overcast as in the states, by dense clouds of corruption. But there too the things started deteriorating and eventually crossed the tipping point.

LN Mishra, a close confidant and Cabinet colleague of Prime Minister Indira Gandhi, came under media focus in the early 1970s as a principal actor on the national stage of high level corruption. But bureaucracy at the senior level was still seen as generally untarnished. Decline started as the concept of committed bureaucracy came to be advocated vigorously, although its principal proponents, such as PN Haksar, did not intend to promote corruption. Their objective was different; they wished to strengthen the personal rule of Indira Gandhi. In a parliamentary democracy like ours the bureaucracy needs to be committed to the Constitution and not to any individual or group. Civil servants understood this but saw an insidious trend of favours bestowed on those who contributed to the promotion of the personality cult. The neutrality of civil service was itself being neutralised. Loyalty to the Ministers enjoying the confidence of the Prime Minister became a substitute for commitment to the Constitution and the rule of law. Critical examination of policy issues on files was frowned upon if it did not favour the intended result.

The Minister's desire came to be treated as Government's order. Corrupt politicians found it easy to manipulate the government machinery for wrong purposes and unscrupulous civil servants became their allies, willingly or otherwise. The Emergency regime contributed greatly to the growth of this culture, though some demonstrative action was taken, like summary dismissal of a state Chief Secretary known to be lacking in integrity, to give an anti-corruption veneer to the regime that was throttling democracy. The Janata Party government of Morarji Desai brought hopes of restoration of values in governance, but it was disunited in action and its tenure was brief. It failed to leave any lasting impact, like the Clean Governance slogan failed in Orissa in 1967.

By the time Rajiv Gandhi became Prime Minister the ground was fertile for the growth of corruption in high value government procurements. After a brief political interlude, he was inducted to the highest office in the government in the extraordinary situation of his mother's assassination, almost airlifted from the cockpit of an aircraft of Indian Airlines where he earlier worked as a pilot. He came with a fresh mind, unpolluted by corruption in public life. But he had colleagues and confidants who were ready with plans to milk the system. The methods they applied were innovative. They focused attention on large value government purchases that offered the opportunity to collect funds at source in bulk, instead of having to rely on diverse channels to make smaller collections in the name of Party Fund.

Allegations of corruption against him, though muted, first came in the purchase of Airbus A320s, where CBI later registered a case naming, among others, a Secretary to the Government of India. Other instances also surfaced, particularly in the Petroleum sector. But Defence purchases, shrouded in secrecy, provided attractive opportunities. An early instance of corruption of high value that came to light in that sector was in the acquisition of submarines. But the case that shook the conscience of the nation was bribery in the purchase of Bofors guns. It not only dealt a severe blow to the image of the Prime Minister but also led to criminal prosecution of the then Defence Secretary, among others. The cover-up extended over a period of almost twenty five years and culminated, during the regime of Prime Minister Manmohan Singh, in the infamous de-freezing by the government of the bank account of Quattrocchi, who was the middleman when Bofors guns were purchased. The cover-up involved a large number of persons in high office who were all rewarded in different ways.

Ordinarily, criminal cases against a Secretary to the Government of India, mentioned above, should have struck terror in the higher civil services but that did not happen. The reason was simple. Criminal prosecution came to be instituted long after the event and only after change of government. Meanwhile, there was elaborate cover up and the concerned officers remained well protected, even rewarded with post-retirement elevation to high offices. An impression was first sought to be created that the allegations levelled against them were baseless. A Joint Parliamentary Committee that examined the Bofors bribery matter did not get to the bottom of the pay-off. Criminal investigation was patchy and the prosecution which followed was interminable. The CBI, ever willing to be helpful to the government in office merrily closed the cases. Higher echelons in practically all services came under malefic influence of unscrupulous forces and the pervasive culture of corruption in high places took its toll on moral values of younger officers.

While corruption was spreading its tentacles and administration was losing credibility and sense of purpose, another dangerous force at work was the increasing criminalisation of politics in the country. Each was feeding the other and both together were gaining in strength with potentially disastrous consequences for the nation. Yet the leadership did nothing to contain the problem. Anti-social elements that committed heinous crimes against thousands of innocent Sikhs in the Delhi massacre of 1984 were identified as Congress workers acting at the behest of well known leaders of the party, including Ministers of the Rajiv Gandhi Government. Some of them were prosecuted for their role after change of government but they were capable of manipulating the criminal justice system to the point of denial of justice to the victims for decades.

Prime Minister Narasimha Rao was able to preside over a minority government for an entire five year term by bribing some Members of Parliament, including one who later, as a Minister in Manmohan Singh's Cabinet, was prosecuted for murder. An infamous god man, who wielded enormous power under Narasimha Rao's government, fixing deals and getting senior officers posted to desired positions, went to jail. Those who sought his help in the days when he could swing decisions in the government regretted that they had prostrated before a criminal who masqueraded as a god man. Criminalisation of politics reached such an extent that the Parliament and state legislatures were packed with Members having criminal record, many of whom became Ministers. The Criminal Justice system in the country no longer inspired confidence among the people.

With the abolition of the much-abused License Permit Raj, one expected corrupt practices to decline. But the forces unleashed by economic liberalisation, far from arresting corruption, only gave greater opportunity to unscrupulous elements. The levers of power came to be operated more for the benefit of those in office and their favourites, who became enormously wealthy, leaving common people to suffer exploitation at the hands of corrupt officials. Governance became conspicuous by its absence. The depth to which governance fell revealed itself in the form of mind-boggling amounts of wrongful losses to the exchequer which surfaced one after another. When the corruption involved in organising the Commonwealth Games (CWG) in 2010 and it was alleged to be of several thousand crores of rupees, it appeared incredible at first, yet it was true. The Telecom Spectrum Scam, that came to be known as 2G Scam, surpassed it and involved larger loss to the exchequer.

The biggest loot came to light thereafter in the allocation of coal mines given away to private parties, referred to as the Coalgate scam. In each of these cases the government first ruled out any wrong. But the truth has an unfailing tendency to emerge. Public outrage led to the intervention of the Supreme Court. The Law started taking its course and persons occupying high offices, including the Minister and the Secretary of Telecommunication, went to jail. In the case of Coalgate, the saddest part was that it happened under the direct watch of Prime Minister Manmohan Singh, who also held the Coal portfolio. The long series of scams in government only became longer with unearthing of Tatra trucks deal, Westland helicopter deal and scam in Railway Board appointments.

While the scams were in progress on such massive scale did senior civil servants act in true spirit of adherence to established procedures and mandatory provisions of law? Had they done so, they would certainly have prevented much of the damage. And where they failed to prevent corruption, did they ensure that they left behind written evidence of undue intervention by political masters? Some of them actually did so. By leaving recorded notes they helped the law to nab wrong doers eventually. But alas, such cases were few and the predominant tendency became one of inert acceptance or active collusion.

It is my conviction, based on personal experience, that a Minister or Chief Minister can be restrained, if not prevented, from wrong doing if a senior officer under him unequivocally puts across a contrary view with clear reasoning; Secretaries to Government have a crucial role in this. I also believe that no large corruption is possible in the government without the support of a section of the higher bureaucracy. A further belief I hold is that a Minister or a Chief Minister, unless he has a criminal disposition, would ordinarily refrain from causing harm to a civil servant of proven integrity if his advice is an impediment to the attainment of a sinister objective.

All that such a civil servant of character and integrity may face is a transfer which, in my view, should be accepted as an occupational hazard. The bureaucracy, the senior civil servants in particular, are duty bound to curb corruption and promote good governance. This duty cannot be subordinated to carrying out the behest of political masters in pursuit of wrongful gain at public cost. An order which is not given lawfully does not become lawful merely because it comes from a lawfully appointed authority like a Minister. The order itself must be lawful intrinsically. It is no doubt difficult and indeed inadvisable for the lower bureaucracy to question orders that are formally communicated to them but senior officers, particularly those in the secretariat, are required first to make sure that what is intended to be implemented is legally in order, morally justified and is unlikely to be abused. In the event of any doubt, the matter would need to be re-submitted, clearly pointing out the questions involved. And if the same order is reiterated by the Minister without giving cogent answers to the questions raised, the officer concerned should spell out the infirmities in the 'order' and record his inability to implement it unless overruled in writing. These are some of the basic principles that the higher civil services are required to observe.

To live up to this however an officer needs to keep himself in readiness to be shunted out and prefer transfer, however inconvenient, to complicity in wrong doing. There have been instances, though not many, of upright officers committed to protecting public interest having acted in such a principled manner and coming out successful without damage to the public interest or even to their own career. They might have gone through testing times but looking back, the experience would be quite rewarding.

In early post-independence days the dominant influence that guided administration was of principled political leadership which acted through a well-structured bureaucracy whose higher echelons were committed to probity. By the time I joined service, some erosion had undoubtedly taken place but the higher civil services as a body was still regarded well. Had we and our successors in service maintained the standard of probity in the bureaucracy at that level and refused to be tempted or bullied by corrupt politicians, the present state of governance in the country would have been far better. Corruption could not have spread its tentacles wide and deep as now. Alas, we failed; if one upright officer resisted wrong doing and paid a price, another stepped in, anxious to please and willing to be misused. Lobbying for positions, frowned upon among civil servants in earlier days, became rampant over time. The politicians saw the opportunity and were quick to exploit it. As Government expanded over the years and areas of patronage grew, especially under the infamous License Permit Raj, corruption increased by leaps and bounds.

With the abolition of that discredited regime, following economic liberalisation, corruption was expected to come down. But that hope was not realised. Economic liberalisation initially unshackled entrepreneurial spirit and led to accelerated growth in Gross Domestic Product (GDP) but it also created hideous disparities in wealth and incomes among citizens that accentuated social tension. Worse was the enormous opportunity it provided to unscrupulous elements, in the absence of transparent public policies, to gain control over invaluable natural resources through bribery and other corrupt practices. Earlier, it was said that corruption was a by-product of misdirected socialist policies whose substitution was necessary to curb the menace by adopting policies that facilitated operation of market forces. People therefore, willingly accepted liberalisation hoping it would bring better economic governance while curbing corruption. Little did the nation expect the massive leap in corruption which unfolded, particularly under the watch of Prime Minister Manmohan Singh, who came with a clean image but allowed it to be mired by humongous scams!

Even in this dismal picture one can still find some bright

spots in the higher bureaucracy, otherwise viewed with disdain for having meekly submitted to if not collaborated with corrupt politicians. From news reports I gathered the impression that in recent years at least one Secretary to the Government of India did make serious efforts to prevent wrong doing of huge proportion. He could not succeed because other senior colleagues in key positions chose to side with wrong doers in higher positions of authority. I refer in particular to the infamous Coalgate where unimaginable corruption was unearthed. At the initial stage itself the Coal Secretary tried to shut the door on deal-making by proposing the adoption of a transparent auction system for allotment of coal blocks. The Prime Minister approved it as the Minister holding the Coal portfolio. But the same Prime Minister, aided by his own office (PMO), subsequently prevented its implementation for years during which a massive scam was perpetrated.

Among the contributions made by the Coal Secretary, who foresaw the clear possibility of the scam and tried to prevent it, was the note he recorded at that time. He might have retired but his note formed the initial basis for the report of the Comptroller and Auditor General of India which unearthed the Coalgate scam. Another case was that of an upright Chief Executive of Air India who tried to bring to the attention of the Prime Minister, through the Cabinet Secretary, how decision-making in his organisation was being subverted by the Minister and the Secretary both. What happened after that is not in public domain but the very fact that the Chief Executive felt compelled to bring the matter of undue interference to the notice of the highest authority in the government points to the extent to which completely unjustified pressure was brought upon him.

Again there is an example of a principled civil servant who took the risk of annoying his superiors to prevent the exploitation of his organisation. The courageous steps taken by Ashok Khemka, an IAS officer, in cancelling illegal transfer of land mutated by unauthorised officials in Gurgaon to please the high and mighty have also been widely appreciated, thanks to media coverage. Likewise, there is the glittering example of courage and firmness shown by Durgashakti Nagpal, a young IAS officer, in confronting the sand mining mafia of NOIDA with its powerful political nexus. It is regrettable that the Government of Uttar Pradesh headed by a young educated Chief Minister, instead of commending her, took vindictive action against Durgashakti. The widespread revulsion one could see in this connection against the Chief Minister's conduct is a clear pointer to unscrupulous politicians and their collaborators in the bureaucracy that the nation is in no mood to forgive them. The exemplary conduct of officers mentioned above should inspire others to awake and arise. Indeed, other instances are coming up in different parts of the country where principled officers of IAS, IPS, IFS and other services are standing up boldly to discharge their public duty unmindful of vindictive action by unscrupulous superiors, whether political or bureaucratic.

These instances, few though they may be, hold promise that all is not lost in the higher civil services. But infusing courage and morality to restore the health of the larger body is a stupendous task, too big for the shoulders of ordinary mortals. The society, of which politicians and bureaucrats are only constituent parts, is itself in need of reform. That calls for leadership of exceptional calibre, pure to the core and burning with selfless desire to lift the spirit of the people and transform the destiny of the nation. Emergence of leaders like Mahatma Gandhi, Swami Vivekananda or Guru Gobind Singh is required for that purpose. Meanwhile, small steps can certainly be taken to contain problems arising from growing corruption in the bureaucracy, particularly in the higher civil services. In my view the following simple and easily implementable measures can go a considerable way in weeding out corruption in higher services.

The prevailing practice of requiring prior approval of Government to prosecute a senior public servant should be abolished when a case of corruption is made out, prima facie.

The exercise of discretion by the executive authority in giving approval before a case can be filed before a Court is the single most abused instrument by which corrupt public servants have been shielded by equally corrupt Ministers. It has been noticed several time that the government sits over the requests of investigating agencies to permit the filing of charge sheet against public servants, against whom clinching evidence had been collected. The provision, intended to protect honest civil servants against vexatious charges, has become totally counterproductive. Abuse of this provision has become so extensive as to make even the Supreme Court pass caustic remarks. Abolition of this provision would plug one major loophole by which the corrupt politician is now able to hold out promise of protection to the unscrupulous civil servant.

The practice of giving post-retirement assignments is yet another instrument to lure civil servants into wrong doing. It should come to an end forthwith. Extension of service, re-employment after superannuation and appointment to high positions after retirement are among temptations offered to senior officers to make them toe the line of political masters while in service and thereafter. It is common knowledge that many able officers compromise at the top not because of any taint of corruption or major flaw in character but for a longing for post-retirement engagement. I was pained to watch on TV a Governor in office tell his interviewer that his ambition, while in service, was to get the high office of Governor after retirement. He surely knew that Governorship could never be a legitimate part of a civil service career.

All that a career civil servant can aim for is the highest position that civil services can offer; not beyond. I pity such persons who shamelessly declare their illegitimate aspirations for the attainment of which they must have had to make themselves malleable when firm and sound advice was required of them. Not that all officers at the top suffer from this infirmity; as a matter of fact most of them do not. But those afflicted by this weakness not only vitiate the process of decision-making but also set bad examples for younger officers. I have observed from close quarters senior officers tailoring their advice to their political bosses, against their own better judgement, in order to come closer to them and qualify for assignments after retirement.

No one is indispensable, nor is there a dearth of talent in this large country. All discretionary appointments including those to Corporations, Boards and other statutory and constitutional bodies should be governed by the principle that the person concerned demits office on the date of his superannuation from his service. It should, in my view, apply also to the appointment of retired judges, whether to Tribunals, Commissions and the like. In case it is felt that the age of superannuation needs to be raised to enable optimal utilisation of human resources, in view of enhanced longevity now in evidence, it should be applied uniformly to all, not selectively.

Strong and independent Lokpal type institutions, with adequate investigative support, need to be set-up in states and the centre without further procrastination so that any citizen with a credible allegation of corruption against a senior public servant can approach that institution. It should also be mandated that sustainability of the allegation must be established within a specified period and, in the event of there being a prime facie case, it should be remitted to a specially designated court for trial with not more than one appellate forum for final disposal within a specified time limit. One of the reasons for spread of corruption is the pervasive impression that the enforcement of anti-corruption laws in our country, apart from being lax, is so dilatory that a corrupt public servant can pass off as innocent for decades, until pronounced otherwise by the final court of appeal. Prompt and time-bound action is essential. Earlier, I quoted an example of SA Venkataraman, the disgraced ICS officer, who was convicted of bribery in the early 1950s. The entire case was finally clinched in less than two years. Ironically it is the same country and under the same judicial process that a former Chief Secretary of Uttar Pradesh remained on bail even in 2013 though convicted of corruption by the trial court in cases that date back to 1994. I recollect that the same officer, along with two others, was voted as most corrupt by their colleagues in IAS way back in the 1980s, years before they reached top echelons in service. Political bosses must have found them useful to team up with.

The fight against corruption needs to be fought within the bureaucracy itself. A large part of the higher services, it must be asserted, is still free from corruption. The problem lies not in the dearth of honest officers but in their reluctance to stand up against forces of corruption. My generation of civil servants might have failed to pay adequate attention to this aspect of duty, perhaps under the mistaken notion that the government had enough strength and vitality to control corruption and deliver good governance. An equally mistaken notion, which I could never accept, gained ground that the wishes of Ministers were synonymous with orders of government. Nothing could be more erroneous. The Government is represented by a Minister as much as any official—whatever his station—duly vested with any power of the government. The practice of treating the Minister as the Government and thereby subordinating the lawful exercise of executive authority to whims and fancies of Ministers, in my view, lies at the root of much abuse. Because of this abuse, which grew over time, corruption increased and governance deteriorated. The deterioration is now so deep that people have become restive. Until a few years ago their anger was directed against politicians but lately the civil services are also being blamed, rightly perhaps. Indeed the malady has become so acute that responsibility has necessarily to be shared by both. If the permanent services can have any legitimacy they must, as a body, take up the challenge to restore health and vitality to their service.

The civil services are still attracting talent of high calibre. It may be true that some of them are lured by the opportunity to get rich quickly but a lot more are not inclined to do so. All said and done, the higher services, the IAS in particular, offer exceptionally good opportunity to serve the nation with dignity. The constitutional protection bestowed on officers is formidable. There is absolutely no need for an officer to be partisan, servile or fearful as long as he conducts himself in accordance with well established principles of the rule of law. Conditions have to be created to liberate the higher services from the eclipse caused by ill motivated men in and around power. Dr. Manmohan Singh, on assuming the high office of Prime Minister, made bold promises of administrative reforms to enhance the quality of governance but till today has delivered nothing positive. On the other hand he has the dubious distinction of having presided over an administration considered most corrupt in independent India. This being the performance of a Prime Minister who came with a clean image, there can be no point in expecting a change of heart from those who have a vested interest in corruption. The moral force to fight it needs to emerge from within the services.

Lately, there has been evidence of powerful movements by civil society activists to exert pressure on the government to control corruption. Anna Hazare was able to lead one such movement to great heights. Arvind Kejriwal, a young officer of the Indian Revenue Service, resigned his lucrative job in the Income Tax Department to devote himself whole time to the fight against corruption. The likes of Ashok Khemka and Durgashakti Nagpal are refreshing instances of public spirited officers dedicated to the call of their duty to the nation. It would be tragic if honest officers in the civil services cannot stand up against corrupt elements, howsoever high, when all that may be at risk is a cosy posting.

They, particularly the younger ones having long years of service ahead, and therefore with a greater stake in the dignity of the service, could form themselves into pressure groups to promote a sense of pride in the service and restore fearlessness among colleagues to fight corruption within. The patently corrupt ones in any organisation are not difficult to identify; their subterranean activities need to be exposed. The pressure groups can also play a quiet role in socially ostracising officers who fail to desist from engaging in corrupt practices and thereby become a threat to sound governance and a blot on the image of the larger body of civil servants. They can be named and shamed to great effect in private groups if not publicly. The moral force exerted by these pressure groups can be formidable. No government would have the courage to subdue these groups so long as they remain within the limits of law. I am hopeful that young civil servants will eventually take up the challenge to cleanse the system from within. It cannot be delayed any longer.

If this is too optimistic, I would plead guilty to the charge.

Chapter 22

Epilogue

This narrative started with a quotation from the *Jail Diary* of C Rajagopalachari who not only exercised power and authority with great distinction and enormous prudence as Chief Minister (referred to those days as Prime Minister) of the erstwhile province of Madras, as Union Home Minister, as Governor and Governor General, but was also an eminent thinker, a leading freedom fighter, a farsighted statesman and an abiding Gandhian. I would like to bring the narrative to a close with the following quotation from a piece the same incisive thinker wrote on Vedanta:

> "Everywhere in the civilized world men want a wise allotment of work in individuals as well as groups in accordance with the demand of common interest in place of personal choice or caprice. They feel that they have had enough of the 'divine' right of making unlimited private profit. If it is essential that individual efforts should be regulated and controlled in the interest of society, this vital duty cannot be left entirely to the spy and the policeman employed to keep watch over citizens. We must

> build up a social conscience and a cultural incentive to cooperate from within and create a spiritual yearning which makes a joy of restraint and strenuous discharge of duty.... The spiritual value of things depends on the price paid for them in suffering and sacrifice.... The only thing that can do this effectively is a faith that operates as a law from within and cooperates with State imposed restraints."

The basis of my optimism, if one can have it in the prevailing difficult times, is this 'abiding faith that operates from within and cooperates with State imposed restraints'. For every unprincipled politician and civil servant there are still, I believe, at least ten in the bureaucracy and vastly more men and women in the society who value and practice ethical conduct. The combined spiritual strength of the massive majority, once aroused, would crush under its influence the deleterious forces let loose by corrupt politicians in collusion with self serving bureaucrats who consider capricious conduct their divine right to make unlimited private profit at the cost of common good.

Clear signs are already in evidence of educated youth unwilling to tolerate relentless exploitation of the society by the evil compact of unscrupulous politicians and their accessories in the bureaucracy. It is a matter of time that this unholy combination will inevitably meet its doom. Enlightened democratic leadership needs to assert itself soon to guide governance back to sanity and ethical conduct in order that democracy itself may not be washed away in the tsunami of popular upsurge against the entire political class.

Index